This Must Be The Place

This Must Be The Place

An Architectural History of Popular
Music Performance Venues

ROBERT KRONENBURG

BLOOMSBURY ACADEMIC
NEW YORK · LONDON · OXFORD · NEW DELHI · SYDNEY

BLOOMSBURY ACADEMIC
Bloomsbury Publishing Inc
1385 Broadway, New York, NY 10018, USA
50 Bedford Square, London, WC1B 3DP, UK

BLOOMSBURY, BLOOMSBURY ACADEMIC and the
Diana logo are trademarks of Bloomsbury Publishing Plc

First published in the United States of America 2019

Copyright © Robert Kronenburg, 2019

Cover design by Philippa Thomas
Cover image © Richard Martin-Roberts / Getty Images

All rights reserved. No part of this publication may be reproduced or transmitted in any form or by any means, electronic or mechanical, including photocopying, recording, or any information storage or retrieval system, without prior permission in writing from the publishers.

Bloomsbury Publishing Inc does not have any control over, or responsibility for, any third-party websites referred to or in this book. All internet addresses given in this book were correct at the time of going to press. The author and publisher regret any inconvenience caused if addresses have changed or sites have ceased to exist, but can accept no responsibility for any such changes.

Whilst every effort has been made to locate copyright holders the publishers would be grateful to hear from any person(s) not here acknowledged.

A catalog record for this book is available from the Library of Congress.

ISBN: HB: 978-1-5013-1927-3
PB: 978-1-5013-1928-0
ePDF: 978-1-5013-1929-7
eBook: 978-1-5013-1930-3

Typeset by Integra Software Services Pvt. Ltd.

To find out more about our authors and books visit www.bloomsbury.com
and sign up for our newsletters.

CONTENTS

List of Plates vi
List of Figures viii
Preface xv

1 Introduction: Popular Music, Architecture and the Home 1
2 Music Halls, Variety and Vaudeville 13
3 Honky-Tonks and Juke Joints 35
4 Jazz Clubs, Social Clubs and Riverboats 51
5 Cabaret, Speakeasies and Supper Clubs 69
6 Pleasure Gardens, Ballrooms and Dance Halls 91
7 Pubs, Barrooms and Coffee Bars 109
8 Theatres, Halls and Auditoria 135
9 Festival Stages and Travelling Sets 155
10 Arenas 177
11 Record Scenes 195
12 Conclusion: The Significance and Value of Popular Music Venues 211

Appendix I 241
Appendix II 243
Notes 250
Bibliography 265
Index 275

PLATES

1. The tree of popular music – with roots all around the world, ever growing and continuously being reinvigorated with new branches ©Robert Kronenburg 2012. Source: Robert Kronenburg.
2. A concert by Primal Scream at Liverpool Olympia Theatre, West Derby Road, Liverpool 26 November 2016. Source: Andy Von Pip Photography.
3. Hackney Empire theatre original floor plan. Source: East London Theatre Archive.
4. Robert's Western World interior. Source: Robert Kronenburg.
5. Birds-eye View of New Orleans, La. Postcard from *c.* 1910 with Rampart Street in the bottom-left corner. The District (Storyville) is in the centre of the picture. Source: Postcard published by B. Mason, New Orleans, La. Public domain.
6. Birdland interior (from a pre-1952 postcard). Source: By JPM Associates, New York, Public domain.
7. Copacabana Club in the 1950s. Source: Photofest.
8. The Blackpool Tower Ballroom (photo 2012). Source: Michael Beckwith.
9. We Banjo 3 playing in the Yard Bar, Matt Molloy's. Source: Matt Molloy's.
10. West 125th Street and the Apollo Theater, Harlem, New York in 2007. Source: Rup11.
11. Coachella 2014, the Sahara Tent installed by AG Light and Sound. Source: Shawn Ahmed.
12. Taylor Swift's concert at CenturyLink Field, the Seahawks American Football stadium in Seattle, Washington, USA. Up to 72,000 people can attend a concert here made possible solely by the mobile stage set the artist's road crew bring with them. Source: Michael Langley.
13. T-Mobile Arena, Las Vegas (architects Populous). Source: Populous, photo: ©Jeff Goldberg, Esto Photographics Inc.
14. The Haçienda, as it was rarely seen by clubbers – empty (designer Ben Kelly, 1982). Source: Ben Kelly.

15 Inside CBGB and OMFUG looking towards the stage at the back of the room (photo October 2006). Source: Ted Pink/Alamy Stock Photo.
16 Grand Ole Opry House, Nashville. Pews and replica stage set similar to those found in its former home, the Ryman Auditorium. Source: Robert Kronenburg.

FIGURES

1 The Cavern Club, Matthew Street, Liverpool in 1962. Source: Steve Hale. Courtesy of Dave Jones. xvi

1.1 Location of the Casbah, which occupies the basement of a suburban house at No. 8 Haymans Green, West Derby, Liverpool. The entrance is at the rear – the door to the right in this photo. Source: Robert Kronenburg. 7

2.1 Wilton's Music Hall, Graces Alley, London (1858). Source: Robert Kronenburg. 14

2.2 Georgian Theatre Royal, Richmond (1788), ground-floor plan. Source: Robert Kronenburg. 16

2.3 Wilton's Music Hall interior. ©Peter Dazeley. 19

2.4 Britannia Panoptican, Glasgow, Scotland (1859) (formerly the Britannia Music Hall). Source: Keith Edkins. 20

2.5 Elephant and Castle Theatre, New Kent Road, Southwark, London (1879) (now the Coronet Theatre) (photo *c.* 1920s). Source: London Metropolitan Archives/Collage. 23

2.6 Hackney Empire, Mare Street, London (1901). Source: Ewan Munro. 25

2.7 The Moulin Rouge, Boulevard de Clichy, Pigalle, Paris (1889) (postcard from *c.* 1900). Source: INTERFOTO/Alamy Stock Photo. 28

2.8 The garden stage at the Moulin Rouge. Source: Bettmann/Getty Image. 28

2.9 Postcard showing Tony Pastor's Theatre (1881), at Tammany Hall, 14th Street, New York. Source: Harry Ransom Humanities Research Center, University of Texas at Austin. 31

2.10 The restored Grand Opera House, Meridian, Mississippi, USA (first built in 1890, photo 2012). Source: Katyrw. 32

3.1 Robert's Western World, Broadway, Nashville. Source: Robert Kronenburg. 36

3.2 The John T. Floore Country Store in 1942 – looking much as it does today. Source: John T. Floore Country Store. 40

3.3 Floore's patio stage. Source: John T. Floore Country Store, photo: Mike Berger. 41

3.4 The Broken Spoke, South Lamar Boulevard, Austin, Texas, entrance door. Source: Robert Kronenburg. 42

3.5 The Broken Spoke – Texas Two-Step on the dance floor. Source: Robert Kronenburg. 43

3.6 Juke joint and living quarters Belle Glade, Florida, February 1941. Source: Marion Post Wolcott, Library of Congress. 44

3.7 Jitterbugging in a Clarksdale juke joint, November 1939 (photo: Marion Post Wolcott). Source: Marion Post Wolcott, Library of Congress. 46

3.8 Po' Monkey's, Merigold Mississippi. Source: Michael W. Harding. 47

3.9 Howlin' Wolf on stage at Silvio's Chicago, *c.* 1964. Source: ©Raeburn Flerlage, Chicago Historical Society. 48

3.10 Kingston Mines, 2548 North Halstead, Chicago. Source: Chad Magiera. 49

4.1 The Spotted Cat Music Club, New Orleans, exterior. Source: Robert Kronenburg. 52

4.2 The Eagle Saloon, New Orleans. Source: Robert Kronenburg. 54

4.3 Preservation Hall, French Quarter, New Orleans. Source: Robert Kronenburg. 56

4.4 Perseverance Society Hall (now the Holy Aid and Comfort Spiritual Church of Eternal Life), New Orleans. Source: Kevin McCaffrey. 58

4.5 The New Orleans Brass Band performing in the French Quarter, 2017. Source: Robert Kronenburg. 59

4.6 Fate Marable's New Orleans Jazz Band on the Mississippi riverboat S.S. *Capitol*, *c.* 1920. Source: Photo: A. P. Bedou, Courtesy of the Hogan Jazz Archive, Tulane University. 60

4.7 S.S. *Capitol*, *c.* 1920. Source: Courtesy of the Hogan Jazz Archive, Tulane University. 61

4.8 Plan of Birdland, 315 West 44th Street, New York City. The archetypal jazz club layout with the stage (right) at the focus of the seated audience. The kitchen is at the rear and the bar near the street entrance. Source: Robert Kronenburg. 66

4.9 John Scofield playing at Birdland, 2010. Source: Robert Kronenburg. 67

4.10 Ronnie Scott's, 47 Frith Street, Soho, London. Source: Robert Kronenburg. 68

5.1 The Shakespeare Theatre, Liverpool (photo: *c.* 1920). The decorative panels to the rear of the grand circle are just visible. In the later alterations to convert the theatre to a cabaret club these were covered by curtains, and the raked stalls seating was overbuilt with a level floor for dining tables and a dance floor. Source: Photo courtesy Ross Collins: CollinsVariety.co.uk. 70

5.2 Une Soiree Au Chat Noir Le Chat Noir, Cabaret Artistique, Boulevard de Clichy (*c.* 1920s, from a pre-1930 postcard). Source: Public domain. 72

5.3 Eldorado, Motzsraße, Berlin, 1932. Source: Bundesarchiv. 73

5.4 A Night in the Cave of the Golden Calf. Illustration published in *The Daily Mirror*, 4 July 1912. Source: Public Domain. 75

5.5 Café de Paris after its 2012 renovation. Source: Café de Paris, London. 76

5.6 Ciro's nightclub, Bubbling Well Road, Shanghai, 1936. Photograph by Malcolm Rosholt. Source: Mei-Fei Elrick, Tess Johnston and Historical Photographs of China, University of Bristol. 77

5.7 The Paradise Room, Reisenweber's, Columbus Circle, New York (contemporary post card). Source: Mary Evans/Jazz Age Collection. 80

5.8 The Original Dixieland Jazz Band. A 1918 promotional postcard produced whilst they were playing at Reisenweber's, Columbus Circle, New York. Left to right, the musicians are Tony Sbarbaro (aka Tony Spargo, drums), Edwin 'Daddy' Edwards (trombone), D. James 'Nick. LaRocca (cornet), Lawrence 'Larry' Shields (clarinet) and Henry Ragas (piano). Source: Public Domain. 80

5.9 A Night-Club Map of Harlem, Campbell E. Simms, 1933, published by *Manhattan Weekly*, vol. 1, no. 1, 18 January 1933. Source: Public Domain. 83

5.10 The Cotton Club's Harlem location *c.* 1920s. The entrance area is boarded to represent a rural plantation hut in the American South. Source: New York Public Library. 84

5.11 The Cotton Club mid-town location at 48th and Broadway in about 1937. Source: Lebrecht Music and Arts Photo Library/Alamy Stock Photo. 86

6.1 The Wellington Rooms, Mount Pleasant, 1829. Source: Engraved by Jas. Allen; Drawn by G. & C. Pyne. 93

6.2 The Ballroom at the former Irish Centre, Wellington, Rooms, Mount Pleasant (photograph 2016). Source: Photo by Jacques Joudrey (A.K.A. SpiderMonkey). 94

6.3 London: Interior of the Rotunda at Ranelagh, Giovanni Antonio Canaletto, 1754 (National Gallery, London). Source: Public domain. 96

6.4 The ballroom at the Bath Assembly Rooms, 1771 (photo: 2010). Source: Heather Cowper. 98

6.5 Social dancing at the Olympic Gardens Dance Hall, Halifax, Nova Scotia, 1948. Source: Public domain. 101

6.6 Hammersmith Palais (photo, 1963). Source: Ralph Crane/The Life Picture Collection/Getty. 103

6.7 Boblo Dancing Pavilion, Bois Blanc Island, Ontario (photo: 1914). Source: Public domain. 105

6.8 Crystal Beach Amusement Park – interior of the Crystal Ballroom (1930s). Source: Niagara Falls (Ontario) Public Library. 106

7.1 Matt Molloy's bar, Bridge Street, Westport, Co. Mayo, Ireland. Source: Paul Gregory. 110

7.2 A lively traditional music session in Matt Molloy's. Source: Matt Molloy's. 111

7.3 Piano sing along with entertainers 'Baz and Dave' and London Bobby, Coach and Horses, 29 Greek Street, Soho, London. Source: Sabine Thoele. 115

7.4 The Hope and Anchor in 2016. Source: Philafrenzy. 116

7.5 The Stranglers on stage at the Hope and Anchor, November 1977. Source: Evening Standard/Stringer/Hulton Archive/Getty Pictures. 117

7.6 The Tote, Collingwood, Melbourne. Source: Robert Kronenburg. 120

7.7 Early evening session in the bar at The Tote. Source: Robert Kronenburg. 121

7.8 Hole in the Wall, Guadalupe Street, Austin, Texas. Source: Robert Kronenburg. 124

7.9 A quiet night in the front bar, Hole in the Wall. Source: Robert Kronenburg. 125

7.10 Al Mac's Diner-Restaurant, Fall River, Massachusetts, USA, open around 1910, the diner closed on 23 July 2012. Source: Ken Zirkel. 128

7.11 2i's Coffee Bar, Old Compton Street, Soho, London (photo: *c.* 1957). Source: Photo by Dezo Hoffmann/Rex/Shutterstock. 129

7.12 Screaming Lord Sutch performing with Vince Taylor in the basement of the 2i's, 24 September 1960. Source: Trinity Mirror/Mirrorpix/Alamy Stock Photo. 130

7.13 Café Wha!, MacDougal Street, New York. Source: Robert Kronenburg. 133

8.1 Empire Theatre, Lime Street, Liverpool. Source: Tony Hisgett. 136

8.2 Empire Theatre, view from the Grand Circle, in a photograph commissioned by the Gaumont Theatre Co. in 1934. Source: National Museums Liverpool, Stewart Bale Collection. 137

8.3 The Apollo Theatre marquee, New York, N.Y. (photo: *c.* 1946–1948, William P. Gottlieb). Source: Public domain. 143

8.4 Finsbury Park Astoria, original layout plan. Source: Islington Local History Centre/Islington History Services. 145

8.5 Finsbury Park Astoria shortly after its opening in 1930. Stage with the safety curtain down. Source: Islington Local History Centre/Islington History Services. 146

8.6 The Rainbow Theatre in 1986 five years after its closure. Source: Dusashenka. 149

8.7 Hammersmith Eventim Apollo in 2013. Source: Enmanuelcueva. 151

8.8 Fans in the Hammersmith Apollo auditorium waiting for Kate Bush's *Before the Dawn* show to start, 20 September 2014. Source: Mark McLellan. 151

9.1 Behind the scenes setting up for *The Wall Live* at Manchester MEN Arena in 2010. The rehearsing school children are on the stage, and the stacked-up 'bricks' can be seen to the right, ready to construct the wall as the show proceeds. Source: Robert Kronenburg. 156

9.2 The Beatles live at Shea Stadium, New York, during their second North American tour in 1966. The stadium held 44,600 fans for the concert. Source: Tony Griffin. 157

9.3 The stage at the Woodstock Music and Art Fair, New York state, 1969 (still from the film *Woodstock*, 1970). Source: Entertainment Pictures/Alamy Stock Photo. 159

9.4 Detail of the central part of the site layout plan for Glastonbury 2017 showing the stage areas – as complex as a small city. Source: Glastonbury Festival. 162

9.5 The Pyramid Stage and surrounding support facilities at Glastonbury in 2010. Source: Glastonbury Festival and Jackie Slade. 163

9.6 *The Wall* live performance at Potsdamer Platz, Berlin, 21 July 1990. Source: Photograph Reproduced Courtesy of Stufish. 170

9.7 Preliminary layout drawing for *The Wall Live* tour, 2019, showing the stage with wall assembly structure from behind. Source: Reproduced Courtesy of Stufish. 171

9.8 *The Joshua Tree* anniversary tour stage at Century Link Field, Seattle, US, designed by Stufish and engineered by Tait Towers. Source: Photograph Reproduced Courtesy of Stufish. 174

FIGURES   xiii

10.1 Earls Court Exhibition Centre. Source: Damien Everett. 178
10.2 The Beatles play at the Empire Pool, Wembley, during the New Musical Express Awards concert, 11 April 1965. Source: Trinity Mirror/Mirrorpix/Alamy Stock Photo. 181
10.3 SSE Arena (formerly Wembley Arena) London (photo: 2007). Source: ©Peter Stevens Photography. 182
10.4 Spectrum Arena, Philadelphia, USA, showing its typical sports-style-encompassing seating layout. Photograph taken during the 'last stroll' around the building to allow fans to say goodbye, October 2011. Source: Doug Kerr. 183
10.5 Waiting for the show to begin – Arcade Fire in-the-round performance at Manchester Evening News Arena, 9 April 2018. Source: Robert Kronenburg. 185
10.6 The Dublin Arena in its docklands context (photo: 2010). Source: Tonkie. 188
10.7 The Dublin Arena section through the fan-shaped seating to the performance area (architects Populous). Source: ©Populous. 190
10.8 O2 Arena Greenwich, London. A purpose-built complex of event spaces and other leisure buildings within the converted Millennium Dome, urban regeneration of derelict land polluted by a former gas works (photo: 2012). Source: Danesman1. 191
10.9 The Philippine Arena, Manila, designed by Populous. This is the world's largest indoor mixed-use arena, a 50,000-capacity enclosed event and performance space. On New Year's Eve 2014, 1,000,000 people celebrated in the arena's grounds. Source: ©Populous. 192
10.10 The planned MSG Sphere proposed for a site in Stratford, London. The Las Vegas version is predicted to open in 2020. Source: ©2018 MSG Sports and Entertainment, LLC. 193
11.1 A section of the Bass Odyssey Sound System, Tropical Hut, St Mary, Jamaica, 2012. Source: Yaniq Walford. 198
11.2 The building that housed the Twisted Wheel in Whitworth Street, Manchester, before demolition in 2013. The venue's sign was in the top part of the central window (blocked up in this photograph) with spoked wheel decorations below. Source: Robert Kronenburg. 200
11.3 Empress Ballroom postcard *c.* 1930. Source: Collection of Ron Hunt. 201
11.4 All-nighter at the Wigan Casino *c.* 1980 (photo: Richard Simner). Source: Collection of Pete Smith. 202

11.5 The Haçienda ground-floor plan (designer Ben Kelly, 1982). Source: Robert Kronenburg. 204

11.6 Easy Street Records, West Seattle. Source: Patrick Tyree. 208

12.1 CBGB and OMFUG location in the Bowery, New York City, 1985 (still from *Burning Down the House: The Story of CBGB*, 2009). Source: Everett Collection INc/Alamy Stock Photo. 212

12.2 De Vorstin, Hilversum, The Netherlands (architect: Frits van Dongen with de Archtekten Cie). Source: Photo: Jeroen Musch. 217

12.3 Grenswerk Poppodium (Border Work Pop Stage), Venlo, The Netherlands (architects and planners: van Dongen-Koschuch). Source: Van Dongen-Koschuch. 220

12.4 The Band Room, Low Mill, North Yorkshire, UK. Source: Robert Kronenburg. 221

12.5 100 Club, Oxford Road, London. Source: Robert Kronenburg. 223

12.6 Cavern Club, Liverpool, UK. Plan of the new 1980s building with the new performance space to the left and the reproduction of the older space to the right. Source: Courtesy of Dave Jones. 226

12.7 Bridgestone Arena, Nashville (architects HOK Sport and Hart Freeland Roberts). Source: Robert Kronenburg. 228

12.8 Site plan of the FedExForum, Memphis, showing how it is slotted into the existing street pattern surrounded by existing buildings such as St Patrick's Church, and new development of a similar scale to the older buildings along Beale Street (architects Looney Ricks Kiss with Ellerbe Becket). Source: Looney Ricks Kiss. 229

12.9 Beale Street, Memphis – historic music neighbourhood or tourist attraction? Source: Robert Kronenburg. 232

12.10 Protests at the Tote Hotel, Collingwood, Melbourne, on 18 January 2010 and 15 March 1980. Source: Nick Carson. 235

PREFACE

In 1966 I was twelve years old. Labour had just won a second general election in two years, the football World Cup was about to start in England and London Zoo's panda Chi-Chi had been flown to Moscow to meet An-An for a close quarters attempt at some cultural detente. At my home in Liverpool, my Dutch auntie was visiting her brother, my father. She was his younger sister and mad about The Beatles (even though she was a married woman with children of her own). My father wasn't really a music fan (and certainly not pop music), but he agreed to take my auntie to the Cavern Club, so she could see where her favourite group had first made their claim for fame. It was decided I would go too; however, my elder sister, who was a Cavern regular, realized that I would never get in, as I was too young. So, it was decided that I would be Dutch too. Under strict orders not to speak, the deception was carried out and the family descended the eighteen steep steps into the cellar on Mathew Street during a lunchtime session. The room felt damp, warm, dark and as noisy a place as I had ever been. It was the archetypal underground music venue – exciting, mysterious, slightly frightening. I don't remember who was playing but I remember the feel and sound of the place clearly. The Cavern wasn't my club (that was Eric's, a decade later but only a few steps away on the other side of Matthew Street) but it was my very first introduction to the cocktail of ingredients that make up a successful popular music venue.

Later that year on 29 August, The Beatles would play their very last ticketed show at Candlestick Park, San Francisco. Their first concert at New York's Shea Stadium on 15 August 1965 is often cited as pivotal in the history of live popular music performance, indicating the medium's new commercial and cultural power. And it was – the stadium had only been open since April the previous year, and although sports arenas had been used for concerts before (including The Beatles, who on their first visit to the United States in April 1964 had appeared at the Washington Coliseum before 8,000 fans), this was the first time that an outdoor venue as large as this had been used for a popular music performance. However, the 1966 concert is also important in that the most admired band in the world had decided that they need never perform live again and would henceforth become recording artists only. This was a decision that questioned the necessity of live performance in popular music – perhaps recording sales, radio, television,

FIGURE 1 *The Cavern Club, Matthew Street, Liverpool in 1962.*
Source: Steve Hale. Courtesy of Dave Jones.

film and merchandise were enough, and seeing the band live was simply not that important anymore. There were other seminal acts who would give up touring in the years following such as Kate Bush in 1979, Leonard Cohen in 1993 and Michael Jackson in 1999. However, all would return (or intended to return in the case of Jackson) to live concerts eventually, although for different reasons, financial and artistic. Live popular music performance has therefore persisted and, because of changes in the music industry, is actually stronger today than it has ever been. The shift away from recorded music as the principal income of major artists (led by file sharing and downloads) and changing audience demands (due to the appetite for new leisure experiences) have led to a resurgence in the commercial importance of concert tours, which has in turn led to the creation in the last decade of new dramatic buildings designed specially to cater to this trend. The most publicized are large venues such as the O2 Arena, London (20,000 capacity, 2007); however, mid-sized and smaller buildings are also regularly filled to capacity. In addition, mobile staging for touring acts and festival events, such as the $60 million U2 360 degrees tour set, has reached an unprecedented level of sophistication, with new audio and video technology revolutionizing the way that popular music is presented.

The aim of this book is to be the first architectural history of popular music performance space, describing its beginning, its different typologies and its development into a distinctive genre of building design. Popular music architecture has been developed in ad hoc ways by a variety of non-professionals such as building owners, promoters and the musicians themselves. Professionals such as architects, designers and construction specialists have also had impact, but only in particular venue typologies, usually those that are large capacity. The story told in this book is therefore very different from that found in most other architectural histories (including classical music performance space). Performance venues have an important impact not only on the development of popular music itself, but also on many other aspects of urban life, influencing how a city may be perceived by its inhabitants and visitors. Like architecture, popular music itself is not static or standardized; it continuously develops and has multiple strands. The venue is a building type that is an essential component in the success of this immensely popular and culturally significant phenomenon that describes so clearly (and with, of course, so many apparent contradictions) what people think about their way of life and place in society. The aim of the book is to follow some of these strands in order to determine how music venue architecture has developed. However, this single volume is not an encyclopaedia, and because of the vast range and variety of popular music genres, it would be impossible to look at all the examples of where it is performed. Neither does it include in great depth the many technical issues regarding the equipment essential to the presentation of live popular music performance today as the detailed case studies of selected key venues featured in my earlier book, *Live Architecture: Popular Music Venues, Stages and Arenas* (2012), examined this aspect of their design. Instead, a narrative path has been charted that examines the main building typologies that have hosted some of the key movements in Western popular music. By examining both famous and less-well-known examples from the smallest barroom to the largest arena, the ambition is to chart how the buildings and spaces of live popular music performance have advanced from their beginnings into the sophisticated and diverse venues we see today, and to tell the story of popular music through the architecture that has supported its development.

I am highly conscious that there are many omissions in this book, in terms of not only specific music genres but also places where popular music is played. An example of the former is musical theatre, and of the latter, rehearsal and recording studios. I can argue that for the former, although it is a live event, it is more about the scripted theatrical process of storytelling than spontaneous live performance, and for the latter, the rehearsal and recording process is a very different one from performing and communicating live in front of an audience. Nevertheless, I wish there had been space in this volume to include some aspects of these performance types, as well as more selections from the countless live music scenes and venue typologies that can be found around the world. The book focuses on venues in Europe and North America with excursions to Australia, the Far

East and South America, not because there are a lack of fascinating venues in other parts of the world but because in a volume of this size the scope has to be limited in some way. If this book has a life beyond this edition, I hope I will be able to travel to these places, do the (enjoyable) research and fill these narrative gaps in the future. In the mean time, I hope the reader can appreciate the examples described here as just a sample from the hundreds of thousands of venues that exist, and hopefully some will have attributes that remind you of your favourite place. Please do not chastise me too much for not including them … the fact you value them signifies their relevance in this story.

Although based on a lifetime's experience as a music fan and part-time musician, architect and academic, the comparatively recent research that is the basis of this book would not have been possible without the support of a number of institutions and individuals. The School of the Arts at the University of Liverpool provided vital research support funds to enable visits to venues, archives and research contacts in the UK and the United States and also supported the granting of picture licences. The Tyrone Guthrie Centre, Annaghmakerrig, Ireland, provided a pivotal research retreat during two vital stages of the book's gestation. I would also like to thank the following for giving their time and sharing their knowledge during the interviews and visits that informed this book: Dave Backhouse architect, John Barrow (Populous), Mark Fisher (Stufish), Dave Jones (Cavern Club), Julia Jones (Found in Music), Jeff Horton (100 Club), Susan Lees (Liverpool Events Office), Bruce Raeburn (Hogan Jazz Archive, Tulane University), Jim Ritts (Paramount Theatre), Shane Shapiro (Sound Diplomacy), Jon Perring (The Tote), Dave Pichilingi (Sound City), Dick Vernon/Phil Miller/Jackie Slade (Glastonbury), James White and Carole Zeidman (Wilton's Music Hall). Thanks also go to all at Bloomsbury for supporting its production, including Leah Babb-Rosenfeld, Katherine de Chant, Ally Jane Grossan and Amy Martin. Finally, once again, it is impossible to understate the continuous backing, practical, emotional and intellectual, provided by my wife Lisa.

CHAPTER ONE

Introduction: Popular Music, Architecture and the Home

Music has always been important to human beings. As the musician, music producer and psychologist Daniel Levitin states, it is 'unusual among all human activities for both its *ubiquity* and its *antiquity*. No known human culture now or anytime in the recorded past lacked music ... Throughout most of the world and for most of human history, music making was as natural an activity as breathing and walking, and everyone participated.'[1] However, although an all-pervading activity, there are surprising areas of conflict in terms of its understanding. In industrialized cultures, there is a distinct split between performer and audience (the skilled and talented versus those who are supposedly not) and between classical and popular music (music of value and music of commerce). These splits occurred comparatively recently in the history of human development, within the last few hundred years, and, it can be argued, are paralleled alongside the development of specific buildings for music performance such as concert halls, which have elevated both performer and specific music types into places of higher status. The idea that classical music is serious and has greater merit compared to popular music is because of its history of control and patronage by the social elite. Although also used for popular music dissemination, it is also, at least in part, due to the development of musical notation that enabled its detailed recording by those with formal education.[2] A similar situation occurs in terms of the places of classical music performance – these are the celebrated buildings of the city, erected by those with power and resources at great expense and designed by the most well-known architects. A prime reason for undertaking this study was the fact that the architectural history of classical concert halls is well recorded (in books), but the architecture of popular music is not.

The debate regarding what can be defined as popular music is entangled with this demarcation between experience and type, engaging history, society, geography, technology and commerce. Musical styles are therefore best identified within discourses rather than types, as this accommodates the complex interactions that take place across boundaries between composers, musicians and audiences.[3] Sociologist Simon Frith has proposed that these discourses can be classified as folk, drawing from social function and tradition; art, deriving from an elitist stance where appreciation is formally taught; and pop, where musical experience becomes a commodity.[4] For this study, popular music is characterized as that which appeals to a wide range of people, encompassing a large variety of musical genres that has been disseminated via the media as a commodity through publication, recording and broadcasting. However, although the philosopher Theodore Adorno (1903–69) viewed the products of popular culture as a means to distract people from important social issues by the provision of pleasure, it is now recognized as a sphere of activity in which the public is actively involved in its critical appreciation, sponsorship and creation and is an art form that has real meaning in their lives.[5]

Girouard has pointed out that medieval cities were on the whole hard-working places, and for the vast majority, entertainment happened on the rare religious and civic holidays and as part of events such as fairs. Although music for pleasure might be performed at these times, a dedicated building was not required.[6] The focus of this study therefore begins in earnest in the eighteenth century when the first dedicated popular music entertainment buildings appeared, as did the availability of inexpensive sheet music tied into popular performers and songs. This research will not be restricted to specific music genres, for example folk, jazz, pop, rock 'n' roll, soul, rock or hip-hop, as there are many crossovers between musical movements that often, consecutively and simultaneously, occupy the same venue; however, the gestation of specific music scenes will be a part of the study as the character of the space and place they occupy is frequently part of the sphere of influence that has generated the building form. Music scenes are the subcultures or communities around which a particular cluster of musicians, audiences and other people active in music practice and the industry socialize and operate.[7] As a performance art, popular music necessitates places for events to occur and scenes to develop: 'Every artwork has to be someplace. Physical works, like paintings and sculptures, have to be housed someplace: a museum, a gallery, a home, a public square. Music and dance and theatre have to be performed someplace: a court, a theatre or concert hall, a private home, a public square or street.'[8] Popular music may begin in informal spaces, for example in the home or on the street, but its eventual success and widespread popularity depend on its migration to recognizable venues. This is because its popularity also leads inevitably to the commercial need to formalize a revenue process (initially to pay performers and composers, but as audiences grow, the many others engaged in enabling the performance), such as ticket sales for admission to the event.

As popular music performance became more formalized through the eighteenth, nineteenth and early twentieth centuries, small venues in drinking and eating houses became identified as concert rooms and nightclubs and larger buildings included music halls, variety and vaudeville theatres, ballrooms and dance halls. However, the buildings in which popular music performance has taken place are diverse. Many venues were created in spaces originally built for other uses, sometimes hastily converted by non-building industry professionals including the musicians and venue operators themselves. Despite their ad hoc creation, they may nevertheless be important in cultural terms, if not for their architectural qualities, then for the sometimes-unique activities and events that have taken place there. External spaces such as pleasure gardens and parks featured bandstands and amphitheatres, but also made use of more peripatetic facilities with floating and rolling stages. The large-scale touring arena and stadium stage set of today is a continuation of this development. Popular music also inspired famous festivals such as Monterey (1967), Woodstock (1969) and Isle of Wight (1970) that have a historical and developmental importance that is at least as relevant as permanent buildings. These events were powerful vehicles for communicating non-commercial ideals, demonstrating that popular music artists and audiences are not homogenous and are frequently fractured and rebellious, instinctively resisting rather than accommodating big business ambitions. There is a cultural and political commentary that invests the manifestation of popular music architecture that is expressive of important changes that have taken place in society, particularly since the end of the Second World War: 'It has always been through the live – public – experience of making and listening to music that it has been most deeply embedded in people's everyday lives and their understanding of their personal and social identities.'[9]

Live popular music performance can best be described as an *authentic* experience: every gig is unique; every individual's experience of it is personal, as musician David Byrne states: 'Music resonates in so many parts of the brain that we can't conceive of it being an isolated thing. It's whom you were with, how old you were, and what was happening that day.'[10] Music performance is an art form that is both experiential and transient. Memories that individuals have of attending a particular performance can be incredibly powerful, and there is a special kudos that individuals gain from having 'been there' when it took place. The power of the experience extends beyond the actual musicians' performance to the circumstances of the event, about which the most important factor is often the venue or location. The recorded memories of those who experienced them are especially valuable (made much more accessible in recent years via online forums and reviews), not only in describing the physical presence of the place but also the ambience that was created during the event.[11] Such reminiscences have been crucial for a study like this where so many of the buildings examined no longer exist or have been changed dramatically.

Popular music's relationship to architecture

The design and creation of venues are driven by both functional and non-functional requirements. Their character and form profoundly influence the performances they host and consequently how these performances are received by audiences, obviously because of the acoustics and view but also because of other environmental factors that shape human experience, such as air quality, temperature and smell. Venues are also part of the physical and cultural image of their settings – usually urban – from the street to the neighbourhood, city and region, and so these buildings fit into a city's urban morphology and influence its character and image. Venue activity is an important component in the creation of a scene, representing a coming together of people within specific social groups as well as differentiation from others. In her autobiographical book *Just Kids*, Patti Smith describes the importance of the New York Bowery venue CBGB: 'CBGB was the ideal place to sound a clarion call. It was a club in the street of the downtrodden that drew a strange breed who welcomed artists yet unsung. The only thing Hilly Krystal required from those who played there was to be new.'[12] Such venues are an embodiment of the diversity of the city and encompass all walks of life: social, economic and cultural. The number of venues varies over time, signifying economic and cultural changes, and although they are not immune to national or international influence, for the vast majority their impact is local. This is not to say that there aren't buildings whose influence in musical and cultural terms has not been wide and profound. Venues like the Cavern in Liverpool, UK, to the Apollo Theater in New York, USA, are internationally known for the crucial part they have played in the history of popular music development. It is important that venues like these are examined in this book, but there is also a place for lesser-known places, which may be important locally or archetypal in their design.

Why is this book needed now? Because the economics of live popular music are in transition, with large international promoters like AEG Live and Live Nation Entertainment (which merged with Ticketmaster in 2010) taking a much greater share of the business at all levels. On the positive side this has led to greater investment in higher-quality buildings (e.g. AEG owns and operates over ninety arenas globally, including the O2, Greenwich, London), but on the negative side this has had a significant adverse effect on independent spaces, now not only in competition with these 'branded' chains, but also frequently unable to book the most popular artists, who regularly sign exclusive deals with the promoter for both venues and ticketing. Recent studies have shown that grassroots venues are under threat from increased legislative and economic pressures: 'facing a "perfect storm" of issues which is affecting their long-term viability and sustainability'.[13] Although there have been positive signs that local and national governments are realizing the commercial and cultural value that live music brings to cities (sometimes called the night-time economy), historic venues are frequently still threatened with closure, and unless things change, it may soon be too late to save this disappearing legacy as a working, active musical scene that still supports the influential musicians of tomorrow.

Popular music in the home

Although this book is about live popular music performance venues – those buildings and spaces that have usually been designed or adapted for live music to be performed – there are other settings that have significant cultural and social influence on popular music's development. This happens even though it is perhaps only infrequently that live music performance before an audience occurs in them, for example clubs and events where the music played is from recorded sources (see Chapter 11). Perhaps the root from which all public performance begins is one of these non-venue places – the home – and as a primer to how the architecture of the space is an important element in the development of the music that takes place there, it is useful to examine it in this general introduction. Before radio or recorded music became commercially available, if people wanted to experience music at home they generally had to make it themselves, and amateur musicianship was seen not only as a mode of entertainment but also as an enjoyable pastime and a worthwhile, self-improving accomplishment. Middle-class families would gather around the parlour piano to sing, children would learn an instrument and entertain their parents at parties and groups of relatives and neighbours would form ensembles for their own pleasure. Individuals would be known for their skills and be persuaded to perform in and outside the home at celebrations and gatherings for entertainment or to accompany dancing. Music making in the home has 'played a significant but relatively unacknowledged part in the development of musicianship and local music cultures and communities'.[14]

Home-made music was encouraged and commercially exploited by the manufacture and sale of affordable instruments and sheet music. In the nineteenth-century music hall, variety and vaudeville stars sponsored particular songs during their tours, their names and pictures featuring prominently on the front of the sheet music, which made its way into the homes of thousands of amateur musicians. The advent of radio broadcasting in the 1920s enhanced home performance, providing the opportunity for listeners to hear particular stars more often and thereby enabling them to copy what they heard rather than having to read music. For example the first radio stations in the United States (such as WSB Atlanta, which first broadcast on 16 March 1922): 'More than phonograph records or movies ... showcased country music to millions of listeners and provided hundreds of performers the chance to make a living from playing it. In the process radio profoundly shaped country music.'[15] Cheaper, easier-to-learn instruments such as the banjo and guitar accentuated the notion that anyone could become a performer, and even perhaps emulate the artists they heard on the radio by also becoming a professional musician. Technological developments have changed the format upon which people listen: the Dansette Bermuda record player in the 1960s, the Sony Walkman in the 1980s, the MP3 player at the beginning of the twenty-first century and streamed music and videos via Spotify and YouTube today: but young people still make music in their bedroom, be it rapping along to a beat box, strumming a guitar with a few newly learnt chords or manipulating a software program on a laptop. This may be a familiar trope, but it is a real activity that many well-known artists have practised on their road to success.

However, the home can also be a place for public performance, something that has been enhanced in the twenty-first century through the internet and social media, and elsewhere in this book the way that domestic rooms used for social gatherings evolved into public places for performance is examined: rent parties spawning blues clubs (Chapter 3) and ballrooms inspiring dance halls (Chapter 6). The informal parties in homes sometimes led to parts of houses being converted to a readily available party space so that events could be held instantaneously, it being only a step away from becoming a formal, semi-commercial gathering place. One of the most famous of these is the Casbah in Liverpool, created in the basement of a Victorian villa at 8 Haymans Green, West Derby, Liverpool, by Mona Best, the mother of The Beatles' first drummer.

Created below the family home, the Casbah was inspired by the 2i's coffee bar in London with which the early British rock 'n' roll groups like Cliff Richards and the Shadows were associated (see Chapter 10). This unpromising space was just five narrow, mostly windowless rooms with bare brick walls and some plywood panelling, entered from the rear garden. Opening on 29 August 1959, Mona intended the place to be a safe, local hangout for the young friends of her son, although it was also a commercial enterprise from the start with membership cards and soft drinks for sale. The opening night saw a performance by the early Beatles incarnation, The Quarrymen (featuring John Lennon, Paul McCartney, George Harrison and Ken Brown – Pete had not yet joined, and Ringo was years away). Paul, George, and John and his girlfriend Cynthia (later his wife) had helped decorate the space, painting stars, a spider's web and a silhouette of John playing a guitar on the walls. The entrance room was where the tickets were sold and visitors left their coats, and inside, one of the rooms had an opening

FIGURE 1.1 *Location of the Casbah, which occupies the basement of a suburban house at No. 8 Haymans Green, West Derby, Liverpool. The entrance is at the rear – the door to the right in this photo. Source: Robert Kronenburg.*

through which the soft drinks and snacks were sold. The band would play here throughout their time in Liverpool, including the last night it was open on 24 June 1962. Since 2009, the Casbah has reopened as a heritage venue for visitors and occasional performances, the interior still largely as it was when used in the 1960s.

Home spaces are also used as temporary venues by artists who want to perform but have no venue, instigating 'house concerts'. The 1950s–60s folk music scene was primarily based around informal gatherings at small venues, often organized peripatetically, moving from place to place as somewhere suitable became available. Home concerts were an important part of developing a regular audience, both for the folk genre and for particular artists. Jacqueline McDonald and Bridget O'Donnell in (Jacqui and Bridie) were the first British professional female folk duo, and they founded their own folk club in 1961 in an early nineteenth-century coach house in St Michael's in the Hamlet, Liverpool, which was also their own home. Running their own club gave them the freedom to perform: 'In those days, as a woman on your own, you couldn't just go and sit in a pub ... You could do bits here and there, but we weren't welcome in a lot of the clubs. They were for the men, and women weren't expected to get involved' (Jacqueline McDonald as quoted in Wright, *Liverpool Echo*, 19 January 2011). On a Monday night, up to 100 people would cram into the Coach House Folk Club, until after three years its popularity outgrew the small room and it moved to a church hall. The duo later toured North America and Europe, performed before the Queen and regularly filled the Royal Liverpool Philharmonic Hall. Persisting for more than fifty years at numerous venues until 2011, the Coach House Folk Club featured sessions from famous artists including Ralph McTell, Tom Paxton, Christy Moore, Peggy Seeger and Ewan McColl, as well as other local musicians besides Jacqui and Bridie.

House concerts can also be created specifically as 'insider' events performed primarily to friends and fans, although they are also intended to create a buzz of excitement around the artist indicating that something special is happening, and the desire among those not involved to be a part of this evolving scene. Events like this have an authentic aspect to them that stands apart from the conventional commercial activity put on in normal venues with its attendant advertising, ticketing, queuing, fighting for the bar and the toilets. One group of musicians whose reputation grew substantially via such guerrilla gigs was the London-based band, The Libertines. In 2002–3, they would send out a text to everyone they knew to meet at a specific location and those who arrived first would be taken off to the gig location, often the Bethnal Green flat of band members Pete Doherty and Carl Barat.[16] Although without many of the trappings of normal gigs (and perhaps because of this), these events feel special and unique. Undoubtedly those who attend want to pass on the experience they have had, thereby creating a mythology about what happened on the night. These non-venue events have developed further with support systems such as the 'Helpyourself Manchester' network, which developed in that city in the early 2000s putting together a list of unconventional places for emerging acts to play. The internet has made exchange of useful experience and information easier with forums that trade tips on licencing and operation for unconventional gigs and home gig advertising.

Sofarsounds.com (short for 'songs from a room') started in London in 2009 when the start-up instigators Rafe Offer, Rocky Start and Dave Alexander went to a local performance and were annoyed by noise from the bar and impolite audience members. They decided to hold a quiet, informal gig in their North London flat with just a few friends listening to Alexander perform. More gigs were organized, advertised by word of mouth initially, and took place with the concept of two or three artists performing at each event; no headliner; bring your own drinks; supported by a modest fee (sometimes on a pay-what-you-want basis), most of which went to the performer. This strategy developed into a global online business with over 500 gigs performed every month in more than 300 cities around the world.

Most of the performances are in volunteer hosts' homes or non-venue-type premises such as shops and gardens. Sometimes thousands of people may request online for access; however, the shows are always small and intimate, usually maximum around fifty people, and this creates a special experience for the audience, artist and host. Speaking of a performance by Canadian artist Jane Siberry in her London Home, host Kate Godleman said: 'It was amazing, it was one of the most exciting things having her in my front room, with a guitar and a keyboard, and my mates and a few people who were fans of hers too. It felt more like a party than a gig.'[17] The value of the domestic popular music performance experience is that it not only predates the creation of dedicated venues but also provides a contemporary alternative.

The domestic setting has undoubtedly influenced the ambience of the popular music venue, particularly those that are the natural staging post to that first public performance. The practical experience of comfort and intimacy that most people seek in their home environment is a key element that is often generated in small venues such as pubs, bars and coffee shops, even to the inclusion of certain sorts of furniture (sofas and armchairs) and accessories (e.g. books and bookcases, real or artificial). There are also numerous venues that have been named for their association with domestic life (The Living Room, The Kitchen etc.). Also, a common way of identifying a venue is with the name of a person (e.g. Eric's in Liverpool, UK, and Stubb's in Austin, Texas), thereby implying that when you attend that place, you are visiting someone you know, someone who will host you and look after you. This references the fact that the design of popular music venues, unlike many other architectural fields, is not primarily driven by functional necessity, but by the need to create an ambience that reflects the character of the people who visit them – both audiences and musicians. The fundamental starting point of all architecture is shelter – the house, the home – a venue is a home for music. However, the diverse types of music and the different ways in which it is shaped by other cultural and economic influences have led to a wide variety of architectural forms. Some of these have stayed fundamentally the same since their inception (e.g. the home) and some have changed dramatically and continue to do so today. In order to tell this story as logically as possible, it has therefore been important to make some decisions about how to organize the research.

A methodology for examining popular music architecture

In telling the story of the popular music live performance venue, there is an unavoidable structural conflict between the desire to recount a chronological narrative and the need to examine it in terms of its typological development. A story is best understood if a clear path can be established that starts at the beginning (the middle of the eighteenth century has been chosen here) and ends in the present day. And yet building design development does not always work in this way – some typologies (e.g. the British public house), although they may differ in material construction, are very close today to when they were first created hundreds of years ago. Others (e.g. the arena concert venue) are dramatically different, first emerging in the late twentieth century, made possible by new technologies in both building construction and live performance equipment. The problem of developing a consistent chronological narrative is exacerbated further when the multiple strands of musical genres are involved as popular music scenes overlap continuously, emerging, prospering then declining at different times in different geographic locations (Plate 1). A decision was made that the clearest way in which to tackle such a complex, interwoven story was to look at the sorts of venues as they appeared and developed in different parts of the world, often in response to specific types of musical performance and entertainment – a primarily typological methodology.

Nevertheless, the structure of this book also does follow a discernible timeline, beginning with the design of early, dedicated music venues and ending with current and future developments. After this background introduction to popular music's relationship with architecture and the home, dedicated popular music venues primarily from the 1700s and 1800s are examined in Chapter 2: the smaller theatres used for music hall, variety and vaudeville in Great Britain, France and the United States. Chapter 3 looks at considerably humbler, but no less important buildings: the North American juke joints, honky-tonks and blues bars from the 1900s. The initial focus of Chapter 4 is 1900s New Orleans, investigating the street music, clubs and riverboats that subsequently influenced the jazz clubs that now exist around the world. The jazz story continues in Chapter 5, which explores the development of supper clubs, cabaret clubs and speakeasies beginning in the 1920s, continuing with examples in the United States, Great Britain, China, Paris and Berlin. The development of venues designed where social dancing is held is explored in Chapter 6: pleasure pavilions, ballrooms and dance halls from the 1700s to the 1950s. Chapter 7 examines the most common venue of the twentieth century, the public barroom, looking at examples in Australia, Ireland, the UK and the United States. The coffee bar as a venue for folk music, skiffle and early rock 'n' roll is also explored. While the history of theatre design is examined in Chapter 2, larger halls and auditoriums adopted as live music venues in the 1960s and '70s are explored in Chapter 8. The tours that made use of these theatres from the 1950s and the subsequent much larger travelling stages used in stadiums and festivals are examined in Chapter 9. Chapters 10 and 11 explore two recent developments in venue design: the late twentieth-century creation of giant arenas for spectacular live music shows and the history of recorded music scenes that has led to the phenomenon of the 'superclub'. Chapter 12 concludes with an investigation of the significance and value of the popular music venue and a further examination of its typologies, focused around the examination of three archetypal clubs, one that is lost – CBGB, New York; one that has persisted largely unchanged – the 100 Club, London; and one that has been rebuilt and reinvented – the Cavern, Liverpool. Hopefully, the reader will be able to navigate the time slips that have occurred between the chapters, by-products of the necessity to mark crucial developments as they have occurred in different types of performance and the venues in which they took place.

Wherever possible I have tried to find examples of buildings that are still in use today, both for my own first-hand experience and for the reader who is interested enough to go and have a look themselves. Where this is not possible, the descriptions of music venues in this book have utilized contemporary drawings and photographs; however, as stated earlier, the popular music venue is not like most architecture – much of it has not been chronicled in this way. It is not like the polite architecture of the classical music performance venue designed by professionals and recorded in architecture and construction journals and books. It has therefore been necessary to look in the contemporary popular press, in fan media and music papers, in films and videos, blogs and fan forums. Years of asking friends and acquaintances 'what is your favourite venue?' and 'what was the most memorable performance you saw there?' have also played a role in this study. Descriptions drawn from first-hand experience have ultimately played a large part in conveying the qualities of the venues: my own as a passionate music fan for more than forty years, or from others who were there at the time. The reader may therefore detect a larger proportion of Liverpool venues than might have been found in a book written by another author; however, as a cosmopolitan port city with a long and rich musical history, which is also a UNESCO City of Music, I make no apology for its availability as a rich source of good examples of popular music architecture.

Everyone who enjoys live music has felt that thrill of arriving at a venue in anticipation of a performance, either by a favourite artist or to see something new. Audiences and musicians engage with venues in this very specific way – we are there for an event, be it good, be it bad, be it memorable or best forgotten. In his book *How Music Works* (2012), musician David Byrne expresses the special nature of the artist/audience/venue synergy that this book attempts to investigate:

> There's something special about the communal nature of an audience at a live performance, the shared experience with other bodies in a room going through the same thing at the same time, that isn't analogous to music heard through headphones. Often the fact of a massive assembly

of fans defines the experience as much as whatever it is they have come to see. It's a social event, an affirmation of a community, and it's also, in some small way, the surrender of the isolated individual to the feeling of belonging to a larger tribe.[18]

Byrne figures (involuntarily) in the story about why this book's title was chosen: of CBGB, Talking Heads, and a close encounter at this important venue is told towards its end (at the beginning of Chapter 12). However, it also is meant to recall that impression which appears in every fan's mind as he or she crosses that threshold into a place of live music performance with anticipation and excitement … in these circumstances, we all might think that *This Must Be The Place*. Hopefully, this book will also add to the continuously developing narrative on how the many 'places' around the world came to be.

CHAPTER TWO

Music Halls, Variety and Vaudeville

Down a narrow street in a busy part of London there is a lane of old houses spared by the destruction of the Blitz and by the subsequent commercial redevelopment of the last sixty years. Although all around new buildings, roads and railway lines are crammed in, the visitor gets a feel of what the area was like 200 years ago. The houses are tall terraces, warm red brick and wooden sash windows, with stone and stucco detailing on the ground floor, indicating the buildings' fluctuating history from residences to commercial premises. The cast-iron bollards of this lane, which is called Graces Alley, block the path to all but bicycles and pedestrians and the old sandstone flags pave your way.

You enter the place of entertainment that is situated there not through some grand formal hallway but via a public house, pushing past punters having a drink or two before the show begins. With your ticket in hand, you walk up a cast-iron staircase and into the auditorium. It is a small, intimate space, perfectly shaped with the small stage to your right, the entrance placed on one of the sides of the U-shaped seating area. Barley sugar columns hold up a balcony that continues around the edge of the room, broken only by the stage. The arched ceiling is decorated with plaster fittings, once illuminated by 500 gas burners and a spectacular 'sunburner'. Faded decorations fill all the walls; they seem ancient but are in fact left over from a recent film shoot when the building was dressed to recreate its original purpose, a music hall.

Once the bell is rung, it doesn't take long for the audience to fill the rows of chairs set out for that night's show. The lights dim and a strangely dressed figure in a ragged men's suit works her way around the side of the floor, talking loudly to those she passes, passing the time of day, cheeky comments that raise bursts of laughter from those nearby. Climbing the steps at the

FIGURE 2.1 *Wilton's Music Hall, Graces Alley, London (1858). Source: Robert Kronenburg.*

side of the stage, a three-piece band pick up a refrain and she is into her first number, 'Champagne Charlie', amusing the crowd as it has done since it was first performed more than a 150 years ago. This is Wilton's Music Hall (1858), the most complete surviving example of a building type that was once both numerous and popular. Where once there were hundreds of music halls in use, present in every British town and city, patronized by every class of society, their performers well-known stars across the land, Wilton's is now one of only a handful of originals left. Although theatre endures vigorously, the theatrical experience that was music hall is all but gone, although its legacy of live performance of popular song and comedy is of course still very much alive in the music venues and stand-up bars that exist in every city, not just in Britain but around the world.

Theatre development

Musical interludes in dramatical pieces were reintroduced from classical precedents in sixteenth-century Italy. Initially, the music was played at set gaps in the play called *intermedi* and *intermezzi*; however, when merged with the rest of the performance, they developed into lavish musical dramas or *drama per musica*, with the first performances taking place in Italy at the very end of the sixteenth century and in Britain a few years later. In its early period of development, what would become opera was a courtly entertainment provided in private for the Italian nobility; however, in 1637 the first public opera house was opened in Venice, the Teatro di San Cassiano, named after the neighbourhood in which it was built. This new venue was sponsored by the Venetian Tron family, although the entrepreneur and composer Francesco Caletti-Bruni managed it from 1639, popularizing the musical drama as a new commercial entertainment for the paying public. This building was created in the pattern of theatres to come: a U-shaped space with an orchestra in front of the stage, a *parterre* (stalls) behind that could be filled with benches for the general public and galleries around the walls divided into boxes for the higher classes, or those who could pay more. Although the Teatro di San Cassiano was a stone building, replacing a former theatre that had burned down, it too suffered from several fires, and its more rudimentary studio facilities were soon overshadowed by the grander opera houses that were built in Venice to supply this new popular trend (ten by the end of the 1700). It remained in operation until 1807 and was demolished in 1812.

The first British theatres were adapted buildings used by touring performers, usually during special occasions such as fair days and public holidays. Humble buildings such as barns and larger rooms in inns were temporarily fitted out with simple mobile sets and stages. A galleried yard at an inn might provide a larger, open-air space, and it is possible this set the pattern for the great sixteenth-century Elizabethan playhouses in London such as the Rose, and Shakespeare's Globe recreated close to its original site on Bankside in London in 1997 thanks to the dedicated efforts of actor and producer Sam Wanamaker and architect Theo Crosby. Grander theatrical shows for higher social classes were held in great halls such as those at Hampton Court and Middle Temple Hall, again with temporary stages and sets. In the eighteenth century, travelling companies of entertainers worked on a 'circuit' across several counties, necessitating the building of modest theatres each of broadly similar size and scale so that the travelling sets would easily fit in. Although these were numerous, only one remains today in a recognizably authentic condition, The Georgian Theatre Royal (1788) in Richmond, Yorkshire. Commissioned by actor Samuel Butler, the theatre was one of the circuits he established throughout the north of England including other theatres at Beverley, Harrogate, Kendal, Northallerton, Ripon, Ulverston and Whitby. The room is shaped like a shoebox, a typical 'courtyard theatre' with two levels of galleries on each side and a floor (or 'pit') below.

The stage protrudes into the room, which holds an audience of 214 people. Productions often contained music. The Ballad Opera included sections of dialogue interspersed with lyrics set to popular tunes, and Pantomime included dancing and silent mimicry to music. Scenery, costumes and special effects were important parts of the show. Theatre going was a noisy business

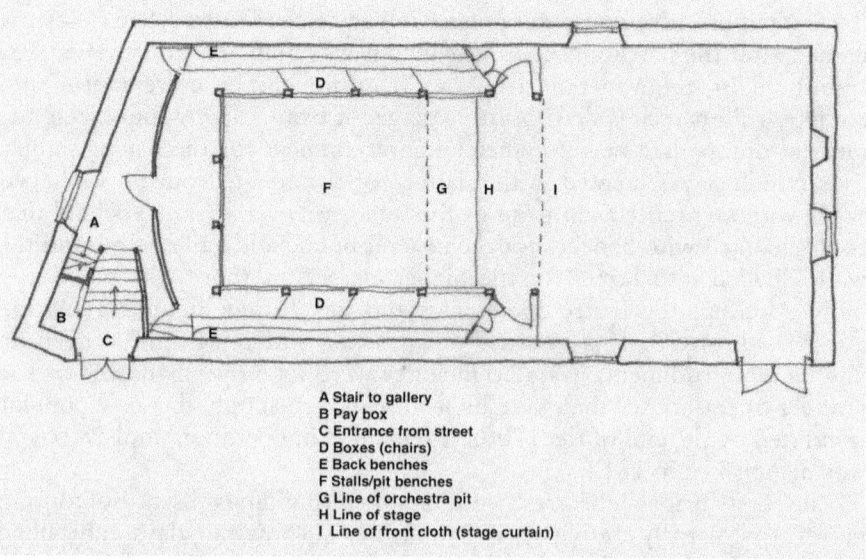

FIGURE 2.2 *Georgian Theatre Royal, Richmond (1788), ground-floor plan. Source: Robert Kronenburg.*

at this time, with patrons drinking and eating during the performance, and behaviour could become unruly with unappreciated participants in the show being bombarded with both comment and projectiles from the audience. The headquarters for the circuit theatres were usually larger and more prestigious venues and were sometimes granted a Royal patent such as the Bristol Theatre Royal (now known as the Bristol Old Vic), originally founded in 1766, although altered in 1790 and 1800 and reconstructed in 1881 to seat over 600 people. The grand Palladian entrance to this much-altered building predates the construction of the original theatre as it was originally the Coopers' Hall, built in 1744, and passed through many more uses before becoming the theatre's foyer in 1972. The theatre is still a vital part of the city's cultural life, redeveloped by Stirling Prize-winning architectural studio Haworth Tompkins in 2018.

The design of early dedicated theatre spaces followed the pattern of the informal spaces that had been adopted to house the travelling theatrical shows – a raised stage area, with a flat seating area in front for standing or movable benches, surrounded by boxes for more wealthy patrons. Construction followed the pattern of the day: early-seventeenth-century timber-framed buildings giving way to eighteenth-century brick structures supporting a wooden trussed roof to provide an open span space. The front façade was usually treated differently – dressed with stone details to create a grand façade. Columns supported the galleries and boxes, wood at first, then cast and wrought iron as construction technology advanced. Safety was a concern in building interiors that were shut off from natural light, which relied on open flame torches for illumination and special effects in the close vicinity of flammable stage props and scenery. In 1794, the Drury Lane Theatre in London was the first to introduce both a large water tank on the roof for fighting fire and an iron safety curtain, a device that is still in use today.

Economic decline and the growth of industrialization (and therefore cities) led to the end of the theatre circuit system, and by 1900 most of these buildings were either demolished or no longer in use for their original purpose (The Georgian Theatre in Richmond became an auction house), although larger urban theatres still flourished under the Royal patent, which gave them the exclusive right to perform drama. The performances in those theatres without a patent were forced to change their content to the 'burletta' – short sketches sometimes accompanied by music and interspersed with popular songs. These performances were varied, light-hearted and hugely popular with audiences. Ballet, jugglers and tumblers were also included, and although many theatres included sections for all classes (boxes for the well-to-do and the pit for the working class), they were quite rightly seen as places where drunkenness, prostitution and violence regularly occurred. In 1843, the Theatres Act reduced the powers of the Lord Chamberlain who had previously been able to veto any play, although it also required that premises wishing to present spoken drama had to obtain his licence. However, drinking was now banned in theatre auditoriums, changing the ambience and popularity of many establishments, particularly the smaller ones that were financially reliant on the sale of alcohol. This rule did not apply to the light entertainments presented by public houses and their associated concert rooms or 'salons', which could now also be licenced directly by local authorities. This was the legislative spur that encouraged the development of British music hall as a distinct entertainment venue.

Music halls

Wilton's music hall was established behind The Prince of Denmark public house at No. 1 Graces Alley, by permission of the local magistrate who awarded music and dancing licences to non-legitimate premises, such as public houses. Taverns and public houses like this had previously been the venue for casual 'singsongs' and 'free and easies' that gave way to more formal musical entertainment that grew in scale and scope. Concert rooms were built onto the existing buildings to complement other entertainments found at the bigger establishments such as skittle alleys or bowling greens. They were simple rectangular spaces similar to the 'circuit' theatres, with a small stage usually without wings or space above to fly scenery (because drama was not allowed!), benches on a flat floor in front and boxes or a gallery around the three remaining sides. Show times were continuous with people coming and going throughout, and the concerts 'became ever more ambitious, with operatic selections, ballads and male and female comic singers "in character"'.[1] As the entertainment became more and more popular, the original public house to which the concert room was an addition might be demolished and the whole site dedicated to a new music hall.

Wilton's was a grand version of its type, and first begun in 1853, it was developed when the architectural form of such theatres was already well established. Its founder, John Wilton, financed, developed and managed his hall and lived on the premises. Later he became the founder member, secretary and treasurer of the Music Hall Protection Society, which looked after the interests of its members. His first hall was built behind Nos. 1–3 Graces Alley, a small rectangular brick building with a rectangular gallery around three sides. Although a substantial construction, it was completely hidden from the street, with the entrance being through the pub with its famous mahogany bar. The booming music hall business meant that in 1858 he could set about redeveloping this original hall into a new larger building 17 metres (55 feet) long, 12 metres (40 feet) wide and 12 metres (40 metres) high, now built across No. 4 Graces Alley as well.

MUSIC HALLS, VARIETY AND VAUDEVILLE

FIGURE 2.3 *Wilton's Music Hall interior. ©Peter Dazeley.*

Bath-based architect Jacob Maggs (*c.* 1824–1900) designed the new theatre, although the actual construction was undertaken by builder Thomas Ennor and supervised by surveyor S. Charles Aubrey. Originally the interior of the building, which is the one that exists today, would have had brass chandeliers and gilded plaster details. Music took a prominent place in the opening night programme (28 March 1858) with six singers, a duo, a character singer, a pair of comic singers and dancers, and a burlesque singer and dancer. Typical songs of the period included 'Limerick Races', 'The Soldier Tired of War's Alarms', as well as 'Champagne Charlie'. These acts would have had to contend with a brilliantly lit 'supper' room, with much coming and going throughout the performance – waiters delivering food and drink, an audience who were drinking, eating, talking and wandering back and forth to the bar and catching up with friends and acquaintants. Nevertheless, the character of the architecture meant that the performances remained intimate with regular audiences building a relationship with familiar performers.

Music halls were built all over the country and they could often be as big or bigger than legitimate theatres; however, their architectural character was very different. The Britannia Music Hall, Glasgow (1859), now known as the Britannia Panopticon, could hold 1,500 people serving the city's bursting population of dockers and shipyard workers.

FIGURE 2.4 *Britannia Panoptican, Glasgow, Scotland (1859) (formerly the Britannia Music Hall). Source: Keith Edkins.*

Along with Wilton's, it is the only intact surviving 'supper room' hall. The original music hall's floor was a flat and open plan to allow either tables and chairs or benches. At this level, there would be a bar for alcohol sales and perhaps a food servery too. On one side there would be a platform, but of course no wings or flies for stage entrances or scenery. There would be a balcony at the first floor, or as at Wilton's, on three sides. Like many other provincial cities, Liverpool's first purpose-built halls opened in the 1850s, and through the next decade city centre halls such as The Parthenon, Star, Constellation, Liver, Cambridge, Oxford and Gaiety were built, and as the city expanded, music halls were built in the surrounding areas too. The last of these was the Pavilion, which opened on Lodge Lane in 1908, now a bingo hall and the city's last remaining music hall, although it has been so altered that its original purpose is now unrecognizable.

Variety

Throughout the 1870–80s, music hall architecture became more ambitious with the design and construction of larger, opulent buildings. Venue managers wanted to attract a wealthier, respectable, middle-class audience, which the wild and risqué reputation of many establishments had frightened away. Ballet was adopted by music halls from the opera houses where it had fallen out of fashion, and the new buildings that were built were designed to give more space to dancers and more ambitious staging, and therefore became more like legitimate theatres incorporating proscenium arch stages. There was less focus on the provision of supper tables and more on providing space for larger audiences. Many of the new theatres were made possible by the emergence of syndicated businesses (such as Edward Moss and Oswald Stoll, later combined to form Moss Empires), which overwhelmed the single proprietors and small companies such as Wilton's, who struggled to compete.

New safety rules enhanced this architectural trend towards the grand scale. Fire (or the fear of fire) had been a major cause of death in assembly buildings, with many people being injured or perishing while attempting to reach safety. A pivotal event was the Theatre Royal fire in Exeter. Destroyed by fire in February 1885, the building was rebuilt and reopened in September 1886. However, just a year later on 5 September 1887, a scenery drape was ignited by a naked gas flame and a fierce fire quickly caught hold. Of the 800 strong audience, more than eighty people were injured and 186 perished, many suffocating while trying to escape from a single, inadequate upper balcony exit.[2] New parliamentary legislation intended to inhibit the spread of fire and smoke was introduced, and adequate means of escape from all areas of theatre buildings now began to be enforced. Regular inspection of premises by the authorities, who were also interested in the public's morals as well as its physical safety, meant that many of the old backstreet concert rooms could not be brought up to standard and 'hundreds of lesser halls simply disappeared'.[3]

The larger, more salubrious establishments were called variety theatres (though the term music hall still persisted even into the 1950s) and were more family friendly with shows that a mother and her children could attend without fear of corruption. The buildings still had bars, although drinking was not allowed in the auditorium (though some had glazed partitions through which the stage could be seen). Catering to a growing middle class with disposable incomes, there was an increasing demand for dedicated entertainment buildings, and specialist architects emerged who understood not only the practicalities of good sightlines and means of escape but also how to create a vigorous and exciting interior space with generous use of elaborate decoration. Perhaps the greatest of these was Frank Matcham (1854–1920), although other nineteenth-century British architects known for theatre design included C.J. Phipps, Owen and Ward, Hope and Maxwell, and later, two of Matcham's former apprentices, Bertie Crewe and W.G.R. Sprague.

Frank Matcham was one of eight children and the son of a brewery clerk, who, after beginning his architectural apprenticeship in Devon, moved to London in 1875 to work with architect Jethro T. Robinson who had a valuable position as consultant to the Lord Chamberlain's office. In 1877, Matcham progressed from being the boss's employee to being the boss's son-in-law after wooing and marrying Robinson's daughter, Hannah Maria. When Robinson died the following year, the young 24-year-old architect took over the practice, completing his father-in-law's design for the Elephant and Castle Theatre (1879).

This was in fact a new theatre to replace a previous one built in 1872 and destroyed by fire in March 1878. Although not without its own problems (there was much dispute about the strength of the structure as it was being erected and a partial collapse led to a redesign), the new theatre was a huge success. Designed to hold 4,000 people, Matcham made much of the safety features it incorporated:

> The width of the proscenium is thirty feet, and the entire width of the house from side to side sixty-seven feet. There are four rows of stalls, and a very spacious pit, calculated to hold nearly a thousand people. The stalls have two exits, five feet six inches wide, and a spacious promenade extends round the pit, to which there are no fewer than three exits, two being five feet six inches, and the other, the main entrance in the New Kent-road, over seven feet ... One feature in connection with the gallery is a fireproof staircase, running underneath the whole length of the back of the house, in addition to three separate exits in other places. The whole building may thus be considered fireproof, so far as immunity from danger to an audience is concerned; and the same may be said in regard to the actors and actresses, whose dressing rooms are in a building separate from the Theatre.[4]

The theatre had an elephant sculpture above its entrance and was decorated in Moorish and Indian motifs – glamorous and exotic.

The success of the new building meant that Matcham's office became in demand for new commissions, and by 1888 he was supervising five theatres under construction and preparing plans for several more. During his career he completed more than 150 theatre buildings, new and rebuilt – the exact number is unknown, but it is certainly more than any other British architect since. His continued edge over his competitors was due in no small part to the innovations he introduced. He utilized a cantilever system incorporating steel beams in balconies to avoid columns that obscure sightlines, and this also improved the auditorium's appearance by making it appear tidy and uncluttered. He also paid attention to environmental issues, common in buildings designed to accommodate thousands of people and lit by heat-producing gas. He devised new ventilation systems for both the auditoria

FIGURE 2.5 *Elephant and Castle Theatre, New Kent Road, Southwark, London (1879) (now the Coronet Theatre) (photo c. 1920s). Source: London Metropolitan Archives/Collage.*

and the 'sunburner' lighting systems with adaptable ventilation systems including opening roof vents. He was also an extremely competent space planner, making these large spaces feel intimate and comfortable, with good views for all – even those in the cheaper seats. Some of his innovations added substantially to the flexibility of the entertainment space, for example the 4,000-seat Liverpool Olympia (1905) featured

> mechanical contrivances [which] are all that modern engineering, in all its necessary branches, can devise, and in this, as in all other features of theatrical building, the summit of perfection seems to have been reached. The very mat on the arena, which has hitherto occupied the labours of about twenty-six men, is expeditiously and simply drawn upon a roller by touching an electric button. The arena itself sinks by means of a similar contrivance, and 80,000 gallons of water takes its place, ready for any aquatic display which may have been arranged. The stage rises, falls, and moves backwards and forwards at the will of the electrician.[5] (Plate 2)

Despite his prodigious achievements, Matcham was never elected to the Royal Institute of British Architects.[6] Victorian decoration could be wild and garish, and Matcham's designs were undoubtedly in this category. However, he also took great pride in its quality, designing his own fibrous plaster system, from which many decorative features were made, so that he could be in greater control of the product. The architectural character of his theatres could not be categorized as they were decorated in a range of eclectic styles ranging between Baroque, Louis XVI, Italianate, Renaissance, Eastern and Oriental styles. Although these were not perhaps recognized as the height of good taste, they were vigorous, exciting and entertaining. As well as theatres, he designed many other entertainment buildings including circuses, opera houses, cinemas and, perhaps his most opulent creation, Blackpool's Tower Ballroom (1899) (see Chapter 8). Good examples of Matcham's Variety theatres remain in use today (including the Gaiety Theatre, Douglas, Isle of Man (1900), London Coliseum (1904) and London Palladium (1910)), although their survival has often been the result of long-fought campaigns by local enthusiasts; otherwise, beautiful buildings like Blackpool's Grand Theatre (1894) would not have survived. The local council approved its demolition in 1972 even though it was listed as of historic importance. Thanks to a concerted campaign, a public enquiry reversed this decision in 1973 and for a while it became a Bingo Hall, before reopening as a theatre in 1981 under the ownership of the Grand Theatre Trust.

Among the many impressive Variety theatres designed by Matcham was the Hackney Empire, Mare Street, London (1901). The theatre was commissioned by Oswald Stoll with the brief to hold a twice-nightly variety show, although it also had film projection facilities. The auditorium, which

FIGURE 2.6 *Hackney Empire, Mare Street, London (1901). Source: Ewan Munro.*

exists largely in its original condition, has three balconies, boxes at the dress circle level and seating for 1,500 people. The entrance elevation is a brick and terracotta mix of flamboyant Victorian Oriental design with twin domes, decorated arches, a balcony and a wrought-iron canopy. The foyer is decorated in Flemish Renaissance designs using alabaster, marble and vitreous tiles illuminated with electric lamps reflected in mirrors and gold detailing. When built, the auditorium was one of the largest in London, 24 metres (80 feet) wide and 23 metres (76 feet) deep (Plate 3). A sliding roof could be opened up for ventilation. Upholstered tip-up seating on Wilton carpet was used in the ground floor, dress circle and balcony. Entry to the 'gods' was at the back of the theatre with a long brick staircase to climb before paying the entrance fee to sit on the hard benches high up above the stage. There would also have been a pit with benches. Variety theatres were open to anyone who could afford the entrance; however, the different sections were strictly divided so that those in the pit and gallery never met the wealthier patrons in the more expensive seats.

Popular music was at the heart of the variety show. Dancing girls accompanied by the orchestra often opened the bill, followed by a comic who usually also sang a comic song or two. A speciality act that could fit on a stage, but might have had its roots in the circus followed – acrobats, balancing acts or juggling. The first half finished with a musical performance, usually a singer or perhaps a gifted instrumentalist. The interval would be a chance to go for a drink or to listen to the orchestra playing popular tunes in instrumental arrangements. More dancing girls started the second half, followed by either a comedian or singer depending on which of these was topping the bill. Each act was given a set number of minutes depending on their position on the bill (twenty at the top), and there was only fifteen minutes between the first and second houses during which the audiences would be changed round and the auditorium cleaned out (and ventilated by opening the roof if like the Hackney Empire it had Matcham's innovation).

A favourite act at the Hackney Empire was the comedy dance trio, Wilson, Kepple and Betty – Danney Varney recalls: 'The pair of Ancient Egyptians with their Cleopatra could always be relied on to bring the "ouse" down when making a welcome return to the Empire.'[7] One Variety star who transitioned the world of popular music and emerging media technologies was George Formby, who began on the stage then transferred to cinema but still performed live in Pantomime- and Variety-type shows almost until his death in 1961. Taking after his father, who was also a Music Hall star, Formby first began as a comedian, taking up the ukulele in 1923 and introducing it to his act that year. Largely under the supervision of his wife Beryl, Formby reinvigorated his act merging music and comedy, and by 1926 he had his first recording contract with Edison Bell/Winner. In 1932 he was with Decca recording the first of his major comic song hits immortalizing Mr Woo in 'Chinese Laundry Blues', one of more than 200 he would eventually record.

Variety continued until the 1950s when television began to have an increasing debilitating impact on audience numbers; however, even then the Hackney Empire continued to stage twice-nightly Variety shows that recreated the classic Music Hall era promising, 'LET THIS BE AN EVENING

YOU'LL NEVER FORGET – SING the CHORUSES YOU KNOW SO WELL! JOIN IN THE FUN! With the Ever Popular OLDE TYME MUSIC HALL.'[8] After an award-winning restoration and extension of backstage and front-of-house facilities in 2004 by Tim Ronalds Architects, the Hackney Empire continues today as a commercial theatre featuring a wide range of popular entertainment including touring opera, stand-up comedy and Christmas pantomime.

French music hall and vaudeville

The essence of music hall and variety – popular entertainment with music at its heart – was transported overseas. Although cabaret-style dance venues had existed in France since the eighteenth century, Parisian music hall began in the 1860s with famous venues like the Folies Bergére (1869) and the Moulin Rouge (1889). The Folies Bergére (originally Folies Trévise until 1872) was named after the street near where it was situated, rue Bergére (Shepherdess Street), and opened as a light entertainment venue, mixing comic opera, operettas, popular song and gymnastics. Designed by the architect Plumeret, its lavish Moorish-style building was based on the Alhambra music hall in London. In 1886, Édouard Marchand developed the show, moving it closer in character to music hall with a repeating revue mixing music and comedy, and wild dancing girls. This latter became the hallmark of the venue, enhanced under its long-running manager Paul Derval, with eroticism and nudity a staple of the typical Folies Bergére show.

The Moulin Rouge (Red Windmill) was created as a popular entertainment venue for the rich in a dubious yet fashionable Parisian district, Pigalle, close to Montmartre. The original 1889 building was full of incongruous yet entertaining features. Along with the windmill that sat over its main entrance, an open-air garden had a giant elephant sculpture alongside the stage and supper tables. The main hall was a large flat floor, which could feature dancing or shows, with the orchestra on a balcony above and the provision for quick changes of décor. Although comedy and singers featured, it is dance and its accompanying music for which the venue was famous, particularly the Can-Can, a highly energetic and potentially revealing dance (depending on what underwear was worn), which, although it was originally a mixed dance done by men and women as couples or alone, became the centrepiece of an erotic performance by elaborately dressed female dancers. The original Moulin Rouge burned down in 1915 but was rebuilt in a similar form and reopened in 1921. Risqué performers like singer and dancer Mistinguett (who debuted in 1895 but continued to perform into the 1930s) and the American Josephine Baker (who debuted with the show *La Revue Négre* in 1925) became huge stars earning large

FIGURE 2.7 *The Moulin Rouge, Boulevard de Clichy, Pigalle, Paris (1889) (postcard from c. 1900). Source: INTERFOTO/Alamy Stock Photo.*

FIGURE 2.8 *The garden stage at the Moulin Rouge. Source: Bettmann/Getty Image.*

sums and gaining celebrity status. Baker famously performed erotic near-naked shows at the Folies Bergére in the 1920s and 30s. Cinema was both a challenge and a saviour to French music hall buildings: many halls closing but also many converting to show the new moving images from the 1910s on, but also publicizing popular stars such as the singer Maurice Chevalier who played at the Casino de Paris in the 1930s while also acting and singing in Hollywood. As in Britain, television closed the vast majority of the music halls, although some still operate today attracting regular tourist audiences.

Although both music hall and variety were terms used in North America, vaudeville, a term perhaps deriving from the French phrase *voix de ville* (voice of the city, although other meanings have been proposed), was often used instead. However, all these terms described the same form of popular entertainment consisting of music, dance, comedy, 'alley oops' (acrobats), jugglers, short plays and sketches. As in Britain, vaudeville's emergence was as a commercial enterprise entertaining a growing population of relatively comfortably off urban workers and their families. It grew enormously popular with grand theatres built across the country, such as the 3,748-seat Koster and Bial's Music Hall built on Broadway and 34th Street, New York City, in 1893. Also similar to Britain, an important ancestor of vaudeville was the concert saloon where alcohol, gambling and free, often risqué, entertainment were combined (see Chapter 7). In the 1850s–60s, every town and city had concert saloons (as many as 300 in New York City). The concert saloon was usually a simple barroom with a flat floor with tables and an area set aside for performance, often retrofitted with a simple stage, and perhaps even a means of staging scenery. Some grander establishments took over theatres, and some had private boxes or 'rooms' often associated with unsavoury activities.[9] Although travelling entertainment in nineteenth-century America was diverse with wild west shows and medicine shows, the main influences on vaudeville-style entertainment were burlesque and the minstrel show. Early burlesque shows from the 1840s were modelled on the British version that mocked high culture with short sketches that made fun of opera, ballet and legitimate theatre. It developed by the 1880s to focus on the female form with beautiful female performers dressed in alluring minimal costumes transforming by the 1920s–30s into striptease, whose most famous exponent was Gypsy Rose Lea. The minstrel show or minstrelsy was a touring performance that emerged in the early 1800s and peaked in the 1830s–40s. Largely performed by white people made up as blacks (although some outfits did incorporate African American performers, usually under white management), the shows consisted of music, dancing and short comic sketches, mocking African American people. Despite these drawbacks, 'The minstrel show was once the only way into the theatre for blacks, and they perforce took it over, with all the cruel stereotypes, as a main outlet for their talents as professional entertainers.'[10] Undoubtedly racist, even at the height of their popularity, the shows had their critics among slavery abolitionists. However, they have also been described as the first uniquely American form of theatre, and when spirituals (called jubilees at the time) began to be included in the 1870s, they were responsible for introducing the first unarguably original African American music to a general audience.

Like variety, vaudeville was a 'cleaned-up' version of these types of shows devised in order to widen the audience to include women and children and thereby increase the size of the house. The first impresario to stage shows of this nature was New York theatre manager Tony Pastor, a former ringmaster and minstrel show operator who in 1865 took over the Volks Garden, a concert saloon at 201 Bowery, and renamed it Tony Pastor's Theater, with entertainment promising 'fun without vulgarity'.[11] Pastor moved uptown to the more respectable entertainment district of Broadway in 1875, and then finally to New York's emerging theatre district on 14th Street in 1881, leasing the smaller of the two auditoria in Tammany Hall on Union Square.

Completed in 1868, this was a grand four-storey, multifunctional building designed to be the headquarters for the Tammany Society, a political association centre of the Democratic party. However, it also contained multiple entertainment facilities, including a gymnasium, barrooms, an oyster saloon and a ladies' café. After a relatively unsuccessful theatrical show, Pastor created a variety show featuring female singers such as Lillian Russell, affecting and feminine rather than raucous and rude. The theatre, which Pastor styled as 'the Great Family Resort of the City', later featured Buster Keaton, before he became a famous silent film star, and the then new ragtime music performed by Ben Harney. By the 1890s, several vaudeville circuits were established throughout the United States and Canada, initially created by Boston entrepreneur B.F. Keith; however, others such as Martin Beck (Orpheum Circuit) and Alexander Pantages (Pantages Circuit) expanded further until the movie business saw vaudeville's audiences gradually dwindle in the 1920s and 30s.

One theatre that was built to host the travelling vaudeville and minstrel shows that still exists today is the Riley Center (1890) (originally Grand Opera House), Meridian, Mississippi. Begun in 1889, the building exterior was designed in a Victorian Romanesque style by local architect Gustavus Maurice Torgerson, who also designed the city's town hall; however, the auditorium was designed by experienced theatre architect John Bailey McElfatrick (1826–1906) who, with his sons William and John, designed more than 200 theatres across the United States. The McElfatricks' buildings emphasized simplicity and elegance as well as safety, and in the United States, they were 'the first in the city to be built on the ground floor, the first to have multiple exits, the first to have proper dressing rooms, the first to have sprinklers'.[12] Meridian's Grand Opera House was, however, on the first floor, the ground floor given over to commercial retail space, shopping also being a new pleasure pastime for the middle class. The developers

FIGURE 2.9 *Postcard showing Tony Pastor's Theatre (1881), at Tammany Hall, 14th Street, New York. Source: Harry Ransom Humanities Research Center, University of Texas at Austin.*

FIGURE 2.10 *The restored Grand Opera House, Meridian, Mississippi, USA (first built in 1890, photo 2012). Source: Katyrw.*

and owners, I. Marks and L. Rothenberg, engaged staff who would work in both the department store and operate the theatre, selling tickets and managing the stage. The auditorium was cleverly designed with good sightlines (although the balcony columns obscured these somewhat) and acoustics and was lit by a 'sunburner' chandelier. The theatre was not used between May and September because it was too hot in the summer months. Although the theatre opened with two German-language operas and on occasion hosted highbrow presentations including Sarah Bernhardt in *Tosca* and Henrik Ibsen's *Ghosts*, the stock fare was travelling shows: vaudeville, minstrel shows and melodramas.[13] A provincial theatre such as this served the whole community including farmers and other working-class people including African Americans, whose seating was in a segregated 'crow's nest' balcony at the very top. However, when the African American touring company of trained opera singer Matilda Sissieretta Jones, the Black Patti Troubadours, gained popularity, their seating for this vaudeville-style show was extended to the dress circle.[14] From 1902 the Grand Opera House also showed moving pictures and eventually installed fans to compete with the other movie houses that were beginning to open in competition; however, inevitably the growing popularity of cinema led to the theatre's closure in 1927. Because of legal complications, it sat vacant for decades, used for storage by the adjacent department store, and as has often happened, by accident rather than design, in due course the building was still intact enough to be considered for restoration and reopening. After decades of delay and fundraising, the building's future was secured by a $10 million donation from the local Riley Foundation to eventually become a centre for the performing arts and education.

Music hall's legacy

Though cinema and new forms of popular music like rock 'n' roll had an effect, variety finally ended in theatres primarily because it was taken over by a remarkably similar form of entertainment on television: the variety show. Many of the most famous entertainers transitioned to television on shows such as the BBC's *The Good Old Days* (1953–83) in Great Britain and CBS's *The Ed Sullivan Show* (1948–71) in the United States. *The Good Old Days* was performed in Leeds City Varieties (1865), one of the few music halls still in original condition, and all the performers and audience dressed in 'period' Victorian costume. *The Ed Sullivan Show* (originally the *Toast of the Town* show) was originally broadcast from the Maxine Elliott Theatre (1909) on Broadway, which had been converted to a television studio in 1948, before moving to the former Hammerstein's Theatre (1927), then CBS Studio 50, which was later renamed the Ed Sullivan Theatre. The theatre is situated on the ground floor of a thirteen-storey brown brick and terracotta office building designed by the prolific theatre architect Herbert J. Krapp (1887–1973) in neo-Gothic style, as was the interior of the theatre. Any form of entertainment could feature from ballet and opera to comics and popular music, and this traditional approach with resident dancers (The Toastettes) and orchestra included many appearances by former stage stars – Sullivan even tagged the new show 'vaudeo', combining vaudeville with television.[15] Sullivan's approach made it easy to respond to changing audience tastes, including adding beat and rock music to his lineup – famously, The Beatles were introduced to an American audience with a Brian Epstein-negotiated top-billing slot on three Sundays in February 1964. In 2005, the theatre was refitted to bring it up to standard for high-definition broadcasting covering some of the original 1920s fittings and removing others for storage so that in the future they can be refitted, which was fortuitous as in 2015 the theatre was restored to its 1927 appearance (though with fewer seats) including revealing its dome and reinstalling its stained glass and its wooden chandelier.[16]

Some variety-style artists became television stars in their own right hosting hugely popular programmes featuring comedy and music as integral interwoven components. The double act of Eric Morecambe and Ernie Wise, who were variety stage artists from 1941, became the basis for the *The Morecambe & Wise Show*, which was broadcast on radio and then television from 1954. In 1959 they topped the bill on the Boxing Day edition of *The Good Old Days* and continued working in television into the 1980s. Similarly, Dean Martin and Jerry Lewis, who debuted on Ed Sullivan's first show in 1948, utilized slapstick and vaudeville jokes in their musical comedy club act, before becoming television and film stars in the 1950s–70s. Martin hosted his own variety show, *The Dean Martin Show*, on NBC from 1965 to 1974.

The reason so few early music hall buildings survive today is that they were purely commercial enterprises. They were created by entrepreneurs who managed them to make money – if they were popular they thrived, if not they died. If they could not be made to pay, then the building was either converted into another use (such as a cinema in the early twentieth century or a bingo hall later on) or demolished to make way for something else. If they were successful and the building in which they were established became too small for the potential audience, they were torn down and a bigger one built. Fashion also played a part in this exercise as audiences turned to newer establishments with new decorations or other improvements. These grander buildings stood more chance of finding other uses and consequently significant theatres designed by Frank Matcham and other architects working in the field have survived, in no small part due to the high standard of functional design, which meant they could still operate as usable entertainment spaces, even if the nature of the show had changed significantly – for example as a television theatre, or as a popular music venue (see Chapter 8). Good sightlines, good acoustics, efficient ventilation and good means of escape could be improved upon with modern technology to reach contemporary standards of comfort and safety. For the contemporary theatre or concert goer, these buildings with their opulent, often eccentric decoration provide an instant, immersive time machine to a past era of entertainment, when going out for the evening was a passport to another brighter, more exotic world. It was also a world where to be entertained was to be actively involved with what was happening on stage, to boo the villain, cheer the heroine, laugh out loud and sing along. The theatre auditorium was not decorated just to provide an attractive space in which to sit while waiting for the lights to go down – it was to extend the performance space into the audience, who participated in the show.

CHAPTER THREE

Honky-Tonks and Juke Joints

The band are already up when I enter the bar. Before I entered, I could see them through the window from the street, crammed together on a small stage right next to the door. Outside, although the street is wide, the buildings are mostly just two or three stories, and there is something about it that makes you feel it has seen better days – a street in transition, its continuous line of brick-fronted buildings and storefronts changed dramatically by the addition a few years earlier of a large sports and events arena. Inside the bar on this Sunday afternoon there may be some tourists, but it seems mostly a local crowd. The band aren't playing as the frontman is leaning on his guitar and talking through the 'mic', halfway through some story, which at least a part of the audience is listening to. It's a long oblong-shaped room with the stage and door on the short side and the bar stretched along a good portion of the long side. The place isn't full but there are enough people there to make it convivial, and worth the musicians' getting started ... but they are in no hurry. By the time I have bought a drink and found a place to sit at one of the small tables near the front, they still haven't begun a tune – then someone walks up from the back and passes the talkative guitarist a few dollars, he leans down away from the 'mic', listening, then nods, stands up and says a few words to the band. 'This one's for Lisa', he says, and away they go with a Hank William's number played so sweetly with acoustic guitar, double bass, fiddle, a three-drum set and harmonies that a tear comes to my eye. The singer is Jesse Lee Jones, and the band is Brazilbilly. They are the house band because Jesse owns the bar: Robert's Western World, on Lower Broadway, Nashville.

On the opposite side of the room is a wall of shelves filled with cowboy boots, some with price tags on, and as it gets darker outside, the neon beer advertisement signs reflect off the pressed metal ceiling, and more people start to filter in. Jesse's band play song after song for hours, each with a pause in between, getting shorter as the bar gets busier and people (after a

FIGURE 3.1 *Robert's Western World, Broadway, Nashville. Source: Robert Kronenburg.*

few drinks) loosen their wallets, allowing the requests to come faster. There is no cover charge at Robert's – the band earn their keep from the tips for playing your song, and their repertoire is consequently huge, turning down a tip because you don't know the tune isn't going to pay the bills. The crowd get noisier, particularly over on the bar stools, but the band get louder, and there is always loud applause at the end of every song. A few couples start to dance in the tight space in front of the stage, and although I'm here on my own I fall in with my neighbours sitting at adjacent tables and I too start talking as well as listening (Plate 4).

When I finally head out onto Lower Broadway, its dark and all the Honky-tonk bars' neon signs are lit. Music is coming out of every door, live and recorded. The record store is still open, Ernest Tubb's Record Shop from which his famous *Midnite Jamboree* radio show was broadcast from 1951 – Patsy Cline and many other stars sang in there and the show is still broadcast on 650AM WSM every Saturday night. The transition of this street is now clear, from an urban, working-class entertainment area to an internationally recognizable music history destination, striving to attract business not just from the city of Nashville, but around the United States and the world.

This transition has been a long process. After the Second World War, the building that Robert's inhabits was a warehouse and office space for the merchants whose business interests lay in the river traffic that operated from the Cumberland River port at the bottom of Broadway. By the 1950s the city had become synonymous with country and western music, and the building was being used by the Sho-Bud Steel Guitar Company manufacturing and selling Dobro-style guitars. In the 1980s Sho-Bud's interests were taken over by Gretsch guitars and the building became a liquor store, squeezed in among rundown bars and porn shops, a sign of the depressed state of the area. By 1992, however, the building housed a Western boot and clothing store and was called Rhinestone Western Wear, soon to become Robert's 3 Doors Down as the owner, Robert Wayne Moor, added a juke box and began to sell beer and cigarettes to boost his income. In 1999, Moore sold the bar to Jesse Lee Jones, and what had now become Robert's Western Wear Bar and Night Club finally went global with its current name.[1] In 2017, Robert's Western World sits next to Layla's (Nashville Hillbilly Music), two doors away from The Stage as well as The Second Fiddle, and three doors from Tootsie's Orchid Lounge. Its location is literally just around the corner from the Ryman Auditorium, the birthplace of country music's commercial success where the syndicated Grand Ole Opry radio show began in 1925. It's fair to say that the primary business strategy for Broadway residents is running a honky-tonk.

Honky-tonks

The story of vaudeville is primarily one of influence from Europe via Music Hall and variety; however, the story of honky-tonks and juke joints is clearly the reverse, for in the years before and after the First World War, it was in these small, informal, sometimes barely legal venues that the principal strands of global popular music performance would be forged – blues, country, jazz and rock 'n' roll. Although Robert's Western World is an urban venue, juke joints and honky-tonks began as rural places of relaxation and entertainment.

The term honky-tonk does not have a reliable source, although it was first found in Texas newspapers such as the *Daily Gazette* (Fort Worth, Texas), 24 January 1889; *Morning News* (Dallas, Texas), 6 August 1890; and *Galveston Daily News*, 26 July 1892, describing bawdy places of entertainment with alcohol and dancing – an entertainment recourse for the poor white population of the Southern states.[2] Honky-tonk is also a style of music derived from ragtime, upbeat and played on the piano like boogie-woogie, although it also became a style of country music from the 1930s. However, the home-made music of the rural South was 'hillbilly' made with the fiddle, banjo and guitar, closely related to the Irish and Scottish traditions from which it was drawn, telling tales of home, love, hardship and grief. Artists like the Carter Family presented the sort of music that was being made by people who worked in the field by day and then entertained each other by night. One of the roots of the honky-tonk is in the harvest dances and roundup parties that took place on special occasions when skilled local amateurs provided the entertainment, especially for dancing. The rural dance hall is still a common type of honky-tonk venue, a building used regularly but not nightly for musical and dance gatherings, essentially a community centre and local meeting place. However, the archetypal honky-tonk is a more ambiguous place, where alcohol and sex play a large part along with the conversation, music and dance. In the 1930s, changes in the rural economy instigated by the Great Depression, industrialization and the oil boom led to an uncertain income and transient lifestyle for many rural businesses, consequently putting pressures on family life. This fed into the subject matter of commercial country music, which became nationally and internationally popular via Nashville's WSM radio station. The honky-tonks became places where this music could be developed, but also where audiences could go to hear the radio stars in person. For example, Ernest Tubb championed a new sound in the 1940s merging traditional country with Western swing played with electric guitars, which he continued to play in concert halls and honky-tonks touring consistently into the 1980s.

The honky-tonk was generally placed on the outskirts of towns where both low property values and lack of neighbours were advantages. Surrounded by a large area of land for the cars and trucks that the rural population needed to access the venue, most were and still are unprepossessing buildings, functional rather than beautiful, the only indication of their purpose being a sign by the highway. A typical location is 'Frontage Road', a strip of gravel and tarmac that lies parallel to the main highway that passes by the town on which truck stops, gas stations and cheap motels can be found. On the border between counties where it is illegal to sell alcohol on certain days, the county-line venue is common. Texas newspaperman Bill Porterfield recalls a typical venue, Rob's Place in Robstown:

> a long, low rectangle of a building, white slapboard, which faced U.S.77 south of town ... As you entered, the front part of the building had a bar on the right side and on the left, tables and chairs and a couple of pool tables and marble machines and a shuffleboard ... If you wanted to dance, you had to walk through a gate in a little wooden fence that cut off the dancefloor from the front.[3]

Honky-tonks were frequently open all day to cater for those who worked shifts during the night, and you could drink and eat and dance to the jukebox without paying for entry. A local band playing in the evening usually required a cover charge, and when one of the bigger stars came through, the price went up. Dancing is a key part of the honky-tonk experience, with specific dances such as the Polka, Waltz, Two-Step, Scottische and the Cotton-Eyed Joe, the latter inspired by and usually accompanied by the traditional folk song of the same name, which dates back to the 1880s. Honky-tonks were not necessarily places of disrepute; however, they were for working people: 'farmers, laborers, truck drivers, and displaced rural dwellers', and bad behaviour and fights were not unknown, in which case 'the best bet was to keep dancing'.[4]

One of the most famous rural honky-tonks is the John T. Floore Country Store, in Helotes, Texas, which opened in 1942 as a grocery, meat market and dance hall. Although open only three days a week (the store used to be opened seven), all the great country music stars played at Floore's, including Hank Williams, Patsy Cline, Ernest Tubb and George Jones. Porterfield describes Floore's as: 'One of the greatest dance floors in Texas, bar none.'[5] The founder of the venue, John T. Floore, was a music promoter and manager of San Antonio's Majestic Theatre who had access to the big up and coming acts that passed through the South, so the artists and musicians who played there are more out of the ordinary than many other similar venues, including Elvis, Little Richard, Jerry Lee Lewis and Bob Dylan. Willie Nelson, who has played regularly at the venue since the 1950s, still returns. It is an unpretentious building with green painted cinderblock walls, a low corrugated metal ceiling and a concrete floor. The outside of the single-storey building is covered with signs: 'DINE AND DANCE', 'WORLD'S BEST HOME MADE TAMALES' and 'BIG NAME COUNTRY WESTERN SWING BAND SAT.9.00PM'. Inside, the decorations are the ubiquitous illuminated beer signs together with old boots, hats and the odd lariat suspended from the trussed metal rafters that hold up the roof. A row of steel columns runs down the centre of the dance floor towards the stage, which is only knee height from the floor due to the low ceiling. Larger

FIGURE 3.2 *The John T. Floore Country Store in 1942 – looking much as it does today. Source: John T. Floore Country Store.*

concerts take place outside on the 'patio', although this is actually a much larger stage with room in front for a thousand people or more. A metal and wood lean-to with a corrugated roof covers the stage, and picnic benches provide the seating (when it's used, as the more famous artists frequently sell-out).

A special feature of Floore's, as with other honky-tonks, is the informality of the venue. All tickets are general admission, and the audience can get as close to the artist on stage as they can manage. If you want a seat at a table, its first come, first served, and for many, the dancing is as important as the music. As well as the big-name concerts, there is free-entry family dancing to a live local band every Sunday. Today, the vast majority of the audience still arrive by car; however, they are as likely to be office workers from San Antonio as farmers or oilmen, and because of the more varied styles of country music, the type of crowd varies, with a quieter, older, respectful audience for traditional artists such as Nelson and Dwight Yoakam and a rowdier kind for young country rock bands such as Whiskey Myers.[6]

A honky-tonk can also be an urban venue, such as Robert's in Nashville; however, at least inside, the architecture has the same character and

FIGURE 3.3 *Floore's patio stage. Source: John T. Floore Country Store, photo: Mike Berger.*

atmosphere. The buildings they occupy are simply adapted from whatever use they had before, whether a warehouse and office building such as Robert's or a community hall such as Rob's. Where they have been built for the specific purpose, the design is not done by professionals – the buildings are constructions rather than works of art. And after all, they are simple in function – a single open space within which there is a place to dance, a place to sit and a place for the musicians to stand. Ancillary support spaces such as kitchens, bar stores and toilets are add-ons – either separated from the main space by a cinder block or wooden wall or tagged on to the outside. The outside appearance of the out-of-town building is not important, its purpose conveyed by signage, and even here the venue's name is less important than what it purveys – music, dance, food and alcohol, writ large in big letters so it can be seen from the road down which its clientele arrive. Urban ventures must compete harder to attract their customers so large neon signs and gaudy decorations are common. The Broken Spoke, situated a couple of miles south of Austin's city centre on South Lamar Boulevard, is typical. Built in 1964 and still operated by its original owner James White, it is a low one-storey shed with a wooden façade illuminated by neon signs proclaiming 'Dining & Dancing'; there is also another in the shape of a steer. A large residential project surrounded the building in 2013, leading to fears the famous old venue would disappear; however, the Transwestern development company's Vice President Ty Puckett instead integrated the honky-tonk into the project and extended its ground lease, not wanting to be responsible for seeing another one of the 'great spots that made Austin get torn down'.[7]

After passing through the venue's entrance (which proclaims 'Through this door pass the best country music dancers in the world'), you enter the restaurant area, which has tables covered with plastic gingham tablecloths, with a full-size stuffed cowboy dummy sitting at one of them. A small

FIGURE 3.4 *The Broken Spoke, South Lamar Boulevard, Austin, Texas, entrance door. Source: Robert Kronenburg.*

bar separates this room from the dance floor beyond, and passing beside this, in exchange for a few dollars, you get an ink stamp on your hand and pass through. Signs tell you not to stand on the dance floor but plenty do, keeping clear of the whirling couples doing the Texas Two Step to a hot country band. The room is low and the décor rustic, a low, patched suspended ceiling with illuminated beer advertisement signs and fluorescent tubes providing the ambient lighting. On either side of the floor is an open frame made from pieces of untreated sawn wood, which separates off the sitting area, more simple tables, plastic tablecloths and unmatched chairs.

The band play energetically at the end of the room, on a stage just a few inches high, not letting the dancers rest, playing throughout their two- to three-hour set without a break. The Broken Spoke has seen many country music greats including Bob Wills, Kitty Wells, Kris Kristopherson, George Strait and Willie Nelson and in March 2017 Garth Brooks gave a secret show there. Although it has had its moments of fame, the Broken Spoke is a local venue, supporting local musicians catering to a knowledgeable enthusiastic crowd. It is a traditional honky-tonk in which dancing is a huge part of the experience and the dancers part of the show. It's a venue that provides friendly, loud, exuberant entertainment that has hardly changed in the five decades the place has been going.

FIGURE 3.5 *The Broken Spoke – Texas Two-Step on the dance floor. Source: Robert Kronenburg.*

Juke joint

While the honky-tonk origins are as an entertainment venue for white Southern rural working people, the juke joint has a similar reason for developing, although for African Americans. The historic roots of the juke joint may well be in the rooms occasionally erected on plantations for the slave workers in the nineteenth-century American South, a practice that migrated to remote rural work camps for industries such as logging and turpentine manufacture. They were an essential, although humble, place for the workers to relax, with drinking and gambling being the main attractions. Juke or jook is thought to be derived from the Gullah language word *joog* for disorderly. Gullah is a language that developed in the eighteenth century among enslaved Africans transported to the coastal regions of the southern American states of Florida, Georgia and South Carolina. Other names for these venues were barrelhouse (because of the barrels used for containing beer but also, perhaps, subsequently their use in the construction of cheap furniture) and chock house (chock being a cheap form of home-brewed alcohol).

By the twentieth century, juke joints could be found at convenient locations by the side of roads – at crossroads, on the edge of town, away from authority and the law. They were a place where hard-working African

FIGURE 3.6 *Juke joint and living quarters Belle Glade, Florida, February 1941.*
Source: *Marion Post Wolcott, Library of Congress.*

Americans could spend time socializing away from white authority, which was usually harsh and driven by prejudice. Although a version of the urban bar or nightclub, the juke joint was usually a ramshackle building adopted from another function or erected at minimum cost from materials that were easy and cheap to obtain. The 1930s/40s photographs of Marion Post Wolcott, who worked for the Farm Security Administration (FSA) during the Great Depression, depict the harsh lives of African American rural workers.[8] The juke joints she photographed were crude wooden shacks, usually no bigger than a sharecropper's cottage.

The original building had usually been built at minimal cost by a landowner, which came as part of an agreement including the provision of land, tools and seed, enabling the landless farmer to scrape a living by keeping a part of the profits from the crop he raised. The simple wooden-framed building would be built on a slightly raised wooden platform, with wooden board siding, a shingle or metal roof, and a brick chimney to one side. Some were reused slave cabins. Conversion work was minimal. Inside, the wooden walls would be decorated with advertisement posters and there would be a simple bar area with the drinks stacked on shelves behind and some wooden seats or booths. External decoration might consist of a beer advertisement, announcing that this was now a commercial establishment rather than someone's home. Alan Lomax, who travelled through the Mississippi Delta in the 1930s and 40s making field recordings of local musicians, describes one such juke joint:

> Hamp's Place was a shack in the middle of an enormous Arkansas cotton field. A country store in the daytime, night transformed it into a dance hall and gambling joint. The light blue walls were plastered with brilliant snuff, baking powder, and roll-your-own advertisements. But the main business of the store was selling country moonshine, as clear as springwater and as fiery as the 4th of July in West Hell. The price was reasonable, so we bought a jug and passed it round, and the crap game in the corner broke up and the Arkansas folk gathered round quietly to hear Willie Brown [a Blues musician who recorded with Son House and Charley Patton in the 1940s] perform.[9]

The music of nineteenth-century juke joints was made by the fiddle and banjo – reels and jigs, an Irish/African American hybrid sound. The acoustic guitar became more dominant from the 1890s. As ragtime and boogie-woogie emerged in the early twentieth century, the piano might be introduced. All this was dance music, as the juke joint was not necessarily a place to be entertained but a place to let off steam and have fun.

Before recorded music was available (or even after, as a phonograph or Victrola machine could be expensive), live musicians were necessary, often drawn from the audience although gifted individuals rose to the surface and

FIGURE 3.7 *Jitterbugging in a Clarksdale juke joint, November 1939 (photo: Marion Post Wolcott). Source: Marion Post Wolcott, Library of Congress.*

began to earn their keep from playing for the crowd. Inevitably, live music leads to interpretation, and different sorts of music began to emerge – barrel house, slow drag music and the blues. The great early innovators of blues music travelled between different juke joints living on tips, free meals and the occasional payment from bar takings. Robert Johnson, Muddy Waters and Howlin' Wolf (Chester Burnett) were all Mississippi blues musicians who performed in juke joints. The juke joint, although a fertile place for musical development, was a rough and often unsafe place to be for its patrons, where alcohol, gambling, prostitution and other criminal activities might take place.

Juke joints are still an important part of African American culture in the Mississippi Delta and, like most active popular music venues, are subject to change, closure and reopening. One venue that has persisted largely unchanged for decades is Po' Monkey's (Poor Monkey's), situated on a roadside outside Merigold, Mississippi.

The joint was created in an old sharecropper's shack in the early 1960s (the owner himself couldn't remember exactly when) by Willie Seaberry whose family nickname gave the venue its name. Farmworker Seaberry opened his house as a venue two nights a week – Mondays were an impromptu strip club with dancers arriving from the nearby town, and Thursday was 'Family' night focusing on blues music, recorded or live, as the entertainment (Thursday

FIGURE 3.8 *Po' Monkey's, Merigold Mississippi. Source: Michael W. Harding.*

became the sole night of operation from the late 2000s). The single-storey building, which was also Seaberry's home before he passed away in 2016, is clad with vertical wooden planks, partly covered outside with signs and posters and old beer advertisements. The owner's code of entry is posted with signs indicating 'No Loud Music, No Dope Smoking, No Rap Music', and the inside is decorated with the inevitable beer signs, and myriad random objects such as stuffed animals, Christmas lights and old dolls, and furnished with odd chairs and home-made tables. On Thursdays the bare plywood floor became a place for dancing while the owner, dressed in his usual loud suit, circulated, handing out $2 beers.[10] Po' Monkey's rich, highly personalized decoration is far different from the original juke joints, which were minimal shacks that reflected the poverty of those who frequented them; however, it is nevertheless a special place, with its eccentric, engaging image – one that resonates with how people imagine a juke joint might be and consequently an exemplar for those who seek to reproduce that character in the design of newer places (see below). In 2009 it was marked on the Mississippi Blues Trail, a largely grant-funded project that aims to identify important historic places that relate to the founding and development of blues music, and therefore it is now a tourist as well as a local's destination.

The economic crises of the 1920s and 30s that impacted on developing the style and presentation of country music also influenced the country blues styles, as many rural African Americans were forced to move to cities to find employment. A second wave of migration occurred in the post-war boom of the 1940s and 50s, where for the first time African Americans had some disposable income and the leisure time to spend it. Cities like Chicago, Detroit and Memphis became centres for a new style of blues using electric instruments, particularly the guitar. 'This floodtide of bittersweet, sexy sound swept the big cities of the Midwest, and soon all America became a land of jazz and the blues, paying tribute to its capital city.'[11] Some of the key musicians who had played in the rural juke joints of Mississippi moved to Chicago, such as Muddy Waters and Howlin' Wolf. The new venues that opened up in the city served as meeting places to share experiences and information between the new immigrants, as well as somewhere to relax and provide a stage to develop the music they brought with them. Clubs such as Silvio's, The 708 and the Flame Club opened in the 1940s, although music also happened on the street in the markets along Maxwell Street.[12]

Muddy Waters recalls playing in the blues clubs of Chicago's South side: 'When I went into the clubs, the first thing I wanted was an amplifier. Couldn't nobody hear you with an acoustic. Wherever you've got booze, you're going to get a little fight. You get more of a pure thing out of an acoustic, but you get more noise out of an amplifier.' He played late and long: 'Mostly we had a late hour licence – three and four and five o'clock in the morning. On Saturday might go to about five. Summertime it was daybreak. Go in there in the day and leave in the day – next day.'[13] As well as the paid work in bars and dance halls, another reason for the musicians

FIGURE 3.9 *Howlin' Wolf on stage at Silvio's Chicago, c. 1964.*
Source: ©Raeburn Flerlage, Chicago Historical Society.

to travel to Chicago was the chance to make records, which were in turn redistributed back home to the Mississippi Delta (then the rest of North America and eventually the world), although Alan Lomax, who surveyed all the commercial records from the period, states that many of the recordings do not fully represent the quality of the live performances as musicians were '"going through the motions" in the commercial recording studios'.[14]

All of these original blues joints have gone; however, Chicago has many newer venues that are the continuing legacy of the original urban juke joint. Kingston Mines is a town in Illinois where the father of one of the actor members of the Chicago-based Kingston Mines Theatre Company worked. The Company was only short-lived, founded in 1968 and ending in 1973; however, the café, which they allowed to open on their premises, thrived, moving to the blues venue's current location at 2548 North Halstead, Lincoln Park, Chicago, in the 1970s. The venue's founder is Lenin 'Doc' Pellegrino, whose daughters are still in charge today with his son as MC. Pellegrino introduced folk music into the café, but eventually decided to change the character of the venue by establishing it as the first blues bar on Chicago's North side.[15] By 1982, the bar was hosting blues music every evening. Originally occupying a single shopfront, the venue has expanded over the years and now has two stages with bands playing on both every night. Although it couldn't be in a more urban location, the appearance is strongly reminiscent of the old rural juke joints, not by design but by how it has developed over the years.

FIGURE 3.10 *Kingston Mines, 2548 North Halstead, Chicago. Source: Chad Magiera.*

The two-storey plain brick façade has a single illuminated sign, with a translucent canopy below that covers the sidewalk. As with the rural joints, signage is well regarded by Kingston Mines' management – 'LIVE BLUES MUSIC 7 NIGHTS A WEEK TILL 4AM' and '2 BANDS 2 STAGES CONTINUOUS MUSIC'. Large wooden signs also indicate who's playing that night. Inside, there is no pretence at coordinated design, except perhaps for the horizontal wooden boards behind the two stages that are perhaps meant to emulate the inside of someone's shack. Large painted murals fill some of the walls, and there are pencil portraits of blues greats, some of which have played in the club. Both stages are small, with two sets of steps leading up to the one in the main room and the other so low as to require none at all. When an artist takes to the stage, a large banner is strung from the ceiling with their name on it. Although the venue attracts criticism from some locals as somewhere that is now catering to tourists, it also won Chicago Readers Best Blues Club 2016 and the 2016 Torch Bearer of Blues in Chicago Award.

Although Kingston Mines, and many other small music venues like it across North America, continues the tradition of the original rural juke joints and honky-tonks, the image of this important musical heritage has also been appropriated in the contemporary commercial world because their recognizable motifs can be used to create a 'ready-made' atmosphere. Juke joints' reputation as edgy, transgressive venues has added to their historic appeal, and a romanticized recreation of their appearance has been adopted by large multinational companies. The juke joint is the clear model for the House of Blues hotel, restaurant and venue chain, founded by Isaak Tigrett, co-founder of the Hard Rock Café, and actor Dan Akroyd, who appeared in the popular cult moving picture *Blues Brothers* (John Landis, 1980). Owned by Live Nation Entertainment since 2006, the company runs twelve operations across the United States. Similarly, you can find a honky-tonk saloon within the Treasure Island hotel and casino complex in Las Vegas – Gilley's, named after a honky-tonk that once stood in Pasadena, Texas, that featured in the 1980 movie *Urban Cowboy* (the original closed in 1989), is the 'reincarnation of the famed honky-tonk cowboy (and cowgirl) saloon from Texas'.[16] The nature of 'authenticity' and the acquisition of traditional venue imagery found in places like Floore's and Po' Monkey's for touristic reproduction are discussed later in this book (see chapter 12); however, despite these ersatz copies, the importance of these humble places in the gestation of crucially important strands of popular music cannot be overestimated. As Alan Lomax states: 'Three centuries of African-American experimentation gave rise to the hoe-down, the spiritual, the minstrel tunes, ragtime, jazz, the blues, rock, and gospel – each genre with a galaxy of strophic melodies that first fascinated America and then the world.'[17]

CHAPTER FOUR

Jazz Clubs, Social Clubs and Riverboats

At the Spotted Cat Music Club, in the Faubourg Marigny district of New Orleans, the music starts early and finishes late – tonight, it's the Shotgun Jazz Band. The double-bass and six-string banjo players sit in the window seats that face onto Frenchman Street and the front-line trombone, clarinet and co-leader Marla Dixon's trumpet (John, her husband, plays the banjo) face the dancers squeezed in between the bar and the tiered benches that line the opposite wall. The piano player can be heard but not seen until the music dies down and the dancers rest for a minute, as the upright sits against the wall behind a line of bar stools. The venue occupies a street front lot adjacent to an empty site (used for open-air art markets on some nights) and a nine-storey apartment block; however, the building is an old New Orleans, wooden, two-storey clapboard structure built over a hundred years ago and only improved when absolutely necessary (e.g. the ramshackle lean-to balcony recently replaced with a steel structure).

L-shaped in plan, with an apartment and workshop to the rear, the Spotted Cat occupies the ground floor with the stage at the front next to the entrance and the bar alongside a sidewall. Operating twelve hours a day, the first show often begins at 2.00 pm and the last doesn't quit until 2.00 am. The music style revolves around traditional jazz and blues but often with a contemporary twist so funk and klezmer creep in. People wander in from off the street attracted by the music and the lack of cover, but then stay as the bands are high quality and bar selection comprehensive.

This informal venue seems essentially New Orleans, a city intimately linked with the birth of jazz, but also blues and zydeco. Today, popular music is quite rightly considered to be a global phenomenon, with styles and genres disseminated via recorded music across countries and continents. However, popular music is also very much a local art form, and most of its

FIGURE 4.1 *The Spotted Cat Music Club, New Orleans, exterior. Source: Robert Kronenburg.*

most well-known sounds have emerged independently within a home-grown scene before becoming globally familiar. For this reason, some cities have a particular link to particular styles of music: Liverpool, UK, for beat music; Nashville, USA, for country and western; and New Orleans, Louisiana, USA, for jazz. The local music of New Orleans had a crucial impact on all jazz and yet has also retained its own distinctive sound, which emerged in the last part of the nineteenth century influenced from its African roots by ragtime, blues and spiritual music.

At the turn of the nineteenth century, New Orleans was the South's largest city with over 300,000 inhabitants, an important port on the Mississippi River that had a rich ethnic mix of European, African and Native American people. It was also a relatively tolerant environment compared to that found further north, enabling immigrants and the descendants of slaves, although without doubt still oppressed, to realize both economic and personal improvement. Music was ever present in the African American community of turn-of-the-century New Orleans, a vital part of religious and community life as well as the saloons and brothels. The music that evolved valued improvisation and rhythm, which could both lift the listeners' spirits and provide appropriately mournful sounds. It was also a 'hot' sound track, emotionally charged and syncopated, a vital accompaniment for dancing and other leisure activities.

JAZZ CLUBS, SOCIAL CLUBS AND RIVERBOATS

Although jazz is sometimes said to have originated in the brothel district of New Orleans, it actually began throughout the city's neighbourhoods, emerging out of a fusion of different innovative musicians, in particular Charles 'Buddy' Bolden, who from 1895 led a dance band whose performances were based on memorized parts enhanced significantly by improvisations that expressed spontaneity and excitement. However, the legalized brothel zone of the city identified as 'The District', but popularly known as 'Storyville' after Alderman Sidney Story, and the nearby 'Back of Town' were the entertainment areas where musicians found employment, and the city's residents and visitors to this great Mississippi port often first heard this new sound (Plate 5). Story championed the area's establishment in 1897 as a place where the port city's prostitution could be monitored and managed. The buildings that housed the brothels ranged in quality from wooden shacks or 'cribs' to the Mahogany Hall, a 'lavishly decorated mansion' run by Lulu White.[1] Although the more expensive houses often had a pianist providing entertainment (sometimes known as the 'Professor'), it was in the saloons, bars, restaurants and nightclubs that jazz music was heard and developed. As well as Bolden, other famous musicians who played there included Jelly Roll Morton, who first began working in brothels as a piano player when he was fourteen years old. Morton described a visit to a New Orleans night spot in 1902:

> Some friends took me to The Frenchman's on the corner of Villery and Bienville, which was at that time the most famous nightspot after everything was closed. It was only a back room, but it was where all the greatest pianists frequented after they got off from work in the sporting-houses [brothels] ... All the girls that could get out of their houses was there. The millionaires would come to listen to their favourite pianists. There weren't any discrimination of any kind. They all sat at different tables or anywhere they felt like sitting. They all mingled together just as they wished to and everyone was just like one big happy family ... So this place would go on at a tremendous rate of speed – plenty money, drinks of all kinds- from four o'clock in the morning until maybe twelve, one, two, or three o'clock in the daytime.[2]

When Storyville was originally founded, the venues were segregated; however, as Morton describes, white musicians visited the area and were increasingly influenced by the African American music they heard there. Although much of this part of New Orleans was destroyed when the Iberville public housing projects were built in the 1940s, a small number of the historic entertainment buildings remains, including the Eagle Saloon. Situated on the corner of Perdido and South Rampart Street, this three-storey building was built in 1850–1 in the neoclassical style. Built from brick faced with stucco decorations, the building has a glass shopfront supported by cast-iron columns.

FIGURE 4.2 *The Eagle Saloon, New Orleans. Source: Robert Kronenburg.*

South Rampart Street was part of a racially segregated area established in the 1800s where African American, Jewish, Italian and Chinese residents established their businesses. As well as places of entertainment, there were tailors, pawn shops and general stores. From 1897, the top floor of the building was a 'ballroom' for the Masonic and Odd Fellows Hall Association, an African American fraternal club that often held dances and meetings there. The ground floor of this building contained a pawn shop, Jake Itzovich's Eagle Loan and Pledge Company, a frequent recourse for local musicians who would pawn their instruments between engagements, but it later became the Eagle Saloon, started by Frank Douroux (who also ran the Little Gem Saloon a few steps away on Poydras and South Rampart Street), where the musicians who played upstairs would gather to drink and sometimes jam: 'everybody from all the other clubs would come to the Eagle Saloon'.[3] This was an area filled with music and nightlife, one in which the young Louis Armstrong was born and thrived: 'On Liberty, Perdido, Franklin, and Poydras there were honky tonks at every corner and in each one of these musical instruments of all kinds were played. At the corner of the street where I lived was the Famous Funky Butt Hall [Union Sons

Hall] where I first heard Buddy Bolden play. He was blowing up a storm.'[4] The area around the Eagle was also called the Battlefield as it was a tough neighbourhood with illicit gambling and prostitution. A not untypical event would have been what happened on New Year's Eve 1913, when the teenage Armstrong was arrested outside the Eagle Saloon for shooting a pistol.

Storyville was shut down in 1917 as New Orleans became a staging post for the US Army embarking for Europe during the First World War, and prostitution was made illegal. The area, and the adjacent Back of Town neighbourhood, continued as an entertainment zone with dance halls, cabarets and restaurants and later in the century during prohibition with speakeasies and gambling houses. After more than fifty years of decline, places like the Little Gem, which was refurbished in 2012, and the Eagle Saloon, which is now scheduled for restoration as a performance venue, with a museum and education facility on the upper floors, are located in a landscape of empty building lots having only just survived wide-scale, edge-of-downtown, urban decline.

Although New Orleans is now full of live music venues such as the Spotted Cat, there was a period in the city's history when its own particular style of jazz was perceived as a music of the past, the musicians who made it famous now mostly gone. In the 1950s, rock 'n' roll was immensely popular and traditional jazz had developed into new, more contemporary styles such as bebop. Beginning in a small gallery run by Larry Borenstein at 726 St Peter Street in the French Quarter, a preservation movement began with regular informal traditional jazz concerts featuring the remaining original musicians, many of whom were contemporaries of early-twentieth-century innovators like Buddy Bolden. When the concerts began to run six nights a week, Borenstein moved his gallery next door, and after a short period of operation by the not-for-profit group The New Orleans Society for the Preservation of Jazz, the former gallery became a permanent venue. From its inception in 1961, Preservation Hall was identified by Allan Jaffe (whose son Ben Jaffe still runs the venue today) as a 'a non-commercial, living museum, dedicated to the preservation of an original local art form'.[5] Although at first focused around preserving both the original music and the original musicians who played it, the Preservation Hall Jazz Band (which has always consisted of a pool of rotating musicians from which the nightly lineup is assembled) has since toured extensively in the United States and abroad, and also collaborated with other artists not normally associated with New Orleans Jazz including hip-hop (Mos Def), bluegrass (Del McCoury Band) and indie rock (Arcade Fire). The Preservation Hall Jazz Band have played at Carnegie Hall, the Hollywood Bowl and at the contemporary music festival Austin City Limits. Preservation Hall's high-profile approach has achieved what it set out to do, preserving a profoundly local musical form by ensuring it is regularly performed. Although the audience at the now twice-nightly shows at Preservation Hall are undoubtedly dominated by tourists, it is nevertheless a place where gifted local musicians play with the objective of preserving a living tradition, not to be a pastiche of the past.

The building on St Peter Street, although in the centre of the lively and touristic French Quarter, seems out of place – a sombre stucco façade with the typical balcony at the upper-storey level, although all the windows are shuttered with wooden boards. The building dates from the first half of the nineteenth century, rebuilt after the original tavern burnt down in 1817. To the right of the façade is the venue's only advertisement, an old weathered sign in the form of a cornet with the words Preservation Hall. An iron-grated gate leads to a side passage with the concert room on the left. The interior is unprepossessing, apparently undecorated since the venue was opened. Some old posters and framed pictures of jazz musicians are hung at random on the walls, and a line of benches faces one end, with a large wooden column inconveniently placed in the centre of the room. There is no bar, and the only items for sale are the band's recordings and a few merchandising items you pick up from a table by the door on the way out. When it's time for the performance, the musicians walk in from the left and sit with their backs to the street wall; the audience are crammed in with two rows sitting on the floor in front of the first of the benches and many more standing at

FIGURE 4.3 *Preservation Hall, French Quarter, New Orleans. Source: Robert Kronenburg.*

the back or crowded around the doorways. Although the musicians who make up today's band are obviously not those from the founding days of New Orleans Jazz, there is a strong tradition that they are upholding, and they make that felt through the way they approach the music and the performance. Nevertheless, this is no conservatoire show – the music is wild and addictive and the links by the band members funny and entertaining. Audience members engage by shouting out requests (for the obligatory tip) and even join in singing the lyrics to well-known tunes. The typical music bar in New Orleans hosts a peripatetic audience, wandering in and out from the street, or to the bar. Waitresses rush to and fro with food and drink, and people talk and laugh during the performance. At Preservation Hall, the audience is locked in, hanging on every note, listening carefully to each word of introduction, and applauding enthusiastically at the end of each tune – mournful when the last encore fades away and the musicians rise and walk out the way they came. The ambience wasn't like this in the saloons of Storyville or Back of Town a hundred years ago, but the music probably was.

New Orleans social clubs

A key element of African American society in New Orleans was the social and community clubs that were founded in the second half of the nineteenth century. These societies were associated with the benevolent organizations, which were formed during the nineteenth century as mutual aid groups to support members in times of hardship and illness. The societies were hugely popular as an estimated 80 per cent of all local residents belonged to such groups, paying a small amount each week as a form of insurance in case they fell on hard times, but also simultaneously helping others in that situation.[6] At the turn of the nineteenth century, there were at least 200 such groups in New Orleans. Many societies set up permanent premises in which members could host social events, which also formed an important way of raising additional funds. Through these activities, the societies also fulfilled an important role in creating a community focus and sense of unity for African Americans, Creole and other ethnic groups.[7] Although many of the original society halls have been lost to both redevelopment and the severe weather that often hits New Orleans (Economy Hall, home to the Economy and Mutual Aid Association, where Louis Armstrong played with Kid Ory's band, was destroyed by Hurricane Hilda in October 1964), a few still remain. These buildings are diverse in form as many were adapted from other uses, such as churches or dwellings. The Perseverance Society Hall, 1644 Villere Street, New Orleans (not be confused with Perseverance Hall No. 4, a former Masonic Lodge now in the care of the National Park Service), was built by the Perseverance Benevolent Mutual Aid Association in the 1880s. Unlike

FIGURE 4.4 *Perseverance Society Hall (now the Holy Aid and Comfort Spiritual Church of Eternal Life), New Orleans. Source: Kevin McCaffrey.*

many of the existing halls that have changed appearance dramatically under new ownership, the Holy Aid and Comfort Spiritual Church of Eternal Life worked with preservationists to retain the building's appearance from 1927 when it was extended at the front with a Spanish mission-style arched parapet. The wooden hall is single storey, with a two-storey service wing at the rear. Many important early jazz musicians played in the hall, including Buddy Bolden, Joe 'King' Oliver and Sidney Bechet.[8]

Besides playing in the halls, musicians would often take to the streets with the social club as the starting point. Parades were social occasions for dressing up, dancing and listening to music. The bands would accompany the club members, sometimes dressed in elaborate costumes, stopping at each other's houses for drinks and food, before meeting up by chance or arrangement. Sidney Bechet recalled:

> Sometimes we'd have what they called in those days 'bucking contests' ... One band, it would come right up in front of the other and play at it, and the first band it would play right back, until finally one band just had to give in. And the one that didn't give in, all the people, they'd rush up to it and give it drinks and food and holler for more.[9]

Another aspect of street music firmly associated with the social clubs was the funeral parades:

There used to be a lot of clubs in New Orleans, social clubs. They used to meet regular ... They would have a brass band, the Onward Brass Band or Allen's Brass Band, and they would go from the club to the house of the member which was dead, and would play not dance music but mortuary music until they got to be about a block from the residence of the dead person. Then the big drum would just give tempo as they approached. The members would all go in to see the corpse, and then they would take him out to the cemetery with funeral marches.[10]

The band was nominally the 'first line'; however, the 'second line', consisting of club members armed with improvised weapons to fend off rival gangs, often headed up the parade.[11] Live street music with brass bands is still a familiar experience on New Orleans streets, either as street buskers or during the city's festivals such as the New Orleans Jazz and Heritage Festival. Some of the social clubs, and their traditions of street parades and 'jazz funerals', still survive in New Orleans.

The Zulu Social Aid and Pleasure Club, chartered in 1916 but formed a decade earlier, is an African American society created to 'unite in the bonds of friendship; protection and progress, to improve the conditions of its

FIGURE 4.5 *The New Orleans Brass Band performing in the French Quarter, 2017.* Source: Robert Kronenburg.

members by judicious counsel and timely aid ... prompt attention to its sick, and burial of its dead'.[12] The club has moved between many buildings in its history, eventually settling in 1978 in an Italianate shotgun house on North Broad Street, although its main musical focus is parades and outdoor events for which it has hired some of the best known jazz musicians including, in 1949, Louis Armstrong and his Esquire All Star Band. The club's annual Lundi Gras Festival takes place in New Orleans' Woldenberg Park on the Mississippi's river bank and features parades, dance troupes, live brass bands, jazz and zydeco artists, with the high point being the arrival of the Queen and King Zulu.

Mississippi riverboats

Earlier in his career, in the early 1920s, Armstrong played on the New Orleans riverboat *Capitol*. The *Capitol* was the largest of the Streckfus line's boats, and no doubt it was the quality of bandleader Fate Marable's musicians that led to their new prestigious berth. Marable worked for John Streckfus

FIGURE 4.6 *Fate Marable's New Orleans Jazz Band on the Mississippi riverboat S.S.* Capitol, *c. 1920. Source: Photo: A. P. Bedou, Courtesy of the Hogan Jazz Archive,* Tulane University.

(whose riverboat company was, throughout the first half of the twentieth century, the largest and most successful) from 1907 to 1940, beginning as a piano player but soon forming dance bands, including the New Orleans musicians of which Armstrong was one. The *Capitol* and others like it were outfitted for the excursion trade, pleasure rides focusing on leisure and entertainment, which grew in popularity from 1900.

Riverboats had travelled on the great river (3,860 miles in length including its most northern fork, the Missouri) since the beginning of the nineteenth century. The first steamboat was the *New Orleans*, launched in 1811 at Pittsburgh; however, by 1830 there were 1,200 boats working the river transporting coal, wood, cotton, rice, tobacco, molasses and people. Riverboats from the nineteenth and early twentieth centuries were primarily wooden vessels of up to 91 metres long (300 feet) and 24 metres (80 feet) wide. The boats had very shallow drafts of about 1.5 metres (5 feet) to be able to navigate the tricky river passage that was an intrinsic hazard of the Mississippi River and its tributaries. This meant that the craft's strength was based on a structural iron truss using a system of kingposts and chains along the length of the boat, rather than a traditional keel. The wood-burning boiler (coal later) was positioned to balance the vessel depending on whether it was a sternwheeler (engines at the rear) or side-wheeler (engines amidships). The upper deck (Texas deck) contained passenger areas, cabins and lounges, and in the better boats these could be very ornate with polished

FIGURE 4.7 *S.S.* Capitol, *c. 1920. Source: Courtesy of the Hogan Jazz Archive,* Tulane University.

or gilt wood details, soft furnishings, bar and dining areas, and a galley. The main ports on the voyage from New Orleans north included Memphis, St Louis, St Paul and Pittsburgh.

The excursion boats were designed as entertainment vessels, a travelling club, in which all the space normally given over to cabins or cargo was made into a large ballroom with tables, a stage for the band and a dance floor. The largest of the boats could accommodate over 4,000 passengers. Like most riverboats built for the excursion trade, the main polished dance floor on the *Capitol* spanned the entire width of the boat, with benches and tables to each side and a bandstand at one end. Another common feature was a steam calliope that was played to signal the boat's arrival or departure. Marable recalled he would often need to wear special gloves to protect his hands as the keys overheated.[13] Many of the boats' journeys were local, a day trip or evening excursion; however, seasonal excursions were longer, travelling up river to the major cities *en route*, taking on different groups of passengers and day-trippers. On some boats, the musicians for these longer trips had to find their own on-shore accommodation, but on the *Capitol*, the top deck had 'the smallest bedrooms in existence' where they could sleep.[14]

The riverboat musicians' job was a demanding one, with both the band leaders and their employers requiring extremely high standards of playing. Compared to the hot, free music found in the clubs and parades in the city, the repertoire was more conventional with the standards of the day, waltzes and rags forming the main fare, although the popularity of the New Orleans bands, and their ability to up the tempo and include impressive improvisation, still made them favoured musicians. The riverboats also enabled New Orleans jazz to be disseminated more widely as audiences (and musicians) from other cities heard their performances outside the city. All musicians valued their riverboat jobs, not only for the steady money but also for the musical experience and training it involved. Although Streckfus was the largest line on the river, there were others operating riverboats out of St Louis or Cincinnati, Ohio. In addition, there were steam boats, such as the S.S. *Dixie*, that ran up the coast from New Orleans to New York with bands on board providing lunchtime concerts and dancing at night.

The Great Depression, the Second World War and the improved reliability of smaller diesel tugs towing barges hastened the decline of the commercial steam cargo riverboats on the Mississippi. Similarly, the popularity of the excursion traffic dramatically reduced, challenged by cinema and television, although a small number of boats kept running, such as the *President*, built in 1944, converted to diesel in 1978 and captained by Verne Streckfus, the original Streckfus company founder's grandson. Perhaps the most well-known riverboat is the *Natchez*, the first version of which was built in New York City in 1823 as a side-wheeler. The current *Natchez* is the ninth version and a sternwheeler, built of steel to United States Coast Guard rules in 1975.

The boat's engines, steering system and paddlewheel shaft were built in 1925 and came from the steamboat *Clairton*. Operated by the New Orleans Steamboat Company, she is docked on Toulouse Street Wharf close by the French Quarter, and her calliope sounds regularly as she takes tourists and locals on daily jazz cruises featuring live jazz bands.

Another type of floating entertainment vessel that was created for use on the Mississippi was the showboat, a mobile theatre that had its heyday in the nineteenth and early twentieth centuries. Unlike the showboat romantically depicted in the 1951 MGM moving picture *Show Boat* (the third to be based on the 1927 Ziegfeld stage musical written by Jerome Kern and Oscar Hammerstein and the 1926 novel by Edna Ferber), these theatres were actually built on barges that were pushed by a separate steam-powered towboat. To place an engine and boiler in the centre of the showboat would have spoiled the layout of the performance space. The first dedicated showboat was probably the *Floating Theatre* commissioned by British-born actor William Chapman for his family-based theatre company who performed plays, music and dance for a small fee in the 1830s. Launched in Pittsburgh in 1831, the enterprise was successful and was therefore redesigned and improved in 1836 to become the *Steamboat Theatre*. Many other showboats followed in Chapman's wake, some providing circus shows and wax museums as well as minstrel shows, vaudeville and burlesque. At this form of entertainment's peak around 1910, there were twenty-one boats cruising the river. The 1,400-seat *Goldenrod* was the culmination of the showboat concept, visiting fourteen mid-west states during her show tours during the 1920s. Built in 1909 at Parkersburg, West Virginia, she had an auditorium 49 metres (162 feet) long and 14 metres (45 feet) wide, with a balcony, proscenium arch stage and twenty-one private boxes. The auditorium was lined full-length with mirrors and had five thousand lights as well as gilt and red velour draperies and friezes.[15] As with the riverboats, the Great Depression, moving pictures and eventually television led to her initial demise, moored by the St Louis riverfront by the late 1930s although still in use in the 1950s. By 1965 she had been sunk, refloated, barely survived a fierce fire and then refurbished, and was not long after registered a US National Historic Landmark. The boat was moved to the Missouri city of St Charles in 1989 and rebuilt and used as a popular dinner theatre until 2001; however, she ran aground when river levels dropped below normal, was severely damaged and, after a number of calamitous events, was destroyed by fire in October 2017.

Jazz clubs

Although jazz began in New Orleans, it spread all over the world, changing and developing in sound and performance, formed by both local practices and international influences. However, throughout this diversity, there remains an archetypal image of the jazz club venue stemming from the musical form's original risqué beginnings as an entertainment heard in brothels, saloons, dance halls and bars. As with the blues musicians of the Mississippi Delta, New Orleans musicians migrated away from the city to other parts of the United States, away from increasingly restrictive race laws and in search of new opportunities when their local working conditions became more difficult. Sidney Bechet went to play in Chicago and New York in 1917, Joe Oliver left in 1918 and Louis Armstrong followed in 1922. The jazz scenes in places like Chicago, Kansas City and New York developed exponentially as a result of this influx of new talent, along with new audiences anxious to hear what they had to offer. By the 1940s, New York City was understood as a world centre for jazz development, new forms appearing not in conservatoires or concert halls but in the many vibrant small venues across the city: clubs such as the Spotlight, the Three Deuces, the Famous Door, the Yacht Club, Kelly's Stable and the Onyx. These were often located in the once grand brownstone mansions in the area around midtown Manhattans' 52nd Street. The influential and famous jazz musician Miles Davis recalled in his autobiography: '52nd Street was something else when it was happening. It would be crowded with people, and the clubs were no bigger than apartment living rooms. They were so small and jam-packed. The clubs were right next to each other and across the street from one another ... That scene was powerful.'[16]

Birdland is one of the most famous New York jazz clubs. Named for Charlie 'Yardbird' Parker, the immensely gifted bebop saxophonist who sometimes headlined the club, it opened on 15 December 1949 and was situated in midtown Manhattan at 1678 Broadway and 52nd Street. For less than a dollar's entrance fee, patrons could see and hear jazz greats like Count Basie, John Coltrane, Miles Davis, Stan Getz, Dizzy Gillespie, Thelonious Monk and of course 'Bird' himself. Birdland, although situated in the basement of a large commercial building, was not very large itself, seating up to 500 people crammed into a single room with a low stage, although there was room (although not all on the stage) for a jazz orchestra if required, unlike many of the other clubs. Tables were arranged in long rows down the centre away from the stage with booths set against the walls. There was also a small drinks-free area nicknamed 'the peanut gallery'. Patrons were served meals and drinks although there was also a long bar (Plate 6).

The layout of these jazz venues undoubtedly shaped the sort of music that was performed there:

> The clubs got real popular during the 1940s when the small bands took over from the large bands. Those clubs were too small to hold big bands. The bandstand couldn't hardly hold a five-piece combo, let alone one with ten or twelve people. So this kind of club created a new kind of musician, who was comfortable in a small-band setting.[17]

Although the original Birdland was a mecca for jazz enthusiasts and celebrities during its early period up to the mid-1950s (with several important live recordings made there including Lennie Tristano Quintent, *Live at Birdland*, 1949; Art Blakey, *A Night at Birdland*, 1954; and Count Basie Orchestra, *Basie at Birdland*, 1961), it was not long before this area of the city's importance in terms of jazz venues declined and the scene moved elsewhere. The rising popularity of rock 'n' roll hurt the club further, and it eventually closed in 1965. However, like many small venues that go through phases, the club would reopen at a new uptown venue still on Broadway but at 105th Street in 1986, and then move again in 1996 back to midtown at 315 44th Street.

The new Birdland, which is still at its 44th Street location, is a good example of how the characteristic jazz club ambience can be created in a new home. Previously a pre-theatre restaurant, the new club was established by Ryan Paternite, who was at that time running another famous, although much newer, New York jazz venue, the Blue Note, situated in Greenwich Village. Only minor building alterations were carried out to the basically rectangular room with a new cloakroom partitioning the entrance area off from the performance space and the creation of a raised stage along one wall in the centre of the space.

The room was furnished with new soft furnishings, carpets and curtains to aid acoustics, and although it is small enough for non-amplified performances, there is a sophisticated amplification system. A bar to the right of the entrance provides a waiting area for patrons waiting between shows, and to the rear of the room is the kitchen and sound desk. All the seating is focused on the stage in semi-circular tiers providing an intimate, relaxed setting. Like many others, the club serves dinner to its patrons before the show and the best seats go to the diners; however, this does not mean that the music is any less exciting or those who listen to it less passionate or enthused. This recreation of Birdland has seen performances by Oscar Peterson, John Scofield, Pat Methany and Diane Krall.

A club with as important a reputation in the UK as Birdland had in the United States is Ronnie Scott's in London. Scott, himself a jazz saxophonist, had visited New York in the 1940s when a member of the band on the transatlantic liner *Queen Mary*, and he set out specifically to recreate a similar venue in London's Soho neighbourhood. First established in 1959 in a former taxi drivers' tea bar and restroom, the club succeeded by bringing in star American musicians (such as Zoot Sims and Sonny Rollins) supported by quality UK talent. By 1965 the club was well established and able to move to larger premises not far away in Frith Street. The club is located in part of a four-storey nineteenth-century brick terrace that would have been two houses when first built, although probably converted to a later date to accommodate commercial premises (such as a shop) on the ground floor. Although extended and refurbished in 1968, in 2005 and again in 2013, the ambience of the club has changed little since the 1960s.

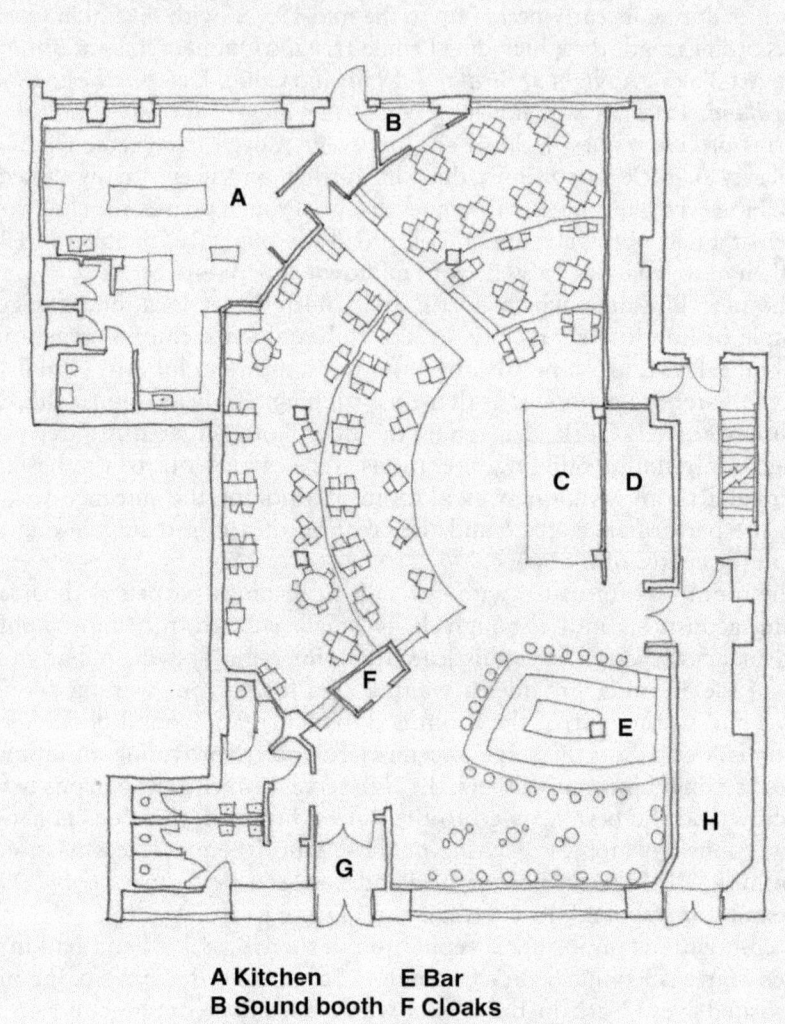

A Kitchen
B Sound booth
C Stage
D Office
E Bar
F Cloaks
G Street entrance
H Loading/Fire escape

FIGURE 4.8 *Plan of Birdland, 315 West 44th Street, New York City. The archetypal jazz club layout with the stage (right) at the focus of the seated audience. The kitchen is at the rear and the bar near the street entrance. Source: Robert Kronenburg.*

FIGURE 4.9 *John Scofield playing at Birdland, 2010. Source: Robert Kronenburg.*

The main performance space seats 220 people at tables surrounding the stage. A bar opposite has some stools, but most of the patrons eat dinner as well as see the show. Low ceilings, soft red furnishings and good acoustics make this an intimate venue, although some inconvenient columns and a few seats crammed into areas without a good view are also part of its idiosyncrasies. Like Birdland, the list of international musicians who have played in the club is long (including, surprisingly, Jimi Hendrix, whose last performance was at the club in 1970) as is the list of live recordings (e.g. Ben Webster, *Live at Ronnie Scott's*, 1964; Ella Fitzgerald, *Ella in London*, 1974; and Chet Baker, *Live at Ronnie Scott's*, 1984).

Jazz clubs such as Birdland and Ronnie Scott's are no longer the edgy, underground establishments they once were. As musical genres have developed, jazz is no longer viewed as the challenging form of popular music it once was, and its proponents (even the young and radical ones), the sort of people out to subvert society and its morals. The jazz club is now associated with an engaging musical experience, but also a comfortable one, often in which dinner is served and cocktails are readily available. However, the jazz club is interesting in that it is undoubtedly a venue with a sharply defined typological identity, a set ambience that can be recreated to provide the optimum environment for the enjoyment of its type of music. And although it is a venue typology that can be visited in almost every city around the world, it nevertheless still retains the essence of a Louisiana red-light district in those early days of the twentieth century.

FIGURE 4.10 *Ronnie Scott's, 47 Frith Street, Soho, London. Source: Robert Kronenburg.*

CHAPTER FIVE

Cabaret, Speakeasies and Supper Clubs

In the late 1960s, a night out at the 'Shakey' cabaret club was a stylish treat for Liverpudlians. As a young teenager, the place seemed really glamorous. My family would have dinner while the warm-up acts were on, a three-course meal served by waiters with white aprons and ties. Local comedian Pete Price was the compere, and he sang popular songs and told jokes making the most of his local knowledge. There was a house band that backed the singers and did covers for dancing in between the acts and after the show ended. One of my favourite headliners was The Black Abbots (whose frontman Russ Abbot later went on to become a familiar figure on British television as a comic in the 1980s), almost a local band as they came from Chester, who merged pop music with comedy.

The club was in the former Shakespeare Theatre, one of several in Liverpool at that time, such as the city-centre She club, the Wookey Hollow in Anfield or Allinson's in Litherland. Built in Fraser Street, central Liverpool, in 1888, it was a beautiful building with interiors lined with carved oak panels featuring scenes and characters from Shakespeare's plays; however, except for a brief period of serious drama during 1957–59 when the American actor and director Sam Wanamaker (who later went on to champion the recreation of the Globe Theatre in London) was artistic director, the theatre hosted popular entertainment such as pantomimes and variety theatre.

After this, the Shakespeare became a dance hall before finding a role as a successful cabaret club. Following a fire in 1963, a major restoration was completed in 1966, which built a new floor, designed for dinner tables and dancing, over the stalls. Illuminated curtains were draped around the walls behind the balconies to give the interior a more contemporary feel (incidentally covering most of the beautiful panelling and paintings that

FIGURE 5.1 *The Shakespeare Theatre, Liverpool (photo: c. 1920). The decorative panels to the rear of the grand circle are just visible. In the later alterations to convert the theatre to a cabaret club these were covered by curtains, and the raked stalls seating was overbuilt with a level floor for dining tables and a dance floor. Source: Photo courtesy Ross Collins: CollinsVariety.co.uk.*

lined the old auditorium). Under the ownership of local millionaire George Silver, the Shakespeare became the largest cabaret club in England, hosting many of the most famous comedians and song and dance artists of the day including Tommy Cooper, Bob Monkhouse, Dave Allen, Bruce Forsyth, Freddy Starr and Larry Grayson.

The cabaret show at the Shakespeare was like variety but influenced by television and the hit parade. It had a local feel to it, with the audience knowing some of the performers and of course each other well. New local talent would get its try-out on the stage, in much the same way it had happened since the 1880s. The crowd could be tough (especially on boxing nights when the local gangsters came in), but it was a hugely popular venue. Pete Price recalls that when it went out of business in April 1975, he was forced to make a stage announcement that this was the last night, and after a riotous evening, the staff split the takings and the audience walked out with souvenirs, stripping the club bare – the receivers had virtually nothing to sell when they arrived the next day.[1] A year later the club reopened under different management; however, just two weeks later it was burned down by an even more disastrous fire than the one in 1963 and the remains of the structure were demolished later that year.

Cabaret and kabarett

The 'Shakey', although undoubtedly local in character, was also a very typical cabaret club. The venue's focus was on the entertainment, primarily music, comedy and dance, which happened on stage, while the audience drank and ate at tables. It was a very adult venue, not aimed at young people or cutting-edge music, although the comedy was often subversive in that it challenged and made fun of authority and social norms. The word cabaret derives from the Middle Dutch word for tavern – *cambret* – and it can equally mean a form of entertainment and the venue in which it takes place. Cabaret emerged in France as a distinctive type of venue from the sixteenth century, selling food and wine with informal entertainment, although the first clubs that follow the modern pattern were established in the nineteenth century, initially *café-concerts* or *café-chantants* with food, drink and professional musicians, singers, dancers and magicians. Cabarets were popular in Paris with a bohemian mixed crowd coming from all walks of life, and the entertainment was provocative and satirical.

Le Chat Noir, a famous cabaret of this period, began in a rented two-room space at 84 Boulevard Rochechouart, Montmartre, in November 1881. The club is synonymous with its impresario Rodolphe Salis, who – acting as a master of ceremonies – began each night's performance with a satirical monologue on current events. The club became so popular that after three and a half years it moved to much bigger premises close by in the former house of the artist Alfred Stevens who had rebuilt the interior with architect Maurice Isabey, incorporating old furniture, sculptures, paintings and bric-a-brac.[2]

The club was as famous for its audience as it was for its performers with the Parisian *avant-garde* attending the nightly shows including composers Erik Satie, Claude Debussy, the artist Henri de Toulouse-Lautrec and the poet Paul Verlaine. Although Salis died in 1897, the club remained popular until the 1920s after further moves to the rue Laval (now rue Victor Massey), and finally the Boulevard de Clichy (where the building and club sign remain, although now operating as a boutique hotel). The popularity of traditional bohemian cabaret in Paris was undermined by competition from the much grander music hall venues such as the Moulin Rouge and the Folies Bergére (see Chapter 2).

Closely linked in style to Salis' Le Chat Noir is German kabarett, which, as well as being an entertainment featuring song, dance and comedy, is also strongly connected to political and topical comment and satire. The very

FIGURE 5.2 *Une Soiree Au Chat Noir Le Chat Noir, Cabaret Artistique, Boulevard de Clichy (c. 1920s, from a pre-1930 postcard). Source: Public domain.*

first German kabarett venues were established at the turn of the twentieth century, for example the *Überbretti* (Superstage) in Berlin founded by Ernst von Wolzogen in 1901 and Munich's *Die Elf Scharfrichter* (The Eleven Executioners). Because of an official ban on public comment in German theatres until the end of the First World War, these had to be private clubs.[3] They were nevertheless a focus for both artistic and political expressions with chansons, costumed dance, recitations, poetry and short dramas, sometimes *avant-garde* in tone. The expressionist art movement Dada began in Zurich, Switzerland, at the Cabaret Voltaire as an effort, via nonsensical and childlike forms of communication to comment on an apparently senseless world that had great social unrest and was involved in a pointless war. The physical space of the Cabaret Voltaire was a back room in the Holländische Meierei at Spiegelgasse 1, Zurich, which opened in February 1916, although Hugo Ball and the other artists who founded it had moved on to other locations by 1917. Recently, the original building has been refurbished and opened as a space for art events that reflect the spirit of Dada. Dada reached Berlin in 1918 and became a highly politicized movement with events, marches and art works used to challenge the authorities on the streets. As a public venue, kabarett found the political space to become popular in Germany from 1918 when the Weimar Republic was declared. Berlin became a permissive city where hedonistic pleasure and entertainment were now easily found.

One of the most famous Berlin kabaretts was *Die Katakombe* (The Catacombs), a venue situated in the basement of the Association of Berlin Artists, Bellevuestraße 3. Werner Finck was co-founder of the club and its *conférencier*, a kind of master of ceremonies, although the role was more wide-ranging, part comic, part bully, part hero, willing to challenge the performers and insult the audience. Typical shows focused on acidic wit, often aimed at public figures, coupled with music, erotic dancing and comic songs. Transvestites and ambiguous sexuality were also common features of many kabarett shows, and one of the most fashionable venues was the Eldorado, initially opened in 1922 at Kantstraße 24. The venue was so successful it took over a dance hall in 1927, and then moved to its final home in the former Grand Café Luitpold on Motzstraße in 1930, although the dance hall building also stayed open until 1931.

This was a large concrete and brick building with apartments above the ground-floor entertainment space. A large sign over the entrance proclaimed '*Hier ist's Richtig!*' (This is the Right Place!). The Eldorado attracted transsexual and transvestite clientele, and patrons could purchase 'chips' to exchange for dances with the transvestite hostesses. The club was highly fashionable with all classes of Berlin society and the shows featured the great stars of the day, including Marlene Dietrich. In July 1932, the new authoritarian government established by Franz von Papen began a series

FIGURE 5.3 *Eldorado, Motzsraße, Berlin, 1932. Source: Bundesarchiv.*

of measures enforced by the police to limit transsexual activity, and by the end of the year the Eldorado was closed. After the Nazi party's seizure of power in January 1933, the situation deteriorated quickly for gay culture and many individuals were arrested and sent to concentration camps. The kabarett clubs were also suppressed, and although the political aspect of the entertainment at *Die Katakombe* was necessarily absent after 1933, the club was nevertheless closed down on 10 May 1935.

The first British cabaret clubs were influenced by the continental model. The Austrian writer Frida Strindberg opened the Cabaret Theatre Club in the basement of a draper's shop at 9 Heddon Street, London, in 1912. Soon retitled The Cave of the Golden Calf, Strindberg intended the venue to be a centre for *avant-garde* artists and writers to meet; however, it instead became a highly fashionable club where patrons were expected to arrive in fashionable evening dress. Decorated by the artist Spencer Gore with contributions by Charles Ginner, Jacob Epstein, Wyndham Lewis and Eric Gill, the club's motif was a golden calf, a Biblical symbol of hedonism and idolatry, which was the main (and least explicit!) emblem in the sign that hung outside the club. Ginner painted semi-abstract wall decorations *Chasing Monkeys, Birds and Indians, Tiger Hunting* (a triptych). Lewis painted a drop curtain for the stage depicting raw meat, and Epstein carved decorative columns and capitals on a sexual theme. The *Times* of 27 June 1912 recorded:

> The club house is dubbed 'The Cave of the Golden Calf', and it is certainly cavernous to the extent that it has to be entered by a sort of man-hole; within there is a small stage and mural decorations representing we should not care to say what precise stage beyond impressionism – they would easily, however, turn into appalling goblins after a little too much supper in the cave.[4] (Upstone 2012)

Despite its rapid leap to fame, the club went bankrupt after just two years, although it set the trend in London for fashionable nightclubs with dining and entertainment.

What a night out at the cabaret was like for the upper classes in London in the 1930s can be experienced from a British Pathé film made in 1932: *London's Famous Clubs and Ciro's*. Ciro's was opened in 1915 and was one of a chain of fashionable upmarket restaurants with branches in Monte Carlo, Nice and Paris. The London club was situated in a converted public bath house, which provided a large two-storey space and a roof that could be opened in summer. This 1932 sound film encourages its viewers to 'Leave the Depression Outside'.[5] Filmed mostly from the upper gallery, it shows customers dancing to the Jacques Jacobs Orchestra before the show starts at midnight in the club's luxurious interior. The soprano Doris Yorke sings 'Memories of Yore', followed by novelty numbers by Esme Neville who

FIGURE 5.4 *A Night in the Cave of the Golden Calf*. *Illustration published in* The Daily Mirror, *4 July 1912. Source: Public Domain.*

sings and dances to 'Ta-ra-ra-boom-de-ay', and Gerald Kirby Junr and Doree Gabelle, who perform 'Daisy Bell' while mimicking a bicycle ride. There are also sing-a-long numbers such as 'You Made Me Love You' and 'All the Nice Girls Love a Sailor'. Also included in the film is a tumbling act by Jumping George Campo and a fashion show.

Influenced by venues in Europe is the Café de Paris, which still operates in its original location at 3–4 Coventry Street, London. First opened in 1924, the venue was made popular in its early days by the Prince of Wales' patronage, although its long list of famous performers include the bandleader Harry Roy, the actress and dancer Louise Brooks as well as Cole Porter. The venue stayed open during the Second World War Blitz until on 8 March 1941 a bomb fell down a ventilation shaft and exploded in front of the bandstand killing and injuring over 100 people. The club did not reopen until 1948; however, once again with royal patronage (this time by Princess Margaret), it was soon successful with entertainment provided by Marlene Dietrich, Frank Sinatra and Noel Coward. Although the club became a dance hall in the 1960s and 70s, it gradually once more began attracting the fashionable set, but this time rock 'n' roll stars. In 1996, the first of a series of renovations began, gradually taking the club back to its glamorous past, often supported by special events including a secret gig by Prince in 1998 shown on Channel 4 television.[6] In 2012, the venue's interior was refurbished again, this time restoring the stage to its original position flanked by two curved staircases leading up to the balcony tables. The venue is now used at least two nights a week as a cabaret club, although it also operates as a nightclub and party venue.

It is common for new nightclubs to take on the name of famous venues from other cities, and like Café de Paris, the Ciro's name also became ubiquitous with high-class night-time entertainment far from its original location. Sir Victor Sassoon was a Shanghai-based businessman who built an empire of hotels, offices and other major developments, many along the city's Bund facing the Huangpu River. One of these was the Cathay Hotel (now the Peace Hotel), an eleven-storey art deco reinforced concrete structure, architecturally advanced for the time and one of the first high-rise

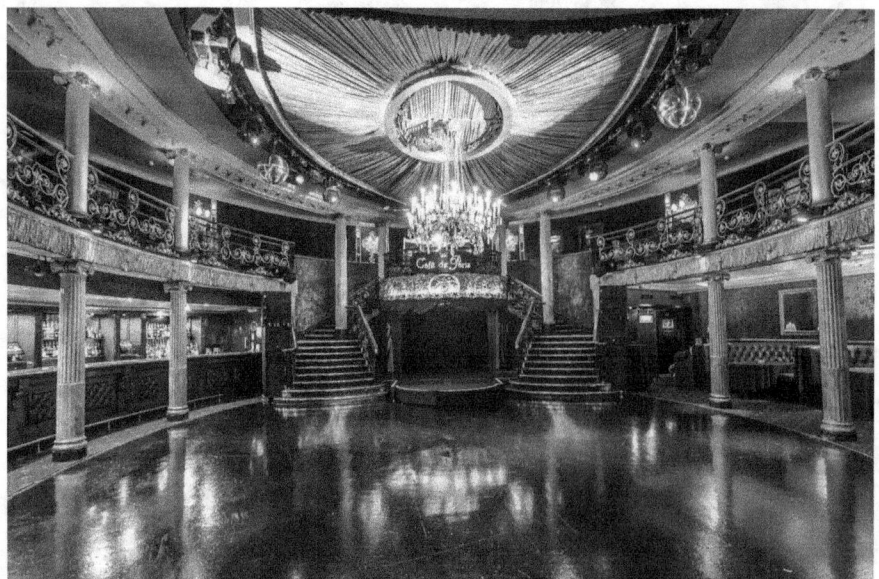

FIGURE 5.5 *Café de Paris after its 2012 renovation. Source: Café de Paris, London.*

buildings in the East. Designed by British architects Palmer and Turner, it was begun in 1926 and completed in 1929. The building is clad in granite, terracotta and copper, and its interior is richly decorated with stained glass and polished stone. The eighth-floor ballroom was the scene of elaborate parties with music provided by a jazz orchestra, presided over by the building's owner who lived in the penthouse above.

Sassoon's most glamorous venue was, however, Ciro's nightclub, built in Bubbling Well Road, Shanghai, in 1936 for 250,000 yuan (US$104,729 equal to US$1.5 million in 2018). Sassoon commissioned the same architects who had built the Cathay Hotel, and although still in the art deco style, it was a more sophisticated, streamlined design, taking advantage of the generous plot, set back from the road behind a large garden, which could also be used for outdoor parties in the summer. Reinforced concrete was utilized to create a cantilevered entrance canopy under which limousines would drop off the club's wealthy patrons, and a tall 'blade' lit up with the club's name in neon lights signed the entrance.

The inside was equally stylish, with the main room built on two levels. Below was the dance floor with couches and the orchestra's stage at one end. Surrounding this space was the elevated dining areas, six in all, with views down to the dance floor and stage. A large kitchen with showers for the staff

FIGURE 5.6 *Ciro's nightclub, Bubbling Well Road, Shanghai, 1936. Photograph by Malcolm Rosholt. Source: Mei-Fei Elrick, Tess Johnston and Historical Photographs of China, University of Bristol.*

was part of the back-of-house facilities as well as a manager's flat and office and changing rooms for the performers, including one room dedicated to the 'premier danseuse'.[7] The jazz music in the club was high quality, usually played by imported musicians. Bao Zhengzhen, who went to Ciro's and other dance halls in the Shanghai of the late 1930s, loved the jazz he heard there and became a saxophonist, playing secretly during the Mao years and as a professional from the end of the 1970s. There was a strict hierarchy in praise of the artists in that white and black American musicians were the most lauded, followed by Russians, and then Filipinos (who were also excellent and willing to pass on their skills to aspiring Chinese students like Bao). In 1941, the Japanese army 'liberated' the city and after that the foreigners quickly began to leave – Sassoon sold up his empire and moved to the Bahamas. After the Second World War ended and before the People's Liberation Army took control of every aspect of public life, there was an opportunity for Chinese jazz musicians to take to the stage, and Bao played in dance halls around the city: 'I wasn't a professional, but I would just go there and play a bit with the band, just playing around. I didn't much care for dancing. I just loved the music. That saxophone sounded so good.'[8]

After the Cultural Revolution, the Peace Hotel's Old Jazz Band was one of the first groups to reappear as a result of China's reforms led by premier Ding Xiaoping. Formed by Zhou Wanrong, who had played trumpet with the all-Chinese Jimmy King (Jimi Jin) orchestra in Shanghai's Metropole and Paramount hotels in the late 1940s, he had been a member of the Shanghai Symphony during the 1950s–70s. Asked to form a band by the manager of the Peace Hotel, he selected all musicians who had played jazz in the old Republic era – their average age was 74. Bao Zhengzhen joined the orchestra in the 1980s and performed regularly with them until 2012 (by which time he was 83). The band (which continues to play in the lavish ground-floor Victor's Café, refurbished with the rest of what is now called the Fairmont Peace Hotel in 2007–10) and others like it were pivotal in building Shanghai's reputation for this type of music. The city is now referred to as the jazz capital of China, with many venues playing the jazz of both the 1930s and 40s, but also contemporary styles with both imported and local artists at venues like the Wooden Box and the JZ Club.

In the United States, cabaret-style entertainment began at the turn of the nineteenth century when New York vaudeville entertainers began to appear in more intimate settings, initially in the roof gardens of the Broadway hotels, although also, by 1911, in the larger restaurants (sometimes known as lobster palaces) such as the Café des Beaux Arts, also on Broadway. Inspiration came from Parisian cabaret, but also from lower class saloons, bars, 'joints' and rathskellers (from the German term of a basement bar or restaurant). The Café des Beaux Arts was established in 1901, close to the theatre district in New York, as a reputable place where men and women could mix late into the night. It was popular with the theatre crowd, audience members and artistes such as the famous singer Lillian Russell, and the latter might be cajoled into an impromptu performance. Dancers Irene and Vernon Castle also performed there. Unlike vaudeville, which welcomed women and children, cabaret was firmly aimed at an adult audience, although unlike its Parisian and German counterparts, simple amusement rather than political satire was the main focus. As ragtime and jazz became more popular, along with the 'vulgar' dancing that came with it, the venues became simultaneously more popular and more suspect to certain parts of the establishment, as for the first time since the 1850s, people from different classes of society, including married and unmarried women, could mix together freely: 'The new amusement trends [including Vaudeville, moving pictures, public dancing and drinking] would come to the fore in the cabaret of the 1910s, where women and men worked out for themselves their attempt to choose new identities.'[9]

Perhaps the most famous New York cabaret venue of this period was John Reisenweber's Café, which, although founded by his father as a small saloon in 1856, was greatly expanded into a four-storey complex and rooftop garden in 1910. The venue featured a restaurant on the ground floor, the 400 Cabaret club on the first floor, a supper club with dance floor on the second floor and a 'Hawaiian Room' on the third floor. Situated on Columbus Circle at 58th Street and Eight Avenue, the venue was located close to Central Park and convenient for local theatres such as the Park, which opened in 1903. The Reisenweber building was in a terraced commercial block and occupied two adjacent buildings. With the expansion, a new entrance was constructed in 1910 in a Tudor style, with a projecting illuminated marquee sign above. Inside, a mirrored hallway led to an elegant curved staircase ascending to the upper floors. The Paradise Room was the restaurant level, with Parisian-style bentwood chairs, wood panelling and an arched ceiling.

The dining tables surrounded a wooden dance floor, which hosted a 'Jim-Jam Revue, A Gorgeously Cultured Entertainment Staged by Edward P. Bowers, with music by Louis Silvers, TWICE NIGHTLY, IN MAIN RESTAURANT'.[10] Entertainment was also provided by artists like Sophie Tucker, the first star to emerge from the Ziegfeld Follies, who would sing risqué comic songs and pull patrons up from the tables to take part in the performance. Tucker was so popular Reisenweber renamed the 400 Cabaret club the Sophie Tucker Room in 1919. In 1917 the Original Dixieland Jass Band began performing at Reisenweber's, an all-white group (although African American musicians also played there), famous for making one of the first jazz recordings on 26 February 1917 ('Livery Stable Blues/Dixie Jass Band One Step'), probably at the Victor Studio on 46 West 38th Street.

From 1912, New York cabarets began to be licensed so that their operating hours and clientele could be monitored and controlled, and in 1913 public cabaret venues were forced to close by 2.00 am. However, a

FIGURE 5.7 The Paradise Room, Reisenweber's, Columbus Circle, New York (contemporary post card). Source: Mary Evans/Jazz Age Collection.

FIGURE 5.8 The Original Dixieland Jazz Band. A 1918 promotional postcard produced whilst they were playing at Reisenweber's, Columbus Circle, New York. Left to right, the musicians are Tony Sbarbaro (aka Tony Spargo, drums), Edwin 'Daddy' Edwards (trombone), D. James 'Nick. LaRocca (cornet), Lawrence 'Larry' Shields (clarinet) and Henry Ragas (piano). Source: Public Domain.

further insurmountable problem was to come for many venues with the National Prohibition Act of 1919, which came into force on 17 January 1920 forbidding the import, manufacture, transportation and sale of intoxicating liquor (although consuming it was not illegal, meaning that those who could afford to do so stockpiled their favourite drinks before the law came into effect). Reisenweber's, like many other establishments, struggled to either enforce the act or to make money when they could no longer sell alcohol, and like the Café de Beaux Arts, which had closed in 1921, the venue shut down in 1922 after a number of police raids.

Speakeasies and nightclubs

Although Prohibition meant closure for many cabaret clubs, it was one of the spurs that encouraged a new form of entertainment venue in the United States, the nightclub. Licencing, which had already enforced public clubs to close at 2.00 am, led to the founding of members' clubs, which could stay open much later, but also enabled patrons to do more of what they liked with less chance of the authorities finding out! After the National Prohibition Act came into force, what they liked to do in private was drink alcohol, and thousands of illicit clubs came into being almost overnight across the United States. Although the speakeasy venue is something that is intimately associated with Prohibition era America, the term is actually British and much older, appearing first as a 'speak-softly' shop in 1823 and then as 'speak-easy' shop in 1847, meaning a smuggler's place of business. The first documented North American use of the word in its more familiar context is in the *Pittsburgh Dispatch*, Philadelphia, in March 1889, in a report concerning Police 'rooting out sly drinking places called "speak-easies"' – these were unlicensed premises as this was many years before Prohibition came into force.[11]

Although ostensibly members' clubs, the vast majority of speakeasies would admit anyone who was able to pay for their drinks, and because of the illegal nature of the business, the venues became synonymous with organized crime, often set up by the criminal 'bootleggers' who illegally supplied the drinks by smuggling or manufacturing it in hidden factories. Music was seen partly as a way of making the venue seem more legitimate (with the audience gathering for entertainment purposes rather than drinking), but as before Prohibition when the cabarets were flourishing, it was also a genuinely enjoyable component of a night out, which served to differentiate the better clubs from the rest.[12] Speakeasies opened up society in that both men and women frequented them, and famously, some women were involved in their operation. Texas Guinan and Helen Morgan were well-known speakeasy operators, who had both previously had a career in show business; Guinan worked in vaudeville, then as a chorus girl on

Broadway, before becoming a 'cowgirl' in silent pictures; Morgan was a star of the stage in the popular musical *Show Boat*. After stints as an emcee at various speakeasies in New York, Guinan opened her own place, the 300 Club at 151 West 54th Street, which featured an elaborate stage show with forty female fan dancers. The club was frequented by many celebrities. One patron was George Gershwin, who would play impromptu piano solos for the crowd, which often included Mae West, Al Jolson, John Barrymore and Rudolph Valentino. Although the club was frequently raided by police and Guinan arrested many times, it is reputed that she earned over $700,000 in just ten months during 1926 (equal to $9.6 million in 2018). Although many speakeasies were in hidden locations (such as Guinan's other operation Club Intime, which was in the basement of the building it occupied but had a hidden bar on the top floor), often they were also out in the open with street addresses and signs over the door. The conceit was that ostensibly no liquor was sold on the premises – Guinan often made the excuse that she never sold an alcoholic drink – patrons brought their own stuff with them! An early sound film, *1928-Toasts by Texas Guinan at Prohibition-era Speakeasy, New York City*, gives a taste of their atmosphere: a crowded, smoky room, with tables bundled around a tiny dance and performance area.[13] The musicians are on a small stage with Guinan up there too, making announcements and jokes for a rowdy audience. The space has been hastily decorated with some cloth ceiling hangings and balloons, and although salubrious it is not, fun it undoubtedly is.

As popular music was a key element in the ambience of a successful speakeasy, it also became a place where performers made their living and popular musical development took place. Although there were many clubs (as a guide published in the *Manhattan Weekly* of 1932 shows), one of the most famous was The Cotton Club, initially located in Harlem on 142nd Street and Lenox Avenue between 1923 and 1935, and then midtown between 1936 and 1940, making it one of the very few speakeasies to transition to a successful existence in the post-Prohibition period from 1933.

Situated on the upper floor of a two-storey commercial building, the club was originally a supper club opened by African American heavyweight boxing champion Jack Johnson; however, in 1923 he sold it to gangster Owney Madden (whose nickname was 'The Killer'). Madden was from Yorkshire, born in Leeds, England, before emigrating to the United States aged 12, and he was a violent and determined criminal. In 1915, he had been sentenced to twenty years in New York State Prison, Sing Sing, for murder, but was released on parole in 1923, and quickly became involved with bootlegging. He began to acquire clubs and speakeasies (he eventually owned more than twenty), including Johnson's place, which he reopened the following year as The Cotton Club.

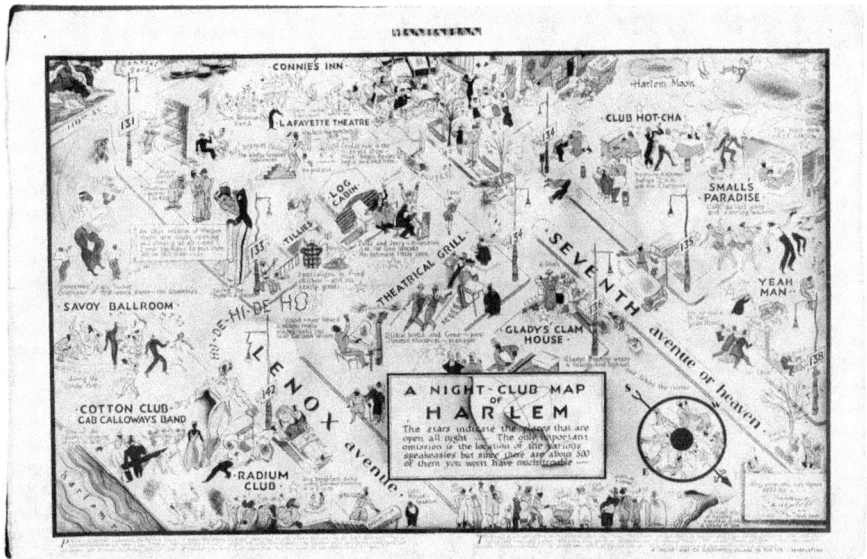

FIGURE 5.9 *A Night-Club Map of Harlem*, Campbell E. Simms, 1933, published by Manhattan Weekly, *vol. 1, no. 1, 18 January 1933. Source: Public Domain.*

The Cotton Club was created as a place where whites could experience African American entertainment in a segregated setting. To add insult to injury, the décor and the show content presented a stereotypical 'primitive' racist image with a dress code for the dancers and other performers as 'jungle natives' or cotton-growing plantation 'darkies'. Cab Calloway, the famous band leader, recalled in his biography that: 'The stage set looked like a "Sleepy Time Down South" stage set from the days of slavery. The bandstand was a replica of a southern mansion with large, white columns and a backdrop painted with weeping willows and slave quarters. The band played on the veranda of the mansion. A few steps down was the dance floor, which was also used for floorshows.'[14] Nevertheless, the high prices charged at the club meant that elaborate high-quality shows could be staged and the performers, African American and white, were well paid. The shows took the form of a review, in which there was a mixture of music, dancing, singers and comedians, which ran each evening from midnight until 3.00 am. The review changed completely every six months with brand new tunes, songs, arrangements and dance routines required for the fresh attraction. Many famous musicians came to prominence via their performances at the club, particularly after live radio broadcasts began to be aired and then syndicated onto the CBS and NBC networks, meaning that listeners across the United States could hear the music that was being created in Harlem, New York.

FIGURE 5.10 *The Cotton Club's Harlem location c. 1920s. The entrance area is boarded to represent a rural plantation hut in the American South. Source: New York Public Library.*

Perhaps the most influential musician to emerge from the Cotton Club was Edward 'Duke' Ellington, whose musicians became the house band on 4 December 1927, and continued through the Prohibition years until 30 June 1931. Increasing his band from a six-piece to an eleven-piece to meet the management's requirements, he composed over a hundred song accompaniments, dance tunes, overtures and transition pieces during this period, developing and perfecting both his own style, but also extending the concept of what jazz music could be. Ellington was already a recording artist and composer when he came to the club, and a recording he made just before his new engagement began, 'Creole Love Call' with Adelaide Hall on vocals, became his first worldwide hit. Cab Calloway's Orchestra first performed at the club in 1930, deputizing for Ellington while he was on tour; however, his exuberant personal style – singing, dancing and gesticulating while conducting – made him hugely popular, and when Duke's band returned, they became 'joint' house bands, allowing both artists to develop their careers with outside performances and tours. After Prohibition ended, the Cotton Club ensured its immediate survival with the introduction of even more elaborate, sophisticated review shows such as *Cotton Club Parade 1934*, fronted by Jimmie Lunceford's band and singer Adelaide Hall – over 600,000 people paid to see the show over its eight-month run.

Although Prohibition had not impeded the club's success, a problem at the root of its organization did. A race riot took place in Harlem in March 1935 during which white-owned businesses were damaged or destroyed. The club's well-known racial segregation policies came under more sustained vocal criticism, and its effect on smaller, local African American owned businesses, which could not compete, was highlighted. Madden had left New York in 1935, and in 1936, the club closed temporarily before reopening later that year at a new mid-town location at Broadway and 48th. The new Times Square venue was a large room over a doughnut shop, on the upper floor of a two-storey building in the centre of the theatre district. Giant neon signs were erected at the corner and over the entrance, enticing customers in by advertising: 'Cab Calloway ... Cotton Club Parade, 50 Sepian Stars – 50 Copper Colored Girls, Dinner $1,50, Never a Cover Charge'. This time the décor was more up to date – a lavish, streamlined Art Deco-themed space with curved booths surrounding a large dance floor spanned by a wide, gently arched, painted ceiling. Nevertheless, a large painted mural on the wall facing the stage still depicted scenes of the Old South with river boats, cotton bales, plantation buildings and negro slaves.

In its final years, Ellington returned to the club as did other stars including Louis Armstrong; however, changing fashions, rent rises and tax evasion investigations led to its closure in 1940. The Cotton Club survived the overwhelming majority of its many contemporaries by taking an innovative approach in providing ambitious, high-quality musical entertainment. However, there is a disturbing contradiction that cannot be denied, although the many African American stars who performed there were the reason for its success, racial discrimination meant that they were not even allowed to mix with the club's patrons.

FIGURE 5.11 *The Cotton Club mid-town location at 48th and Broadway in about 1937. Source: Lebrecht Music and Arts Photo Library/Alamy Stock Photo.*

Supper clubs

After Prohibition ended in the United States, speakeasy patrons were now able to legally enjoy alcoholic drinks during their evening out, and competition for business was once more based on the qualities of the establishment in terms of décor, food, ambience and entertainment. Supper clubs catering to a new, increased audience were established in cities nationwide. One of the most successful was the Copacabana, New York City, which opened officially at 10 East 60th Street on 10 November 1940. Some of the old speakeasy characteristics were carried over into this new venue and, according to Pete Denis – the club's DJ in the 1970s – it was for several years an illegal underground venue before it was legitimized.[15] Its (unofficial) owner was gangster Frank Costello, although the public face of the club was Monte Proser. Initially it had a 'whites only' policy, although this was relaxed a few years after opening, and it eventually became a very important venue for African American popular music artists.

The club featured Brazilian-style décor and Latin-themed orchestras although the food served was, bizarrely, Chinese and Italian. The club was situated in a large brownstone building with its kitchen in the basement, a casino on the fourth floor and the main showroom on the first floor. The building's columns were dressed to look like giant coconut palm trees (Plate 7). Large clubs like the Copacabana were glamorous with formally dressed staff, elaborate cocktails, dancing to a full orchestra and a floor show of well-known acts that frequently transferred to radio, then television and film. Sammy Davis Jr played there in the 1950s and 60s as did Frank Sinatra, Dean Martin and Jerry Lewis. In the 1960s, the club hosted a string of up and coming Tamla Motown artists – The Supremes were discovered there by Tamla Motown CEO Berry Gordy, and they later recorded a hit live album *The Supremes at the Copa* in 1965. Subsequently Sam Cooke, Marvin Gaye and The Temptations all played at the club and recorded live records there. In the early 1970s the club closed temporarily, and although the main showroom and casino remained, a new discotheque was introduced with disco balls, flashing lights and neon representations of the famous stars who had played there. A giant head of Carmen Miranda made in neon fronted a hidden deejay booth behind a one-way mirror wall. In 1992, 2001 and 2007, the club was forced to relocate mainly due to Manhattan development and real estate speculation, which affected many venues as new towers rose around 52nd Street; however, in 2011 the club reopened at 268 West 47th Street in Times Square. Palm fronds were introduced once again to decorate the new location's columns.

Although the show business side of the supper club is clear in big venues such as the Copa, there were also many other smaller venues, sometimes with quite different agendas. Café Society was started by Jewish New Jersey native Barney Josephson on 18 December 1938 in a basement room in a four-storey plastered brick building at 1 Sheridan Square, Greenwich Village, New York City. Although he had no experience at running a nightclub, he had visited places like the Cotton Club, which, while showcasing African American talent, either excluded them or relegated them to substandard seats at the back. The club's name was chosen to mock the smart venues it was meant to challenge, and its motto 'The Wrong Place for the Right People' joked about its mission to be the first fully integrated club in the city: 'I wanted a club where blacks and whites worked together behind the footlights and sat together out front. There wasn't, so far as I know, a place like that in New York or in the whole country.'[16]

The club's interior was decorated with strange cartoon murals painted by local artists that made fun of more conventional nightclubs, either directly or depicting the social scene as a circus. The venue opened with Billie Holiday who played there for its first nine months, often finishing her set with the powerful anti-racial prejudice song *Strange Fruit*. Many famous artists were launched there, including Lena Horne (who later played at the Cotton Club), Sarah Vaughan and Big Joe Turner. Sadly, the club, and another he opened on 58th Street, closed due to the McCarthy-led inquiry into so-called 'Un-American Activities', essentially a witch-hunt searching for Communist sympathizers in the entertainment industry. The club was the setting for numerous left-wing meetings and fundraisers, and when Josephson's brother Leon was subpoenaed by the McCarthy committee in 1947, audiences dropped off and it was forced to close a year later.

Cabaret venues' impact on popular culture

Cabarets, speakeasies and supper clubs have had a remarkable influence on the mainstream arts, both through the careers of the performers they launched whose music and personality have influenced generations since and also as a powerful archetypal image of the risqué entertainment venue where, often, illegal fun can be found. They are found as key settings in fiction writing, theatre and especially films. For such a short-lived phenomenon, speakeasies have a particularly interesting cultural history, depicted in the powerful movies made during the Prohibition period such as *The Public Enemy* (William Wellman, 1931) and *Scarface* (Howard Hawks, 1932) to musical comedies like *Some Like it Hot* (Billy Wilder, 1959) and *The Great Gatsby* (Baz Lurmann, 2013). There has even been a children's film set in a speakeasy: *Bugsy Malone* (Alan Parker, 1976). The Cotton Club itself was influential in popular culture. It featured in moving pictures as early as 1932 (The Cotton Pickers' Club in the 1932 film *Taxi*, directed by Roy Del Ruth and featuring James Cagney), although stage replicas depicting its ambience were used extensively for the many musical shorts featuring artists like Calloway and Ellington from the end of the 1920s. Its most thorough reinvention was in Francis Ford Coppola's 1984 film *The Cotton Club*. The tag line from its trailer set the tone: 'The Cotton Club – where deals were made, lives were traded, and the legends of Jazz lit up the night', although music was a big part of the new film including many of the original songs actually played at the club.[17] Funded in part by Las Vegas casino owners, an arms dealer and a vaudeville and Broadway promoter whose subsequent killing was dubbed 'The Cotton Club Murder', the film lived up to its historic inspiration, but failed at the box office, making about half of its $58 million budget. In 2017, Coppola used $500,000 of his own money to restore the film for limited release, adding in nearly thirty minutes of previously cut material, including eleven songs missing from the original version.[18]

Like the Cotton Club, the Copacabana featured in several moving pictures – the musical *Copacabana* (Alfred E. Green, 1947), which starred Groucho Marx and Carmen Miranda, was supposedly partly filmed in the club. It was also used by film director Martin Scorsese as a classic New York location in his films *Raging Bull* (1980) and *Goodfellas* (1990). Barry Manilow had a worldwide hit with his song *Copacabana* in 1978, which told an imaginative tale of the performer Lola, who worked in the club. This was expanded into a television film in 1985, soundtrack record album

(1985) and a stage musical, which first ran at Caesars Circus Maximus Theatre in Atlantic City, New Jersey, in 1990–91. It then also had successful runs in the UK; Pittsburgh, USA; and Sweden.

Perhaps the most famous depiction of the cabaret club in popular culture, a film that mixed great songs, performances and a realistically vivid image of a turbulent time in recent history was *Cabaret* (Bob Fosse, 1972), based in turn on the 1939 semi-autobiographical novel by Christopher Isherwood *Goodbye to Berlin*, the 1951 stage play by John Kander *I Am a Camera*, and the 1966 musical *Cabaret* (book by Joe Masteroff), which has been revived many times, most recently on Broadway in 2014. The story is set in 1930s Germany as the Nazis increase their hold on the country, and revolves around the performers and patrons of the Kit Kat Club, a typical Berlin kabarett. Each of the main characters represents a person who will suffer from the rise of an intolerant, racist and homophobic regime, and each stage of *Cabaret*'s cultural exposure has reflected this dark moment in world history, reflecting on the terrible effects of prejudice and discrimination in a contemporary context, while simultaneously showcasing the ability of popular performing arts to address such issues and bring them to a wider audience.

CHAPTER SIX

Pleasure Gardens, Ballrooms and Dance Halls

The first thing I am told about the place is that the Guinness is really great, and it's true, it's the best I have ever had, perhaps because it tastes like the stout you get in Ireland. But this is not the only impressive thing about the Irish Centre. First, outside it is a well-proportioned, formal classical building fronting onto Mount Pleasant just up from Liverpool's city centre – it's a bit down at heal, the sandstone dark and stained by years of coal soot, but its quality of design and construction is still clear. Inside, there have been many alterations with new light fittings, signs and carpets, but the walls are covered with beautiful plasterwork details. New stained-glass panels with Irish themes have been inserted into the roof-light openings for this is entirely a single-storey building. It's also a big building, with many rooms offering various forms of entertainment. In the Claddaß room you can sit down for a meal, and we pass by a shop selling souvenirs of the old country. In the Kennedy Room (which features murals and paintings of the US President, an 'Irish boy' made good), there is a session going on, with the tables filled with drinks and people gossiping, and a constant stream of movement to and from the long bar, which stretches entirely along one side of the room. Every so often someone will rise from the tables and begin to sing, and the room will go quiet to listen attentively, followed by loud applause when they finish and then the chatter will resume until someone else stands up.

But on this night in 1987 we have come for the *céilí*, which is happening in the ballroom at the back of the building. Passing through a central corridor to an octagonal ante-space (which also has its own bar), we pay a small fee and enter. The room is about 10 metres wide and more than twice as long. Ornate pilasters divide up the walls with a complex classical frieze featuring dancing maidens across the top. There is a coffered ceiling from which two chandeliers are suspended. On the stage at the end of the room, the band are set up with electric guitars, a full drum kit and a large PA, but are incongruously belting out a furious reel at full speed. Around the edge of the wooden floor are lines of chairs set up against the walls, but not many are in use as there are plenty of dancers on the floor hurling themselves around in time to the music – it seems wild and fun and like nothing I have seen before. It will take me a few more pints before I join them, not knowing any of the steps, but just enjoying the movement and spinning in time to the music.

The Wellington Rooms became the Irish Centre on 1 February 1965 (the Feast of St Brigid); however, it had a long history with dancing and entertainment before that, a history that has mirrored the changes in society that shaped the popularity and operation of dance venues up to the 1990s. Popular music and dance are inextricably linked, throughout history influencing each other in the style and nature of their performance: 'Dance is an example of our active engagement with popular music and its wider social importance ... closely associated with music, ritual, courtship and everyday pleasure.'[1] Its importance is signified by both the range and number of buildings given over to its enjoyment, both as a performance to be perfected and enjoyed as a spectator experience (dance schools, theatres and auditoriums for ballet, musical theatre and modern dance) and as a participatory one. Participatory dance (as opposed to dance performance or dance associated with ritual or religion) first took place on an ad hoc basis in spaces intended for other uses. Folk dancing did not rely on the creation of special venues for its performance; however, as new patterns of formal dance were developed for the gentry, this eventually resulted in the design of special spaces, if not wholly dedicated to dance, still created with this use in mind: 'dance was an essential part of celebration and recreation in both city and country; and of the rich and social context within which music was performed'.[2]

The Wellington Rooms were built primarily for this latter purpose in 1815–16, the result of an architectural competition supervised by the architect Thomas Rickman who, although an expert on Gothic-style architecture, supported the Neoclassical style of the highest placed entry. The winner Edmund Aiken moved to Liverpool, no doubt seeing a prosperous future for a young architect in this rich, port city. His brief was to create a private members' club for dances, balls and parties, to be funded by subscription by the elite of Liverpool society, the wealthy ship owners and businessmen, benefiting from the industrial development of North West England and increasing global trade. This was a lavish Regency building, designed with plenty of references to the classical architecture that these new titans of empire would aspire to, even though the building was a private club rather than a public edifice. A record of the Batchelor's Ball held in 1821 was printed in *The Kaleidoscope*, a weekly magazine published by Egerton Smith:

The Wellington Rooms were ... the scene of this enchanting entertainment ... Passing on to the grand ball-room, the scene became most dazzling; and while the eye wandered 'in fond delight,' the ear was charmed by the harmony of an admirable orchestra, under the direction of Mr. J. Hatton, jun. At eleven, Quadrilles commenced; for till that hour the general attention was too much taken up in admiring and recognising the novel objects which glanced before the eye, to think of dancing.[3]

Among the 'novel objects' was an entrance portico modelled on the Choragic Monument of Lysicrates near the Acropolis in Greece, who was a wealthy patron of music, and the capitals were copied from the Temple of Vesta at Tivoli.[4] The west side of the building had a portico for sedan chairs and the east-side one for carriages. As well as dancing, the building also had a supper room and a card room. Inside, plaster decorations were incorporated throughout to convey an atmosphere of elegant opulence. The venue's form, with its most important space being the substantial ballroom, was designed as a direct response to the newly enhanced enthusiasm for dancing.

As Liverpool society changed after the First World War, the Wellington Rooms became a dance hall (see below) until 1940 when the building began to be used as a youth centre. In 1941 its roofs were badly damaged by bombs falling nearby and many of the ornate ceilings were lost, although the ballroom survived intact. The building's architectural significance was

FIGURE 6.1 *The Wellington Rooms, Mount Pleasant, 1829. Source: Engraved by Jas. Allen; Drawn by G. & C. Pyne.*

recognized in 1952 when it was placed on the historic buildings register; however, its future was still uncertain until it became the new Irish Centre in 1965. This was a very active society, intent on retaining the cultural traditions of their community with plenty of young blood interested in both pipe and *céilí* music and traditional dancing. Such was the quality of the activities that went on there that the Liverpool Céilí Band won the All Ireland Competition in 1963 and 1964 and released two record albums on Decca. In 1973, the community restored the building to be a continuing home for the local Irish Community, but also as a base for outreach charity organizations. During this period, the venue was used on a daily basis for dance classes, rehearsals, music concerts and céilís. However, by 1992, the burden of running a large building, which also had many restrictions on it because of its historic listed status, became too much and the Centre sold it to a local businessman, still occupying the building until 1997. The Irish community moved to new premises in 1999, where traditional dancing and music still happen every week. For years after the Wellington Rooms remained empty, gradually falling into deeper disrepair, despite various proposals put forward for the building's reuse; however, in 2018 repair works began to save it from further decline with a view to bringing it back into public use once more.

FIGURE 6.2 *The Ballroom at the former Irish Centre, Wellington, Rooms, Mount Pleasant (photograph 2016). Source: Photo by Jacques Joudrey (A.K.A. SpiderMonkey).*

Pleasure gardens and ballrooms

Pleasure gardens were a new sort of space for dance and popular music that emerged in the seventeenth century as a part of the Enlightenment, the period following the restoration of the monarchy in England in which the arts, leisure and fashion became more valued in society. The urban environment of cities was in transition at this time, with new carefully designed elegant areas in contrast to the older neighbourhoods of densely packed buildings, served by cramped thoroughfares, often awash with mud and night soil. These places were often dangerous too, with street crime barely under control. The new public pleasure gardens provided safe, well-maintained, fashionable locations for the gentry and burgeoning middle classes to dress up, be entertained and socialize: 'The air was clean and perfumed; the manicured walks were luxurious to walk upon, allowing voluminous skirts and dainty high heels to remain clean; and the romance of sun-dappled bowers allowed heads to spin.'[5] These hugely popular gardens were commercial businesses in which a fee was paid for entry although there were many further opportunities once inside for further expenditure with eating, drinking, shopping, gambling and dancing activities. By the middle of the eighteenth century, there were sixty-four separate venues in London, and most provincial cities also had their own versions. Popular music performance was an essential part of the pleasure garden experience, and the buildings and structures that were provided for this new pastime often took on new architectural forms. One early facility was *The Folly on the Thames*, a floating barge built like a castle with a turret at each corner that was moored near Waterloo Bridge between 1668 and 1720, offering music and dancing, as well as private booths. Despite a visit by Queen Mary (and a change of name to the *Royal Diversion*), its reputation was gained more for gambling and prostitution than gentle leisure activities.

The most famous London gardens were Vauxhall, Spring and Ranalegh. Typically, they would make use of existing major landscape features such as mature trees and water elements like streams and ponds, added to with pathways through formal and informal garden areas, with imaginative and sometimes extravagant buildings and pavilions. Night-time events and activities were especially popular, so thousands of lanterns would be suspended around the grounds, with some areas left darker for potentially illicit assignations. Bands and orchestras would be set up in pavilions or on stages, adjacent to performance or dancing areas. One of the most dramatic of these was the Rotunda built at Ranelagh gardens around 1742.

This massive circular building with a 170-metre (555-foot) internal circumference was modelled on the classical Pantheon in Rome and was three storeys high with a domed roof. The walls were 5.2 metres (17 feet) thick and the rotunda at its centre spanned 46 metres (150 feet). Around the inside were 55 supper boxes where revellers would eat and drink and

FIGURE 6.3 *London: Interior of the Rotunda at Ranelagh, Giovanni Antonio Canaletto, 1754 (National Gallery, London). Source: Public domain.*

watch the parade of fashionable ladies and gentlemen strolling around the perimeter. Marbled columns and gilded caryatids supported the vast olive and rainbow-coloured ceiling from which was suspended crystal chandeliers lit by candles. A central structure was originally meant to support the orchestra; however, poor acoustics meant a new bandstand was built to one side and the central element became a fireplace to provide some warmth on chilly evenings. Horace Walpole described the musical elements of a masquerade evening held at Ranelagh Gardens on 26 April 1749:

> In one quarter was a maypole dressed with garlands, and people dancing round it to a tabor and pipe, and rustic music, all masked, as were all the various bands of music that were disposed in. Different parts of the garden; some like huntsmen with French horns, some like peasants, and a troop of harlequins and scaramouches in the little open temple on the mount. On the canal was a sort of gondola adorned with flags and streamers, and filled with music, rowing about … In short, it pleased me more than the finest thing I ever saw.[6]

Pleasure gardens' popularity continued into the nineteenth century, their design and operation adapting to changing circumstances, adding more extravagant amusements as leisure time and disposable income increased for the general population. The pattern was absorbed into the Victorian public park with bandstands, tea rooms and sporting pastimes, and as a principal element in seaside resort attractions.

The first ballrooms were in large private houses and were used for parties, at first adapted from other rooms such as the gallery or drawing room, but as the social occasion became a method for establishing rank and status, a dedicated grand room, lofty and highly decorated with a smooth wooden floor, began to be designed. A ball (the term stems from the Latin word *ballare*, which means 'to dance') would feature music and dancing, initially in the form of a group with interchangeable partners. The Quadrille was one of these; a dance involving groups of couples who take turns in performing the steps was popular at the end of the eighteenth and beginning of the nineteenth centuries. Although there were some dances at this time involving just two partners (such as the minuet, in which partners would perform side by side), as 'closed hold' dances such as the waltz were introduced, these became understandably popular (with concern and disapproval in some quarters regarding the necessary embrace this entailed). Special music was composed for dancing, paying attention to rhythm and pace but also to the separate stages of the steps so that a new theme or section began in time with the dancers' movements. However, much music also included themes from popular songs or tunes that would be familiar to the audience.[7]

Public assembly rooms in cities and in fashionable resorts were built in the latest architectural styles with high-quality materials that reflected the 'quality' of those who would attend, although 'public' entry was strictly controlled, tickets never went on public sale. The Bath Assembly Rooms were opened in 1771 to the designs of John Wood, the Younger who with his father (John Wood the Elder) had designed many of the new dwellings for the city's fashionable residents and visitors who came to 'take the waters'. Built to complement these ambitious houses that were organized as a series of impressive terraces (e.g. The Circus, Queen Square and the Royal Crescent), the Assembly Rooms were designed in a restrained classical style from local Bath stone (limestone) with a portico entrance supported by Doric columns. This was a grand project, with a tea room for 250 people, an octagonal room with four fireplaces and a ballroom for 500 people at 30 metres (100 feet) long by 14 metres (45 feet) wide and 13 metres (42 feet) high; in 1777, a card room was also added. The interiors were splendid, with elegant plasterwork detailing illuminated by three chandeliers in the tea room and five in the ballroom.

Ballroom events were held frequently, particularly in the 'season' (June to October) with two balls a week in addition to concerts and other social events. If there were no special events, patrons could still come and play cards or take tea. Although severely damaged by bombing during the Second World War, Bath Assembly Rooms were restored in the 1960s and maintain their original function, open to the public for visits and concerts and available for private hire for functions and dances.

FIGURE 6.4 *The ballroom at the Bath Assembly Rooms, 1771 (photo: 2010).*
Source: Heather Cowper.

Dancing was originally a pastime for the social elite at private events; however, as new public spaces began to be included in the designs of large hotels as function spaces for parties and celebrations, and also into other tourist attractions such as pleasure gardens and seaside resorts, the middle classes began to enjoy this leisure activity. One of the most well-known ballrooms still in use today came from a later, more egalitarian era. The Blackpool Tower Ballroom was initially built in 1894 as part of the complex of pleasure buildings that surround the base of the famous North of England seaside landmark. In response to competition from the Empress Ballroom at the nearby Winter Gardens, the present ballroom was designed in 1897 by local architects James Maxwell and Charles Tuke but decorated by the prolific theatre architect Frank Matcham (see Chapter 2). The Ballroom is part of a leisure complex, which as well as the 158-metre (518-feet)-high steel tower, includes a circus, an aquarium and roof gardens with a free-flight aviary, and is part of the rapid development of nineteenth-century British seaside resorts that were aimed at entertaining working people during their increased leisure time.

The Tower Ballroom is on the first floor above a ground-floor café, and its grandeur is spectacular. To the east side is a grand proscenium arch, with a swan-neck pediment featuring a large sculpture of the three graces at its centre (Plate 8). The other three sides feature two levels of balconies, decorated with a wide variety of architectural features including onion domes, curvilinear lattices and rocaille mouldings.[8] The ceiling is painted with Baroque murals and lighting is provided by a giant skylight, and chandeliers that can be lowered to the floor for cleaning. A 1938 programme declared:

> Blackpool is deservedly proud of its famous Tower Ballroom, the beautiful interior of which is second to no other ballroom or concert hall in the world. In addition to the myriads of dancers who have been carried into the seventh heaven of delight whilst dancing on its new parquet floor, the Kings and Queens of song thrill thousands with their singing at celebrity concerts in this wonderful hall.[9]

The ballroom was nearly lost in 1956 after a disastrous fire; however, it was restored to its original splendour by the film and set designer Andrew Mazzei, who diligently researched the original design prior to starting work. The Tower Ballroom's recent fame in the UK has come from its long-standing presence on television, first as the setting for the BBC Television programme *Come Dancing* (1959–88), and more recently selected shows from *Strictly Come Dancing* (2004–date).

Although featuring live performances by dance bands and orchestras throughout its history, the Tower Ballroom is also famous for its Wurlitzer Organ and Reginald Dixon, the venue's third organist, and Britain's most famous popular music organ player. Dixon was a musical prodigy who was already giving concerts at the age 12, and by 17 he was an associate of the Royal College of Music. He began playing in cinemas in the late 1920s, which frequently had organ recitals as part of the show. When he was 25 years old he auditioned for the job of organist on the Tower Ballroom's 2/10 Wurlitzer, with the requirement that the new musician would be able to keep the strict tempo required for dancing (neither of the previous incumbents being able to do so). After a few weeks it became clear that Dixon was the man for the job – not only was his playing style so advanced that it was clear he would need a better organ to fully exploit the role (it arrived in 1935, a Wurlitzer 3/13), but he was also being broadcast on BBC radio, shows that would be extended in both duration and frequency so that a year later he would be on the radio up to five times a week. Dixon's repertoire was wide and eclectic, including popular songs, traditional tunes, jazz standards and classical pieces, both orchestral and from opera. After serving in the RAF during the Second World War (although still being called on to play the organ to entertain the troops and civilians), Dixon returned to the Tower Ballroom, and by the mid-1950s, he had tallied over 1,000 radio broadcasts, with an estimated 6 million people listening to each show, which does not count his live audiences and those who purchased the many recordings he made. Dixon retired from the Tower Ballroom organ in 1970, although he continued to give concerts in the UK and abroad. His replacement, Phil Kelsall, began playing there in 1975 and continues to this day, the building's organ still forming a popular attraction for both concerts and dancing.

Dance halls

The Wellington Rooms was successful in its original role for over a century; however, after the First World War, society was changing and the subscription club around which it was based was no longer viable, finally winding up in 1922. However, these same societal changes meant that there was a new potential clientele who were enthusiastic about dance, and the venue was reopened as the Embassy Club in 1923, where dance classes and tea dances were held, now for a much wider range of social classes. The emergence of dance as an important part of the commercial popular entertainment industry therefore began after the First World War. In the late 1800s and early 1900s, even with the new public ballrooms that were built, social dancing of this type had still not been a widely adopted activity. The upper classes would attend society balls in large private houses, or special events in large hotels (e.g. in London, The Savoy and The Ritz) particularly during the 'social season' (approximately January to June). Wealthy middle classes also attended 'subscription dances' held in hotels and other venues, held to support charity or clubs, for example for cricket, rowing or tennis. The first dance clubs were also for the rich; the dinner dance became a popular evening out at clubs such as Ciro's and the Café de Paris (see Chapter 5). As a popular leisure activity, dance was still restricted for the working class, as it had to be learned via tuition at dance classes, and the event required a suitable venue and trained musicians, all of which was financially beyond most people.

However, during and after the First World War there was significant emancipation in both class and gender – wages for working people rose and the number of hours they were required to work fell, combining to give them more time off and more disposable income. Paid holidays also spread to nearly 50 per cent of the population, giving impetus for the development of more holiday resorts where new pastimes could be tried. Musical styles also influenced this new popularity as jazz, imported from the United States, became both more accessible and popular. Between 1919 and 1925, it is estimated that around 11,000 dance halls were established in the UK.[10] Many of these were conversions from older buildings, and the proprietors of other entertainments, such as cinemas and music hall, recognized this as a threat to their businesses as patronage dropped in favour of this new craze. By the 1950s around 4 million people were attending a British dance hall every week, 200 million per year (compared to 80–90 million attending football matches). Social dancing such as this took place in two primary venues, a public hall temporarily used for dance (church, village and social club rooms) and the purpose-designed dance halls, built specifically to cater to (and develop) this new activity.

Some dance halls were converted from other functions. The Corn Exchange (1862) in Derby, England, was converted into a music hall, the Palace Theatre of Varieties in 1897; however, after the First World War it was converted again, this time into the Palais de Danse. The Palais de Danse title was one that became widely adopted, evoking with its French name something more romantic and exotic, although the influence came as much from the United States as Europe. The new halls not only had improved facilities with good-quality dance floors and an orchestra space, but also had cafés and restaurants that raised additional revenue and made a visit more of an evening out. The North American influence came from the music that was played and the types of dancing that took place – up-to-date jazz bands and orchestras, playing the latest tunes, with dance instructors on hand to demonstrate the new moves.

The first purpose-built Palais de Danse in Britain was developed by Howard Booker and Frank Mitchell, both American citizens (although Booker also held a British/Canadian passport). The Hammersmith Palais de Danse was constructed at 242 Shepherd's Bush Road, London, on a site specifically chosen to have good transport links around the capital. The partners were intent on bringing new popular culture businesses to

FIGURE 6.5 *Social dancing at the Olympic Gardens Dance Hall, Halifax, Nova Scotia, 1948. Source: Public domain.*

Great Britain including baseball, mail order and beauty supplies shopping; however, the Hammersmith Palais was one of their most ambitious projects. The new building began as a part-conversion, as it made use of the structure of a former roller skating rink only constructed in 1910, yet closed by 1915. Booker and Mitchell acquired the site late in the First World War and set about rebuilding it to the designs of theatre and cinema architect Bertie Crewe, who had previously worked with Frank Matcham and W.G.R. Sprague (see Chapter 2). The interior was extravagant and eclectic, completed in a faux Chinese style. A large central dance floor made from Canadian maple was enclosed by a fret-work pagoda with lacquered columns and silk lanterns. In the centre was a model mountain complete with a miniature Chinese village and a fountain. A bandstand was placed at each end to allow the musicians to interchange quickly between sessions. This was a large building and a considerable investment designed to accommodate up to 2,000 people; however, success was quick in coming. On 28 October 1919, the first night saw a huge crowd of 7,000 people turn up to see the Original Dixieland Jazz Band, who were subsequently resident for the first nine months. The importation of musicians from America was a practice that the owners were keen to continue with New Orleans jazzman Sidney Bechet, and later on Adelaide Hall also playing there. The company made three times its £30,000 capital back in the first twelve months of operation (equal to £1.5 million in 2018). Although aimed at the mass market, its fame was such that celebrities also came to experience the Palais, including royalty and film stars like Mary Pickford and Douglas Fairbanks.[11]

The Hammersmith Palais had a long and mostly successful history as a dance hall. Although briefly converted to an ice rink in the early 1930s, a new dance floor was once more back in place by the end of 1934. From 1959, the Joe Loss Orchestra, one of the most popular in its day, was the resident band, playing there almost every night for a decade.

From the 1960s the venue began to host pop and rock bands, in which the emphasis gradually shifted towards concert performance. The Beatles, The Rolling Stones, The Who and David Bowie all played there, followed in the 1980s by U2, The Police and The Cure. The last ever performance was by Manchester band The Fall on 1 April 2007. In 2009, the local council Hammersmith and Fulham rejected plans for demolition of the building and to turn the site into a student apartment building; however, this was overturned on appeal by the Government's Planning Inspectorate, and this historic building that embodied a long and vibrant history of popular music, not just for London but for Britain as a whole, was demolished in May 2012.

Similar venues to the Hammersmith Palais, although not usually as large, were opened all over the country, with the big cities having dozens of Palais' competing for business. Even small towns would have a hall usually with an exotic name, if not Palais de Danse, they might be the Locarno (Glasgow,

FIGURE 6.6 *Hammersmith Palais (photo, 1963). Source: Ralph Crane/The Life Picture Collection/Getty.*

1926), Rivoli (Manchester, 1923) or the Arcadian (Exmouth, 1923). As styles changed, so would the architecture – the Palais de Danse at Dennistoun, Glasgow, was built in an Art Deco style in 1936, and Glasgow's Locarno had a streamlined neon-signed marquee entrance by 1938. Typical was the Oxford Galleries in Newcastle. Originally designed as a restaurant, billiard hall and cinema with seating for 2,000 people, the plans were approved by the council in 1921; however, shortly after the promoters withdrew them, and instead changed the design to a vast new dance hall with a capacity of 2,500. The hall consisted of a large shed built at the back of an older neoclassical house designed by architect John Dobson for himself in 1823. Fronting onto New Bridge Street (although named after the street that ran alongside), the dance hall's entrance was a grand pedimented arch with ionic columns. Inside, a vast, gently arched ceiling covered the large dance floor, with the bandstand positioned in the centre. The hall opened in June 1923 with music provided by the London Sonora Band led by Bobbie Hind. This band played syncopated jazz and were recording artists on the Paris-based Pathé label and in Germany for Favorite. They toured all over Europe and gave a Royal Command performance for Queen Mary in 1923.[12] As well as evening dances, there were afternoon tea dances, and lady 'professionals' could be hired for sixpence a dance. The hall continued as a dance venue throughout the twentieth century and into the twenty-first as in the 1960s it was transformed into the first of a string of discotheques: Tiffany's, the Ritzy, Ikon, The Studio, Central Park, Diva and Liquid Envy. Its final incarnation was Club LQ, which closed in 2015, and the building was demolished shortly after to make way for student apartments.

As with the Tower Ballroom, some dance halls were also used for radio and television broadcasting. An interesting mix of both live music and dance was the *BBC Dancing Club*, which aimed to 'bring the glamour and elegance of good ballroom dancing into your home'. Victor Silvester was both a professional ballroom dancer and band leader who had published successful dance instruction books before the Second World War. His first radio show was broadcast in the spring of 1941 from the Paris Cinema, Lower Regent Street, London, in front of a studio audience. As well as live music from his orchestra, Victor Silvester would slowly read out instructions for the accompanying dances so audiences at home could try them out, a method described as 'the magic way to ballroom dancing'. The radio show transferred to television in January 1948 (becoming the *BBC Television Dancing Club*) and from 1953 it was recorded at the Carlton Rooms, Maida Vale, London.

American dance halls

Between the two World Wars, dance venues in North America ranged from the country and Western music-flavoured local dance halls and honky-tonks such as Floore's (see Chapter 3) to the jazz-focused nightclubs like the Cotton Club (see Chapter 5). Both styles of music were widely publicized via public radio broadcasts. However, in addition to these small- and medium-sized venues, there were also much larger halls that paralleled (and influenced) the Palais de Danse-type establishments that were built in the UK from 1919 onwards. The largest dance halls were built at resorts, locations (like Blackpool in England) where a regular crowd could be guaranteed. The first of these huge buildings was the Dancing Pavilion at the Boblo Island Amusement Park, Bois Blanc Island, Ontario, Canada (although close to the US city of Detroit), designed by the prolific Detroit architect Albert Khan, who revolutionized industrial building techniques with his use of concrete to replace wood. The pavilion was built between 1912 and 1913 and funded by Henry Ford, for whom Kahn had designed many buildings including the Highland Park plant (1908–10) where the assembly-line manufacturing process for the Model T motor car was fully realized. The Boblo Island dancing pavilion consisted of an enclosed, cathedral-like shed, with a lightweight, steel truss frame roof, in the form of a flattened gothic arch, providing a completely open space without columns.

FIGURE 6.7 *Boblo Dancing Pavilion, Bois Blanc Island, Ontario (photo: 1914).*
Source: Public domain.

The Eastern gable end was almost entirely glass, and there was a deep gallery around the interior walls for spectators. In the centre of the South wall was an Orchestrion, made by the Welte company, a type of calliope that was intended to mimic the sound of an orchestra, including percussion. This massive building could reputedly accommodate 5,000 dancers at one time.

The Boblo dance pavilion was only North America's largest for eleven years until the Crystal Beach Amusement Park ballroom was created, also in Ontario, although close to the US city of Buffalo, New York. The Crystal Beach Amusement Park ballroom was designed by the Schultz architectural practice of Brantford, Canada, in 1924 using steel box beams in an innovative manner for the time to create a giant column free hall 70 metres long (230 feet) by 50 metres wide (164 feet). Unlike the Boblo pavilion, this looked like an up-to-date, modern building, with the massive linear beams creating a lofty yet dynamic space and continuous glass doors that opened onto the lake or the formal gardens at each end. Initially the bandstand was located in the centre of the dance floor with reflective wooden panels above to broadcast the music around the large space; however, later, when amplification equipment was added, a large art deco bandstand was created on the south side.

FIGURE 6.8 *Crystal Beach Amusement Park – interior of the Crystal Ballroom (1930s). Source: Niagara Falls (Ontario) Public Library.*

Venues like the Crystal Beach Ballroom became associated with a particular style of jazz that was hugely popular across the world – the big band. Although there are significant differences between the various ensembles, big bands play a type of jazz known as swing that features a more supple and relaxed rhythm, incorporating groups (usually three or four of each) of brass instruments such as the trumpet, trombone and saxophone, plus bass, drums, guitar, keyboards and a singer. Some also include clarinet, French horn, violin or even timpani. Count Basie, Tommy Dorsey (with Frank Sinatra), Gene Krupa, Stan Kenton and Artie Shaw all played at Crystal Beach – as did perhaps the most famous of them all, Glenn Miller (although the band leader himself was not present that night). Audiences for the big bands were discerning about the styles and sound of the particular orchestras and were as much fans of the music, musicians and soloists as the dancing that went along with it. Paul Kassay was a regular at the hall: 'It was just amazing, the reverberation throughout that hall, and the people crammed up to the stages and just enjoying it. There were more people that would be up against the stages [listening to the band] than were dancing – it was that type of thing.'[13] Big bands' popularity began to reach its peak in the 1930s and it is often understood as the soundtrack of the Second World War; however, the advent of the jazz combo and then rock 'n' roll in the 1950s swiftly reduced its impact. Like many other similar venues, Crystal Beach Ballroom suffered a large downturn in its audiences, being converted to a new fad, roller skating, in the 1960s. After a large fire in 1975, the hall was restored and continued for another ten years until it was closed and demolished, along with the amusement park, in 1985.

There are fewer occasions today where a dwindling big band audience can be matched to an appropriate venue, generating a large-enough fee that can be profitably shared between a relatively large group of musicians. However, this music does persist due to its dedicated fans. Some of the live music consists of 'ghost bands' playing the music of long dead artists, for example The Glenn Miller Orchestra and the Duke Ellington Orchestra, and these names continue to draw an undoubtedly nostalgic audience. Mercer Ellington, son of the Duke, insists that: 'I want the sound of everything that was there, including the solos, because I don't think that anyone today can concoct a solo that fits this music better than what Tricky Sam Nanton or Lawrence Brown or Cootie Williams [soloists in the original orchestra] played on it. I want to hear those same notes.'[14] Concerts by the famous ensembles and others who are well known due to their own continuing reputation (such as the BBC Big band) are held in seated concert halls and a few important remaining dance venues, such as Blackpool's Tower Ballroom, enabling the music in these places to do what it was intended for – be listened to and be danced to.

Social dance is an activity that is popular in every part of the world, and although there are some styles that are universal, there are others that are specific to the region in which they have developed, often alongside dedicated musical forms and social practices in which they take place. One dance style that is distinctive in all these ways, but has had global influence, is Argentinian tango. Emerging in the second half of the nineteenth century, tango developed simultaneously both as a musical and as a dance style, and although its origins are obscure, it is almost certainly another example of the influence of African rhythms introduced by slaves and their free descendants, mixed with the music of immigrants from Europe who brought their traditional waltzes, polkas and mazurkas. The word tango may derive from the Italian and Latin verb *tangere*, to touch, which is an apt description of the dance that involves partners (traditionally men and women, although partners of the same gender are also common) walking in intimate embrace in time with the music – it is a sensual dance, and where there are lyrics the accompanying music often shares sad and nostalgic stories of lost love.

Tango was initially a dance of the poor and it was associated with the brothels, bars and cheap dance halls of Argentinian (and Uruguayan) towns and cities. The word *milonga* is crucial to Argentinian tango as it is a description of a type of dance, its associated music and the dance event where people gather to enjoy the pastime. In the Argentinian capital Buenos Aires, districts such as San Telmo, one of the oldest of the city's barrios (neighbourhoods), is the setting for one of the longest running public *milongas*, the Milonga del Indio, which has taken place in the Plaza Dorrego every Sunday for the last twenty years. Funded by voluntary contributions gathered in a hat that is passed around, the dancing takes place on a temporary dance floor to recorded music. Tango also happens in bars, in halls and on the stage as exhibition dancing is popular not just as a tourist show but also with *milongueros* who come to watch the *tangueros* show off the best style and moves. A typical tango orchestra consists of two violins, a flute, piano, double bass and two bandoneóns (concertinas); however, it can also be played on a solo guitar or by a guitar duo. Musical groups in the newer, late-night venues have also introduced electronic instruments and drums. Venues are many and varied, ranging from historic cafés with afternoon tea dances to brand new nightclubs that don't liven up until 2.00 am.

The Confitería Ideal is one of the most beautiful *milonga* venues in the city. Built in 1912 as a pastry and tea shop, it was designed by C. F. González for its Spanish immigrant owner Don Manuel Rosendo Fernández in a Belle Epoque style reminiscent of fashionable nineteenth-century Parisian architecture; however, it did not become a regular tango venue until the 1990s. Downstairs is the tea room selling pastries and sandwiches in elegant and stylish surroundings featuring Italian stained glass fittings, bevelled glass cases displaying the cakes and imported furniture – a grand wood panelled room, its high ceiling is defined by a line of columns on either side of the central space. On the upper floor, accessed via a marble staircase or a brass, wood and glass elevator is the ballroom, with Corinthian columns surrounding the dance floor and an elegant glass roof light above. Although listed as a building of National Cultural Heritage in 2003, the building gradually deteriorated until eventually it was closed in March 2016 for a lengthy restoration. Tango is not just a historic dance, but one that has an enthusiastic and growing audience, both within Argentina and abroad, first beginning in France in the 1980s following the publicity generated by a popular touring show, but also in the UK and the United States. Dedicated tango dance festivals occur in many cities (for instance the annual Boston Tango Festival, Massachusetts, USA), the events taking place in hotel ballrooms, dance studios and, as in Argentina, external public spaces. Like all social dance, the activity of tango is a portable one and not tied to a specific type of dance hall. Its musical heritage is, however, enhanced by the practice of dancing, enabling its character and atmosphere to be readily transplanted into new and widely varying spaces, both inside and outside.

CHAPTER SEVEN

Pubs, Barrooms and Coffee Bars

Although it's still light, its Saturday evening and Bridge Street, Westport, Co. Mayo is already busy. The street is wet with recent rain, although it's gone off now. The mini-buses that have dropped off the people from the various communities around and about have just turned on their lights as they swish down towards the harbour to park up until they take their rides home at midnight or later. Groups of these carousers, talking loudly, wonder up and down, dropping in and out of the brightly painted bars, and we are among them. We've had a pint in O'Malley's and another in the Clock, but now it's time for Matt Molloy's.

Like the rest of the bars, outside it's just a white rendered two-storey terraced building with the inevitable Guinness sign above the entrance. Two Georgian windows are at the first-floor level above a red painted wooden shop front. If anyone is trying to sleep in the upstairs bedroom, it will be a few hours before they do so because it's noisy downstairs. Inside, there is a press at the front bar and everyone is talking loudly to make themselves heard. White painted walls, a stained wooden ceiling and a black painted wood bar with three separate pumps just for the black stuff. There is also a pump for Budweiser, and I wonder if it's in honour of the US Vice President's visit the previous year. From the back there is the sound of a fiddle being tuned and we press through into the snug, which is a sizeable room for what is not a big bar, about 6 metres (20 feet) across. In the corner beneath a sign that requests 'please reserve for musicians when there is a session', three elderly men and a young woman are getting themselves settled – a few words, a laugh, a last sip of the pint and then they are off – the session has started with the lady fiddle player, guitar, whistle and *bhodran*, although others might join as the evening continues.

I'm not an expert but I recognize the jig *Handsome Sally*. There is nowhere for us to sit, we are too late for that, but we are happy to stand by the wall – easier to get back to the bar anyway.

FIGURE 7.1 *Matt Molloy's bar, Bridge Street, Westport, Co. Mayo, Ireland.*
Source: Paul Gregory.

Music can be found in many of the bars around Westport on a Saturday night, and most other nights too – provided, if not by professional musicians, then by those who play for fun (the word amateurs does not do them justice). However, Molloy's has a reputation beyond Westport, and for some, beyond Ireland too, as the place belongs to Matt Molly, who is the flautist and

FIGURE 7.2 *A lively traditional music session in Matt Molloy's. Source: Matt Molloy's.*

whistle player with one of Ireland's most famous traditional music groups, The Chieftains. Although the session music is loud enough, after a while I hear something else in the lulls, and when it's time for the inevitable visit out back, I hear the sound of electric guitars and drums. Poking my nose in through a door I see where the noise is coming from – it's Matt Malloy's Yard Bar, bigger and, tonight, louder for sure (Plate 9). People are dancing and shouting to a rock 'n' roll number pelted out with gusto by a four-piece, crammed onto a small stage in front of a stone wall. This is a bigger function room, the high glass ceiling and the plants hanging from the walls mean it looks a bit like a conservatory, but tonight it's party time, someone's birthday or another celebration. But it's the session music I'm here for, and when I head back inside, my friends have grabbed some seats and we settle in for the night.

From a musician's (and the audience) point of view, having somewhere to play that is affordable with a crowd receptive to what you have to offer is, of course, essential. In most towns and cities this is provided by the small neighbourhood bar or pub, a place where alcohol is sold for consumption on the premises (although coffee bars may also fit the bill), thereby creating a place where people can sit, talk, play cards or something similar, and quite often also be entertained. Music performance is sometimes performed as a way to generate more business, to sell more drinks or food if its offered, but its presence in these small venues is just as likely to be driven by the musicians themselves finding a place to perform, a way to have their music heard, sometimes for free, or a few drinks, or for tips. Music at this level is an arrangement between the bar owner (or pub landlord/landlady) and the musicians – mutually convenient while it lasts. Although bars differ in character and customs throughout the world – a place where people can have a drink, have something to eat and also listen to live music for free or a moderate fee is almost ubiquitous. And yet bars and pubs suffer from many problems associated with their operation, leading to a certain transience. These range from problems with clientele – drunkenness, fighting, stealing – as the worst sometimes comes out in people where alcoholic drink is concerned, to restrictions in licencing by local and national authorities trying to control aspects of their business and consequently limiting the viability of the operation. But the bar/pub is the essential local venue, the place where musicians begin and end their careers. Begin if they are lucky enough (and talented enough) to move on to the next stage (recording, bigger venues, touring), and if they just get fed up with the grind and leave professional performance behind, or if they love it enough to keep playing on and on, never moving up but content with what they have. The barroom venue is the place of discovery of new music and artists and the place of reassurance that the older music with which audiences are familiar is still popular with someone, be it traditional Irish music as found in Matt Molloy's snug or rock 'n' roll from the yard.

Pubs

Based on the Latin term *taberna*, tavern is a word introduced into Britain by the Romans, who had special shops of this name for selling food and drink adjacent to the roads they built. Such useful buildings were a part of British society in Saxon times (fifth to eleventh centuries), and these early taverns, alehouses and inns were for drinking, eating and rest or relaxation. They also were places where music and public singing could be found that was different from that in situations such as the church or in higher-class society. As government control increased over alcohol and the places that made and served it, the businesses were controlled by local licencing laws, requiring more complex systems to operate and maximize income. In 1393, legislation was passed enforcing public houses to display a sign outside so that the King's tasters could identify the building and then approve its product. A survey in 1577 found that in England and Wales there were 16,612 alehouses, taverns and inns, many of these now with rooms to provide a place to rest for travellers. In the eighteenth century, the more potent drink of gin became popular, leading to the creation of 'Gin Palaces' although most establishments were illegal and decidedly not palatial. To counter the perceived increase in drunkenness, ill health and crime that gin consumption was thought to cause, new licencing laws were introduced to encourage places that only served beer or cider. These nineteenth-century alehouses became the foundation of the modern-day brewing industry, as when legislation changed again, the owners of these applied to become legitimate public houses, some brewing their own product.

From the middle of the eighteenth century, special rooms were added to popular houses to provide separate spaces for dining and entertainment, sometimes called the saloon or lounge bar. As well as games such as cards, dominoes and indoor quoits, these might feature singers working a room while diners ate, or musicians accompanied comedians and other acts. In the larger pubs these rooms became concert rooms, which subsequently inspired the development of the music hall (see Chapter 2). Whereas development such as this led to more formal situations for popular music performance, it is the informality of the bar and pub venue that has resulted in its continuing success. A pub or bar is a room or rooms where a neighbourhood's social life happens, a place where you can be at home with local people, or where you can get to know a new location. It is not by chance that they have frequently been used as a setting in literature and drama; in the present day, the local pub is ubiquitous in television soap operas, which rely on both a continuing cast of varied characters and the introduction of new ones to drive narratives forward. The catchphrase and theme song from the popular US sitcom *Cheers* that ran on the Paramount Television Network from 1982 to 1993 (and since on CBS) was accurate in describing the bar is a place 'Where everybody knows your name'.

The architectural style of the pub/bar is diverse, although there are many tropes, which are replicated by lazy design teams seeking to create instant atmosphere. For the pub chain refurbishment teams in contemporary Great Britain, there is a style dichotomy between the archetypal country pub and the urban pub that began to be introduced in the 1930s (when travel by motor car became more common). The country pub style is an ancient building, perhaps thatched, low to the ground, with lots of wood and natural materials like weathered brick and stone although white washed render may also be seen. Inside, there are stone floors, a wooden ceiling, a substantial wooden bar and a big fireplace. The place is often filled with old collectables, antiques and books. The contemporary version is 'dressed' with replicas of these items made specially to order. Although there are real pubs that match this description, there are also countless more designed to covey this image although their much greater size, as well as their style, betrays their age. Located in the suburbs as well as the countryside, such buildings, old and new, form the venues for family celebrations: weddings, anniversaries, christenings and birthdays, where music is played and enjoyed.

It is, however, unfortunate that real Victorian pubs are so often refurbished into a pastiche assembled from random elements from the past.

The truly urban British pub has greater diversity of image. During the nineteenth century there was a boom in public house building led by the large breweries as they amalgamated smaller businesses and set about creating retail venues for their product – tied houses. These Victorian pubs might be small and humble, intended to serve a very local population in the streets around which they were sited, but they were also often grand and ambitious, particularly if constructed in the city centre. Each pub would have at least a lounge bar and a public bar – the former more comfortable and ostensibly more welcoming to ladies. Working men needing a quick (or longer) drink use the public bar. In the smaller venue, the bar from which drinks were purchased occupied the centre of the ground floor with the barrooms arranged around it, although still partitioned off from each other. This efficiency allowed a single bartender to operate the entire premises when it was quiet. Obscure glass in the exterior windows was used so drinkers could not be observed from outside, but large mirrors inside made the place bright and cheerful. Below the bar was the cellar where the barrels of ale were kept, delivered down a metal chute from the street; access to this was sometimes from a trapdoor in the floor of the bar area so the barman could descend to change the barrel without leaving the sales area. The landlord or landlady usually resided in a flat upstairs. This general pattern was followed in the grander establishments; however, the standard of fittings was higher, even extravagant, with arts and crafts interiors of the highest quality – fine wood panelling and bar fittings, often carved with details and figures; sculptural plasterwork and stucco ceilings and wall panels; stained glass panels in both the external walls and internal partitions; marble and alabaster floors, bar tops, fireplace surrounds; and metal work including hammered copper panels, polished brass door and window fittings. These buildings also advertised their opulence outside with cast and wrought iron gates, carved stone details, cast terracotta panelling and elaborate signage. Smaller pubs had a piano for singsongs and for the accompaniment of an entertainer, while larger ones would have a dedicated concert and events room (although rarely a stage). Frequently given patriotic names (e.g. The Queen Victoria, The Prince of Wales, The Duke of Wellington) that identify their place in history, the nineteenth-century public house can still be found in every city in Britain fulfilling largely the same function it has for over hundred years.

It was in just this sort of venue that pub rock became popular in 1970s Britain, particularly London. Rather than a specific genre of popular music, it was a style of presentation that developed in reaction to the complex big stage acts associated with progressive rock and the commercially driven pop music aimed at young teenagers, seen on television, and heard on mainstream radio shows. Pub rock was a back to the roots venture,

FIGURE 7.3 *Piano sing along with entertainers 'Baz and Dave' and London Bobby, Coach and Horses, 29 Greek Street, Soho, London. Source: Sabine Thoele.*

independently funded and operated, which needed local, low-cost venues to emerge – the public house was perfect. The emphasis was on live performance, and although many of the best bands (which featured rhythm and blues, country rock and soul) were scouted by larger labels, they were usually signed by independents such as Stiff Records, who because of the simple recording techniques used, could make a profit on as little as 2,000 copies sold. At its height in 1974–75, gig-goers in London could catch intimate, high-energy performances from Dr. Feelgood, Eddie and the Hot Rods, Ian Drury and Elvis Costello in one weekend. North London was the geographic epicentre of the music, with pubs in Camden Town, Kentish Town and Kensington, although there were others out of town, for instance Canvey Island where Dr. Feelgood came from. Other cities outside London such as Edinburgh and Glasgow had similar, although less-focused, and well-known scenes. In Liverpool, as well as Victorian pubs like O'Connor's Tavern and the Philharmonic Hotel, there was a surprisingly active scene based in the modern pubs: The Sportsman, Star and Garter and The Moonstone, which were located in the 1970s shopping development, St John's Precinct.

One of the most well-known pub rock venues is the Hope and Anchor, 207 Islington Upper Street, London. Although there was probably an earlier public house on the site of the same name, this pub was built in 1880.

FIGURE 7.4 *The Hope and Anchor in 2016. Source: Philafrenzy.*

It's a big building that occupies a prominent corner site, and the outside is architecturally impressive – red brick walls decorated with complex stucco and stone dressings.[1] The ground-floor bar is a lofty 4-metre-high space, designed as if it was an Italian arcaded portico, with grey and pink polished granite Corinthian columns supporting semicircular arched openings decorated with foliage patterns. The first floor is also grand with three linked, arched windows onto Upper Street and five similar ones facing Islington Park Street. This floor would have been the concert or function room in the past, although it was operated as an extra bar and a poolroom in recent years and since 2013 has been a successful independent fifty-seat theatre. A wrought iron decorative railing is in front of the windows. The second floor would have been the house landlord's accommodation, with a more sparsely furnished top floor being occupied by servants and the public house's live-in employees. Refurbished in the late 1980s after a brief closure, the interior of the pub retains none of its historic features; however, the part of the building that is famous in musical terms retains the essence of how it was in the 1970s. You enter the basement by descending a staircase close by the Upper Street entrance stairway. The bar is opposite as you enter the venue and the stage is next to the toilets, with a line of columns to the right framing the performance space. Although it now has smooth walls, framed photos and high-quality lighting and amplification, in the 1970s this was a brick-lined cellar with minimal lighting and ventilation, a famously smelly, sticky floor and a bar lined with chicken wire to protect the staff. It was notoriously difficult to get served here, spawning a hit record called 'Two Pints of Lager and a Packet of Crisps Please' (Splodgenessabounds, 1980), in which these sole lyrics are repeated continuously with increasing levels of frustration to a deaf bartender.[2]

The Hope and Anchor was not the first pub to support rock musicians and audiences at this time – The Tally Ho in Kentish town had regular rock gigs up until a new manager changed the emphasis to Irish show bands. When this happened, the Hope increased the number of shows it had to take up the slack until it became the main pub rock venue in North London.[3] Fred Grainger and Dave Robinson (later co-founder of Stiff Records) managed the venue introducing rock bands like The Kursall Flyers, Graham Parker and the Rumour and The Police who played there four months after they first formed. The pub also became a famous punk venue with performances from The Stranglers, The Ramones, The Damned and The Clash.

FIGURE 7.5 *The Stranglers on stage at the Hope and Anchor, November 1977.*
Source: Evening Standard/Stringer/Hulton Archive/Getty Pictures.

As well as live shows, the venue also had a primitive recording studio, and live albums were recorded there including the *Hope & Anchor Front Row Festival* (1978), a release that compiles excerpts from a series of benefit concerts organized by John Eichler who took over management of the pub in 1977 (The Stranglers, live album *Live at the Hope and Anchor*, bootleg 1977, EMI release 1992, was their entire set from this show). Promotional videos were also made in the venue (such as 'New Rose', The Damned and 'One Step Beyond' by Madness).

The Hope and Anchor is a seminal venue where many of the most famous rock and punk bands of the 1970s, 80s and 90s had their first taste of a London audience, not always to rave receptions. The venue itself could be a disappointment if you weren't prepared. Licenced at that time for 120 (although sometimes packed out with 200), it was a dank brick cellar, with access for equipment through a trapdoor in the pavement, and if you weren't a local act, or not known nationally, then an audience could be hard to attract. On 27 December 1978, thirty people saw Joy Division's London performance paying just 60p entry – the review in *Sounds* magazine stated:

> They stutter on stage wearing sulky, long looks. The vocalist Ian Curtis, seems intensely irritated but he doesn't say anything between songs ... The music is matt coloured, fast HM, often flat and usually undistinguished ... They may have gathered a tight following in hometown Manchester, but they failed to ignite a similar impression in front of a new ... audience.[4]

Joy Division did, however, return to the Hope just a few months later in March 1979. On 12 April 1979, U2 (mistitled the U2's) reputedly had only nine paying customers and left the stage after a couple of numbers never to return.[5] However, for most bands it was a welcome, if exhausting, place to play, held in their affection by simply giving them a stage for what they wanted to do. As well as the Front Row Festival, there were many more benefit gigs with artists playing for expenses only in order to keep the place open.

In the Britain of the mid-1980s, the political scene under a Conservative government led by Margaret Thatcher, which had given punk such energy and relevance, led to difficult economic times for many, and pubs with an alternative social and economic base like the Hope and Anchor suffered. For a short time in 1985, the building became a squat with mattresses on the upper floors, illegal electricity cables hung from ceilings, although still with gigs in the basement. The Islington area of London began to be gentrified in the late 1980s, and this created a new threat for the pub as a venue, as for a time it became a wine bar; however, after a series of goodwill gigs and patient negotiation, its live music licence was returned in the mid-1990s. Since then the venue has continued showcasing new acts and reunions from its punk and rock past with a largely unchanged formula as recorded by a happy punter:

> A damned good Hope & Anchor gig happens down in the basement, just you and the rats it's a regular rat trap where it gets hot and sweaty and it's quite dark. A claustrophobic's nightmare with 300 punters sweating on you and grabbing your family tree and spilling their piss all over you but it ain't quite rape because Wilko Johnson's shoving his Telecaster in your face, the king of pub rock when pubs were king and the sweat rolls down the walls to the blistering feedback guitars.[6]

The public house, although a British institution, is a venue type that is found around the world, although perhaps known by other names. It is known as a pub in those places with strong British ties, particularly countries in the Commonwealth of Nations (until 1949 titled the British Commonwealth) like Ireland, Canada, New Zealand, South Africa and Australia. In nineteenth-century Canada, the word tavern was used to describe a venue where people (mostly men) could relax and drink alcohol; however, after a period of prohibition in the 1920s, many beer parlours were opened. After the Second World War, returning Canadian servicemen had grown used to the concept of the British pub where a wide variety of drinks could be enjoyed comfortably by both sexes alongside entertainments such as games and music. This global homogenization of bar culture happened around the world as travelling servicemen brought the style of pub and bar establishments to wherever they were based, for example American Bars where cocktails and other modish drinks were prepared became popular in the UK.

Australian pubs, although having many of the characteristics of the British venue, were more controlled by licencing laws including restrictions on operating hours that required them to close at 6.00 pm. From the 1950s, these laws began to be relaxed and the traditional pub began to become a viable venue for music performance. Melbourne, Victoria, is a city that is intensely proud of its identity as a place where popular music is encouraged and flourishes. Alongside the large arenas, concert halls and clubs there are venues like The Tote, The Prince of Wales and The Corner Hotel. These pubs feature live music as an integral part of a vibrant cultural scene, valued both by locals and by visitors.

The Tote is a typical Victorian era corner pub (built in 1876 as the Ivanhoe Hotel) in the Collingwood neighbourhood of Melbourne that has been adapted and extended so that three music spaces operate within its walls – the front bar, a main stage with adjoining garden and an upstairs space. The front bar is a typical Victorian pub similar to many found in this part of Australia, but also Britain – a central bar area from which the drinks are served, surrounded by a number of small rooms.

FIGURE 7.6 *The Tote, Collingwood, Melbourne. Source: Robert Kronenburg.*

The rooms above the bar, which once would have been the manager's accommodation, or a dining room, are now a small venue. At the rear of the property through the garden is a larger shed-like space, which, although still only big enough for a hundred or so, is because of its shape and size more like a club in atmosphere. The Tote is not a smart venue but it's a very active one. It cultivates a predominantly rock music image although the bands and artists who play there always seem to be breaking beyond this boundary. It has the image of a place where there is something almost always on so you can just turn up and see what is happening. The pub began hosting live music in 1980 when it became the Tote, and it still exists because its owner Jon Perring, with his partners and helpers, has carefully managed its existence over twenty years fighting detrimental local government policy, financial disaster and changing liquor and health and safety regulations.

The Tote is more than just an active local venue – it is also a pivotal place in the history of popular music performance. When threatened with closure in 2010 due to controversial changes in licencing laws that included forced hiring of numerous security guards, CCTV installation and reduced hours of operation, it formed the centrepiece of a grass roots struggle to preserve live music in Melbourne, with public parades and protests that

FIGURE 7.7 *Early evening session in the bar at The Tote. Source: Robert Kronenburg.*

successfully changed local rules to enable the venue to maintain operation.[7] What happened there had a pivotal impact on the continued existence of music venues across Australia, spurring the state of Victoria to introduce Agent of Change legislation that required the developers of new building projects built next to existing venues to be responsible for the acoustic treatments needed to avoid them being a sound disturbance in the new homes or businesses they were creating. The Australian experience has been a model for pressure groups in cities around the world seeking reforms that will preserve their favourite venues when threatened by gentrification and new commercial development, encouraging the gathering of data that informs the public and legislators about the value of live music industries and potential solutions for their protection (see Chapter 12).

Barrooms

In the United States, as well as regional and typological variations such as the honky-tonks, juke joints, speakeasies, blues and jazz clubs (see Chapters 3, 4 and 5), establishments for drinking alcohol were traditionally called saloons and taverns. As in the public house, the bar was simply the furnishing from which the drinks were served; however, it is now the most common name used for the whole establishment, and although it is also used in the European context, this term is more common in the United States. The contemporary North American bar or barroom responds to the differing regional and city licencing laws, resulting in a greater variety of establishment types than the British public house. It is easy to find specialized places that focus on particular markets such as food, wine or cocktails; particular clientele or demographic profile such as business people, LGBT or bikers; particular entertainments such as sports, comedy or of course music. Although there are now large businesses that operate chains of bars in the United States, often associated with a particular area of activity (e.g. Houlihan's is a Kansas-based sports bar and restaurant chain that operates or franchises about ninety businesses around the United States), the image of the bar is still as an independent, locally managed operation that depends on loyal local patronage from regular returning customers. Because of their less-defined architectural image (unlike British Pubs), the line between what is a music bar and what is a music club in the United States is more fluid.

Austin, Texas, is a city that has a prominent engagement with popular music styling itself as 'The Live Music Capital of the World'. Its national reputation in this regard is based around its broadcast image, hosting *Austin City Limits*, the longest running live concert television show in the United States. The show's pilot aired on 17 October 1974 with local star Willy Nelson headlining, and the show's first full season commenced in 1976. Recorded at the Moody Theatre (ACL Live) in downtown Austin, the show led to the creation of the large music festival that was inspired by this success: Austin City Limits Music Festival. However, there are more than 250 permanent live music venues that underpin these prominent events (and others like South by Southwest and the Urban Music Festival). The city's oldest continuously operating bar is Scholz's Hall, founded on San Jacinto Boulevard in 1866. The owner, August Scholz, was one of the city's early immigrants, creating a German bier hall and garden, which in the early days featured German folk music. Country music became popular in the 1920s with the most famous cowboy singer of the 1930s, 'Tex' Ritter, who started out as local University of Texas law student Woodward Maurice Ritter. In the 1960s, both country and western music and rock music had their own bars in the city (such as the Broken Spoke and the Jade Room, respectively), but Rhythm and Blues also had dedicated venues such as the IL Club on East 111th Street. Downtown's 6th Street became the focus for the live music bars and clubs, a location that is still very active today. Antone's, which opened there in 1975, became famous for gigs by Austin stars like Stevie Ray Vaughan and Double Trouble, and The Fabulous Thunderbirds, before moving to cheaper premises on the north side.

The Hole in the Wall is a typical local bar that seems unchanged since its founding in 1974. Situated at 2538 Guadalupe Street, a main road not far from the University of Texas, many of the nearby businesses are now chain restaurants and stores supplying student-friendly food and items. This local commercial development recently put pressure on the bar to close in 2015 when landlord Will Tanner was asked for a rent rise, while simultaneously hearing the location was being touted as a new site for out-of-town businesses. Opened as a truck stop-type restaurant by original owner Doug Cugini, it was one of the first bars to operate in the area due to a freeing up in the mid-70s of the licencing laws. Musicians were playing on the sidewalk for tips, and it was they who asked him if they could play inside at night under the same arrangement. Cugini recalls: 'It wasn't like I had this idea to open up a club that was going to last 40 years and have all these famous musicians start out there ... I didn't have any idea or vision of that at all. I had these guys coming into me and asking me to play.'[8]

The entrance to the Hole in the Wall is through an unpretentious single-storey shop front, cement render on brick, with two large windows, one directly behind the front bar's stage, so when they enter customers can see who's on, but also have to walk by the tips bucket when they leave. An audacious illuminated sign hangs above the door's canvas awning, advertising some of the bar's attractions. There is also a mural of cowgirls shooting musical notes from their pistols, and the door handle is a recycled baseball bat. Some permanent lettering on the sign gives a clue to the bar's ancient history with the legend 'arcade restaurant' – restaurant there still is, but the arcade was what filled the back room in the early days – pool tables and pinball machines you could play while you drank. Today, a bar stretches the length of the room beneath a wooden beam ceiling, wooden planked walls and old wooden chairs and tables. Posters and beer signs form the main decoration in the front bar, although there are some ancient framed photographs of revered musicians, many of whom (such as Scotty Moore, Stevie Ray Vaughan and Emmy Lou Harris) have played in the venue. One of the first artists to make it big after playing at the Hole was Nanci Griffith who played there in its first year even before amplification was installed. Other past performers that have made it include Lucinda Williams, Lyle Lovett, St Vincent and local band Spoon.

The Hole in the Wall's next manager was Debbie Rombach, an ex-UT student who started working there at the very beginning and kept on coming back, eventually taking over from Cugini in 1998. The back room was opened up by removing an office and swinging doors and installing a larger stage at the rear, now a proper venue but still not huge, capable of holding a crowd of about a hundred. Caricature drawings of the customers were moved around to create space for stylized mural paintings of musical heroes like Johnny Cash. Later on, when new manager Will Tanner took over in 2003, a new pool and pinball area and outside eating and drinking space were created. There is no cover for the front bar and so this is a place where you can pop in for a draft and catch a singer songwriter playing gentle acoustic numbers in the early evening, and then return later on and for a few dollars hear a full band whoop it up in the back with a gang of local fans

FIGURE 7.8 *Hole in the Wall, Guadalupe Street, Austin, Texas.* Source: Robert Kronenburg.

FIGURE 7.9 *A quiet night in the front bar, Hole in the Wall. Source: Robert Kronenburg.*

cheering them on. After its last brush with closure in 2015, Tanner was able to negotiate a lease for a further five years, which will run out in 2020. The Hole in the Wall is now the second oldest venue in Austin (the oldest being the Broken Spoke; see Chapter 3). In a city that puts so much emphasis on its musical integrity, but also one that lost one of the most important venues in American popular music history (Armadillo World Headquarters, 1970–80), it is nevertheless not unusual that a venue with such a long history can be under threat. The pressures facing small venues like The Hole are symbolic of those around the world: 'While every city has its issues with artists losing ground to big business and gentrification, watching it happen in the "Live Music Capitol of the World" doesn't inspire much hope for other places.'[9] To ensure live music remains a part of the city's identity, Austen's city hall now has a dedicated department (ATX Music) to assist venues with permits for both indoor and outdoor music performance and also offers low-interest micro loans to businesses to support their operation; however, commercial pressures are hard to resist when businesses are so small in comparison to the large companies with which they must compete to continue operating in viable locations.[10]

Venues like the Hole are established almost by chance, the result of a range of happy circumstances matching musicians, audiences, locations and a business entrepreneur open to new ideas. Their architectural development is equally fortuitous, the building interiors gradually change over years of operation with improvements that are made based on direct experience of what works, usually with little or no professional design involvement. This architectural ambience is therefore remarkably sympathetic with the music that is played there – unpretentious and homemade, tuned to respond to an activity and people that the proprietor knows well.

The Hope and Anchor, the Tote and the Hole in the Wall are the sort of operations from which musical activity grows, spills into downtown venues, festival stages and, eventually, the arenas. Although they all have a drop-in bar, their operational model is as a destination for gig-goers, whether to see a particular act or just to take a chance on what might be happening because they like its ambience and booking policy. It is this sort of venue that is of enormous importance to popular music development. There is no doubt that the existence of venues like this are a seminal part of popular music activity in any given location (there are another 466 in Melbourne alone), providing places for beginning artist's first gigs, stages on which they can learn their craft and a continuing institution around which older musicians can return to their roots and just keep making music. They also are meeting points for audiences to enjoy the company of like-minded music lovers, to engage by encouragement (and disparity) with musicians they can stand next to at the bar as well as listen to and dance along with. These venues also provide a place that is distinctly local, a community base, a place where shared, intimate events can happen – events that can usually only be found in a small venue. Only a few become famous (and even these are not immune from closure), but without their continued operation it is certain that no city can continue to call itself a 'Music City' or perhaps more significantly, a 'Musician's City'.

Coffee bars

There have been many technical innovations that have affected the development of popular music, including radio, electrical amplification and electronic recording. One of these, beginning early in the age of mechanical sound reproduction, is the jukebox. The jukebox is an automated device that brings a degree of control to the customer over what music is played in a public setting, and although at its peak it could be found in restaurants, bars and public houses, playing an important part in the popularization of commercial musical genres from the 1930s on, it became particularly associated with the coffee bar (for the importance of record scenes on venue development, see Chapter 11).

The ancestor of the jukebox was the player-piano, a mechanical instrument in which melodies were arranged on paper rolls, metal discs or cylinders to trigger the keys to be played in a set order. After the invention of the phonograph, the first coin-actuated device to play a recording was marketed in 1890, although these early machines had just one recording available and had to be listened to via tubes held to the ear. In 1918, the first multiple recording machine was patented, and in 1927 the Automated Music Instrument Company (later known as AMI) introduced one of the first machines in which the customer could select the record they wanted to hear. Other famous jukebox manufacturers began to enter the field such as Seeburg and Wurlitzer, creating more powerful machines with electronic amplification and powered operation; however, it was not until the 1940s that the device began to be known as a jukebox, the name derived from the musical juke joint venue (see Chapter 3). These early machines used shellac 78-rpm records; however, in 1950 Seeburg introduced a 45-rpm record version, with smaller and lighter records, and a louder, more high-fidelity sound. The design of the machines also became more important at this time with glamorous chrome, glass and plastic cases, illuminated by electric lights and displaying moving parts. The machines counted which records were being played the most frequently, thereby enabling operators to leave these discs in place longer when refreshing selections. Record companies also took note of this information, releasing new records to the jukebox operators first. For the music fan, the jukebox provided a source of advertisement-free music they could select themselves, with a better sound quality than most could experience at home from domestic radios.

Jukeboxes were so common because the venue owner didn't need to pay for them as they were provided free by entrepreneurial syndicates who took some or all of their takings. They were placed in bars, small clubs and restaurants, and the style of music was selected to suit the locality, ambience and clientele – this piece of music-making technology was pivotal in developing the record industry, for example in US country music alone, accounting for up to half of all record sales by the end of the 1930s (Peterson 165). From the late 1930s, people who could not or did not want to drink alcohol could frequent diners where the jukebox was an essential accessory. A diner was a place where young people could socialize with just a few coins in their pocket, some for the odd drink or snack but most for the jukebox, which would have the latest records to play. The resonance of these as places associated with youth culture has been reinforced in television and film, for example *Happy Days* (Paramount 1974–84), *Grease* (Kleiser 1978) and *Back to the Future* (Zemeckis 1985). By the 1950s the classic diner style was established with Formica tables, streamlined colourful fittings, bright lights and chrome – pleasant environments that were open to all. Often styled on the railroad dining car, and sometimes even constructed within an old carriage, these buildings were simultaneously fashionable and affordable. Although many individual original diners from this period still exist across the United States and Canada, there are also a number of chain restaurants that utilize

FIGURE 7.10 *Al Mac's Diner-Restaurant, Fall River, Massachusetts, USA, open around 1910, the diner closed on 23 July 2012. Source: Ken Zirkel.*

their nostalgic styling as a marketing ploy (e.g. Denny's and the drive-in chain Sonic).

In Britain, the jukebox was common in pubs, but its image is particularly associated with espresso coffee shops, which, as with North America diners, became popular in the 1950s with the new teenage culture. The increased spending power of young people was expressed in fashion and music tastes, and although it might be argued that the pastimes of the under-21s did not really change much (they still listened to music and went dancing), the places in which they passed their leisure time did, tuned by operators to make them more attractive to this new type of customer.[11] The first Moka premises was opened by the popular Italian actress Gina Lollabrigida in Frith Street, Soho, in 1953, and an image of fashionable youth was established compared to the existing cafés and public houses. The 2i's coffee bar was opened at 29 Old Compton Street by brothers Freddy and Sammy Irani in 1956. Typical of this type of establishment, and one of many similar places in the area, it featured a glass shop front through which the interior could be seen from the street – including the all-important jukebox situated right behind the window. Once past a glass door with a chrome handle, inside there was a long room about 10 metres (33 feet) by 3 metres (10 feet) with a linoleum floor and Formica tables and a bar serving simple meals like cheese on toast with coffee, orange juice and Coca-Cola. On 22 April 1956 two Australian wrestlers, Paul 'Dr. Death' Hunter and Ray 'Rebel' Hunter, took

FIGURE 7.11 *2i's Coffee Bar, Old Compton Street, Soho, London (photo: c. 1957).* Source: Photo by Dezo Hoffmann/Rex/Shutterstock.

over the coffee bar from the Iranis and soon, although quite by accident, its reputation as a place for musicians was established. In July 1956, Wally Whyton and his group The Vipers dropped in:

> We Vipers ordered coffee, sat down and began playing their guitars and even passed our hat and extracted a few coppers from the tourists who'd happened by. As we were preparing to leave, the proprietor intercepted us and said: 'Excuse me, lads, but I really enjoyed that … I'd be happy for you to come in and sing any time you like.'[12]

Within a few weeks the band had a residency at the coffee bar playing there three times a week. The basement was the main place for live music. At the back of the shop was a narrow stairway that led to a room directly under the café. Rick Brown, who was the bass player with the Savages in the early 1960s, recalls:

> From the main coffee bar area you went down some narrow stairs to a dismal, dark and gloomy basement about the size of a large bedroom, lit

by a couple of weak bulbs. At one end were a few milk crates with planks on top of them, which everybody assumed was the stage. And there may have been some sort of microphone system, left over from the Boer War. The nearest toilets were probably Piccadilly Circus Station.[13]

As the venue took off, bands played there every night, sometimes just by turning up rather than by arrangement, and although the comfortable capacity was somewhere around twenty, usually the audience was 50 or more.

In September 1956 singer Tony Hicks was spotted singing with the resident band and signed with Decca Records to become the first British rock 'n' roll star: Tommy Steele. With this publicity, the venue became famous overnight

FIGURE 7.12 *Screaming Lord Sutch performing with Vince Taylor in the basement of the 2i's, 24 September 1960. Source: Trinity Mirror/Mirrorpix/Alamy Stock Photo.*

and a destination for music fans, budding musicians and those out to spot new talent. A second venue, the 2i's Club, was opened nearby at 44 Gerrard Street and Lincoln began to organize tours of the artists who played at the club including an English Channel ferry cruise in June 1957. On 21 November that year, the 2i's reputation was sealed with a live broadcast from the venue on the popular BBC television show *Six-Five Special* featuring London singers such as Wee Willie Harris and Adam Faith, whose skiffle group the Worried Men had a residency at the venue. Other artists who were discovered included Harry Webb (soon to be Cliff Richard) and Hank Marvin and his band the Drifters (who became the Shadows). Cliff Richard and the Shadows appeared in the 1958 film *Expresso Bongo* (Val Guest), which satirized the rapacious music industry, including a scene where the young Bert Rudge (Richard) is discovered in an espresso bar. However, a more accurate recreation of the 2i's also made an appearance in the 1986 rock musical *Absolute Beginners* (Julian Temple), which depicted London in 1958. The 2i's closed in 1967 as mainstream popular music performance refocused towards dedicated clubs and large theatres rather than tiny snack bars.

Coffee bars were also at the centre of the resurgent folk movement in the 1950s and 60s, providing a setting for these intimate acoustic performances. Although the term 'folk club' implies a type of venue (see also Chapter 1), it is more usually just a name for a particular activity, the artists and their audience occupying a bar or café for the duration of the event, although usually on a regular basis. These clubs emerged after the Second World War, as a result of a renewed enthusiasm for traditional music, either from its European roots or North American developments. Amateur music such as skiffle and blues gave it a boost in the late 1950s, but by the 1960s folk had its own devotees who rejected overtly commercial popular music. Many different styles of folk developed, some purists striving for authentic sounds using only traditional instruments, sourcing and interpreting geographically local material, and other musicians who enjoyed the cross-fertilization of different cultures and even different musical styles including rock.

The Topic Folk Club was founded in Bradford, West Yorkshire, in 1956 and is still running on a weekly basis today, although it has been held at thirteen different venues in that time. Its focus was not just the music, but as a place for young people 'to get together and talk politics and sing folk songs or play skiffle'.[14] In its early days, besides music being performed in whatever venue the club met at, members would also provide performances for other local organizations. There was also a library of club books and records. The club values its history and longevity, which is understandable with over 3,000 meetings and counting, as it continues each Thursday evening since 2014 at Glyde House, a former non-conformist church built in 1852, now a café, bar and venue with offices on the floor above.

The local folk club is typically a semi-formal event at which invited seasoned, even professional artists perform, but it is also expected that a large part of the entertainment will come from the audience, performing one or two pieces, usually purely for their own enjoyment, but occasionally as a step on the ladder to becoming professional. Future star Bob Dylan played at the Café Wha! in New York's Greenwich Village on the first night he arrived in the city in January 1961. The small venue on the corner of MacDougal Street also hosted folk group Peter, Paul and Mary and stand-up comedians such as Lenny Bruce and Woody Allen and beat poets Alan Ginsberg and Jack Kerouac. By the mid-1960s blues and rock acts also played there, including Jimi Hendrix, Bruce Springsteen and Lou Reed. In 1968 the coffee bar closed and reopened as the Café Feegon featuring Israeli and Middle Eastern music, which continued until 1987. It then reopened as the Café Wha again as a rock music club (now selling alcohol) that operates on the basis of presenting a distinctive house band with the best local musicians playing high-quality covers of popular songs, often with guests.

From the 1960s to the 1980s, every town in Britain and many in the United States would have had at least one regular folk club, but as with Café Wha, musical trends challenged this local form of popular music entertainment, resulting in a rapid reduction in the number of active traditional folk clubs. However, many still persist (such as the Topic), and new ones have emerged as the genre has changed, drawing in widespread influences from world music to rap, and folk can now reasonably be described as another strand of popular music. Rather than a conduit for the preservation of old traditions, folk is now a term:

> applied to areas of contemporary music, to composers of personal songs such as Nick Drake, Sandy Denny, John Martyn, or more recently Fionn Regan, Alasdair Roberts or Eliza Carthy. Nowadays it's become a signifier of texture and aesthetics as in such descriptive terms as "acid folk", "free folk", "wyrd folk", "anti-folk" and even the ungainly "folktronica".[15]

Folk music now makes use of the same venues as other genres, with performances taking place in pubs, bars and clubs, and more well-known artists featuring in halls, theatres and on festival stages.

Most coffee bars today (and pubs, bars, restaurants etc.) primarily feature piped music over which neither the staff nor the customer has much control; however, some independent places strive for a different identity. In Kyoto, a few blocks away from one of the main shopping streets, down Pontocho Dori, in a narrow alley not even wide enough for a small Toyota pickup truck, there is a bar with very little street presence, just a gap between buildings, a white brick wall, and an illuminated sign stood on the ground outside: 'Majorica, Jazz LP DISC since 1974'. Inside, there are less than a dozen seats and a bar along one wall on which is stacked bottles, papers and other random items. The wall behind the bar is equally packed with postcards, photos, drinks and bottles, although hidden there behind some

FIGURE 7.13 *Café Wha!, MacDougal Street, New York. Source: Robert Kronenburg.*

cupboard doors is what makes this place special – a large stack of vinyl records. After you are settled in with a coffee (or Suntory whisky), the owner will sift through the selection, and carefully place a disc on the turntable – the music precluding talking, enhancing this relaxing retreat from the city outside. The *kissaten* is a jazz café where vinyl records are played on good-quality equipment by a discerning owner. Chairs are arranged for listening rather than chatting, drinks are sold and the barman is usually also the owner and the DJ, selecting the records (and taking requests), which are placed on view each time they are changed. These places are contemplative and restful, and it's not just jazz, but rhythm 'n' blues, and soul you might hear – the playlist depends on the owner although requests are accepted. Emerging after the Second World War, these venues reached their peak in numbers in the 1960s; however, the ones that remain (like Kyoto's Majorica, or JBS, which stands for Jazz, Blues, Soul, in Shibuya, Tokyo) retain a loyal clientele.[16] The *kissaten* replicates the same intimate architectural ambience of a small live jazz venue, only with recorded music, its key feature being that there is an interactive engagement between the music on offer and the customer. It is a primary element in the café's ambience and a prime reason why people go there.

CHAPTER EIGHT

Theatres, Halls and Auditoria

We had queued up since before dawn, crowds of long-haired, loon-panted individuals waiting patiently right around the back of the building on a cold November day, past Lime Street station and then up London Road. The tickets were all one pound each, which perhaps increased the demand a little, but it would surely have been there anyway. After the box office opened, the line moved forward slowly, only turning into a scrum right by the doors, but my friend and I got our stalls seats anyway, which gave us bragging rights in college for the next few days. A couple of months later the night of the concert has arrived, 14 January 1973, and being a veteran of several gigs, I am relaxed about getting to the Empire for 7.00 pm – they never start on time, do they? But as I come in through the door from the foyer the band are already on stage – Led Zeppelin are thrashing through their first number: *Rock and Roll*, Jimmy Page swinging his guitar low through the riff and Robert Plant letting loose pent-up energy as he screams out the verse.

In the 1970s, for the vast majority of popular music fans, you didn't travel to see the big bands, they came to you, taking over your local theatre for a night playing a one-night stand before moving on to the next show, which might only be a few dozen miles away in the next city with a sizable auditorium. This was my first taste of these great artists, and although there were several theatres in Liverpool capacious enough for a 'big' act (particularly the Royal Court, which was a renowned venue into the 1980s), the place where I saw most of these acts was the Liverpool Empire. As well as Led Zeppelin, there was Canned Heat (1970); Yes (1970); Pink Floyd (*Dark Side of the Moon* tour); Genesis (*The Lamb Lies Down on Broadway* tour in 1973); Emerson, Lake and Palmer (1974); Wings (1975); Deep Purple (1976); Queen (1977); and Rainbow (1977, see also below). Although Eric's was the venue in Liverpool where the crucial punk acts that shaped the late 1970s and early 80s music scene appeared, the Empire was the place where rock gods could be worshipped by their fans.

The theatre which hosted all these rock bands was not in fact the first on this site, a prominent location facing St George's Plateau, a grand civic space with one of the 'finest [neo-Grecian buildings] in the world' directly opposite, and its museums and art galleries to one side.[1] Theatres had existed here since 1866; the first was the Prince of Wales, followed by the Royal Alexandra. This building was extensively refurbished in 1879 and 1896 by renowned theatre architect Frank Matcham (see Chapter 2). The new operator was Messrs, Moss and Thornton, soon to become the large theatre chain Moss Empires, and so the theatre was renamed the Liverpool Empire. In 1925 it was altered again, this time in the fashionable classical American style (popularized in the city by the head of the Liverpool School of Architecture, Charles Reilly), with a new angular Portland stone façade with paired Doric columns, constructed on a steel frame, although the sides and back remained plain brick walls. Inside, the architects for this project, W. and T. R. Milburn, created plasterwork designs in the Louis XVI style featuring foliage and elephants. The wide two-tier auditorium, at over 2,300 seats, is still one of the largest of its type in Great Britain.

The programme at this time was a mixture of variety and popular stage shows such as pantomime, all accompanied by a live orchestra in the theatre's extensive pit area, reputedly: 'the finest pits in the kingdom'.[2] The Empire still impresses; a wide, deep stage that extends as far back as the

FIGURE 8.1 *Empire Theatre, Lime Street, Liverpool. Source: Tony Hisgett.*

FIGURE 8.2 *Empire Theatre, view from the Grand Circle, in a photograph commissioned by the Gaumont Theatre Co. in 1934. Source: National Museums Liverpool, Stewart Bale Collection.*

theatre's external rear wall, flanked by two boxes which give a good view of the audience but not the performance! Massive semicircular arches span the stage and the auditorium with the steeply raked circle rising to a projection box at ceiling level. The building was adopted for a rock audience without any special construction work, travelling bands bringing in their own light and sound equipment, which in any case, at least in the early days, was in many cases quite basic.

In the 1940s and 50s, big US stars such as Judy Garland, Frank Sinatra and Bing Crosby performed at the Empire, and when the rock 'n' roll boom began, younger US stars took over including Frankie Lymon and the Teenagers and Little Richard. Little Richard's show on 28 October 1962 was the first performance in the venue for the Beatles, who would appear there twice in 1963 and play their final two shows in the city at the Empire on 5 December 1965. Bob Dylan played there on 14 May 1966 as part of his first 'electric' tour during which an audience member shouted out: 'Where's the poet in you? What's happened to your conscience?' Dylan responded, 'There's a fellow up there looking for the saviour, huh? The saviour's backstage, we have a picture of him.'[3] Jimi Hendrix played there twice in 1967, somewhat surreally the first time as part of a tour line-up that also featured crooner Engelbert Humperdinck.

But it wasn't just rock that was featured on the Empire's stage in this period. The Carpenters, Johnny Mathis, Neil Sedaka and Marvin Gaye were among the many pop and mainstream acts that visited the city, and the first ever show by legendary pop artist Kate Bush (then still only twenty years old) was held there on 3 April 1979, featuring the theatrical elements she became famous for with seventeen costume changes and thirteen performers in the ensemble. In the early 1980s, the city of Liverpool was in recession and many businesses were under threat. The beginning of the end for rock music in the venue was hastened by the famous rock guitarist Richie Blackmore, who, during the performance by his band Rainbow in 1977, climbed up onto one of the side boxes and smashed up a replica Fender Stratocaster, taking a good portion of the decorative plasterwork with it. Moss Empires decided to close the Empire; however, it was rescued by Merseyside County Council who subsidized its operation before transferring it to a local trust in 1986 who kept it running, although its most important years as a music venue had now passed. After an £11 million renovation (equal to £18 million in 2018), which also added a side extension incorporating support facilities, the building reopened in 1999 returning to its previous role as a home for variety, musicals, comedy and opera, although occasional live music concerts do still happen, however, by artists unlikely to cause damage to the building's fabric as part of the show.

The Empire is a typical example of a provincial theatre: large in their day, medium-sized now. Their value was that they enabled well-known musicians to come to your town, an event that somehow cemented a fan's relationship with the music. If a fan was really keen, he or she could hang around the stage door afterwards and wait for an autograph, occasionally even being asked inside the lobby, and sometimes even into the dressing room. Simon Robinson remembers meeting Ritchie Blackmore at the Empire when 'he invited a couple of us backstage for quarter of an hour before the show. I can recall him visibly sharpening when the questions clearly weren't those of fans of five minutes, and he was very receptive.'[4] Otherwise, artists might be seen at a nearby bar having a drink before or after the show (in this case, Ma Egerton's right behind the Empire and closest to the stage door) or continuing their night in the city at a local restaurant or nightclub. The separation between artist and fan seemed less, even though you were not accessing their every thought through twitter. These are big places, usually over 2,000 seats, but pre-video screen, the focus was on the stage, which was a lot closer than it is in an arena or at a festival, and at the end of the night (or earlier), many people left their seats and got much closer. These venues became familiar to the audience as they were visited repeatedly for different concerts, generating unique stories associated with specific performances (in my case when I stood at the back because Rainbow were just so painfully loud, or the time my friend drank so much he passed out in the toilets and woke up all alone early next morning). Fans know which seats to go for, what the drinks are like and if it's possible to get in on the cheap or free. Although experiencing a major band in a small club just before they really made it might be the pinnacle of many people's memories, seeing them once they were at the top of their fame but in a venue ten times larger (as opposed to up to a hundred times for an arena) is an event far more have experienced.

Although the Empire was created as a commercial enterprise from its beginning, venues of this size were also instigated for other reasons. One of the first great town halls to be built in Victorian Britain was in Birmingham, a city that had grown significantly in both size and wealth due to the introduction of new manufacturing industries by 1830. The new hall was created as a meeting place, but also as a permanent home for the Birmingham Triennial Music Festival, which had been founded in 1784, but fundamentally as a symbolic expression of civic pride. Chosen by design competition, the building's architects were Joseph Hansom and Edward Welch, who created a monumental neoclassical building based on the ancient temple of Castor and Pollux situated in the Forum in Rome. The rectangular structure surrounded by a colonnade of Corinthian columns sits on a substantial rusticated podium, constructed in brick but clad entirely in Penmon Marble (although this is actually a white limestone). Its transportation from the quarry in North Wales led to Hansom's bankruptcy and a delay in completion until 1834, and further improvements were still underway in 1835. This grand building was, however, very successful, being extended in 1837 and again in 1850. It also set a trend for other vigorous Victorian cities to build similar town halls, although some would argue (particularly 'Brummies') none so grand.

Birmingham Town Hall's concert space (in classical terms the *cella*) is a shoebox-shaped hall lined with tall glass windows, and it was a successful venue from the start. As well as the festival, regular classical performances took place there including many premiers, as well as recitals by the 6,000-pipe concert organ. However, the town hall was also an important popular music venue featuring regular jazz and rock concerts. In 1957 Sister Rosetta

Tharpe played there with British jazz musician Chris Barber, and other concerts in the 1950s included the Modern Jazz Quartet and Dave Brubeck. Oscar Peterson, Gil Evans and Thelonious Monk followed in the 1960s. Buddy Holly and the Crickets played in Birmingham on 3 October 1958, but there had been rock 'n' roll concerts there since the mid-1950s and all-night rock 'n' roll and jazz balls were held into the 1960s. The Beatles played at the hall only once on 4 June 1963 while touring with Roy Orbison; however, George Harrison returned in 1969 to perform with Delaney and Bonnie. The Rolling Stones, Bob Dylan, Pink Floyd, Led Zeppelin and Deep Purple played there, as did Birmingham's most famous heavy rock band, Black Sabbath. After the opening of Birmingham Symphony Hall in 1991, the Town Hall began an extensive ten-year restoration in 1997. Completed in 2007, the building still fulfils its role as a symbol of the city's cultural and economic life with weekly concerts from touring artists ranging from Cliff Richard to King Crimson.

There are many thousands of similar venues to the Liverpool Empire and Birmingham Town Hall in cities around the world that hold an essential place in local music histories. On occasion, these venues sometimes hosted individual performances that have since gained national or even international fame. For example in Liverpool's case it was perhaps as the first place where Kate Bush performed, or as a place where a world-famous band such as The Beatles once played to their home town audience (Black Sabbath for Birmingham Town Hall). Although looming large in local musical history, they do not have an international reputation. However, there are a few auditoria venues that are recognized worldwide for the contribution they have made to popular music as places that have been particularly important in nurturing its general development.

Apollo Theater, New York

The Apollo Theater in Harlem, New York, is not only a famous music venue that has seen many memorable performances, it is important in African American cultural history because of its role in repeatedly launching talented artists, comedians and dancers as well as singers and musicians, into the national and international consciousness. Jonelle Procope, President and CEO of the Apollo, explains that: 'They appeared there because they didn't have any other place to go … They weren't allowed in mainstream establishments. And so, when they were on the Apollo stage, they weren't legends. So that's why I call it a place of opportunity. They became legends after they appeared on the Apollo stage.'[5] Although the audiences at the Apollo are mixed, with 40 per cent white during the week and up to 75 per cent white at the weekend, this is a place where African Americans have set the agenda for eighty years.[6] However, the Apollo is an artistic institution that also engages with all races and is therefore a model for coexistence and cultural integration. As Billy Mitchell, Apollo Theater employee for over fifty years and in-house historian and tour director, states: 'One might think this is a black theatre because they always show black people. The truth is that every race, every culture, every ethnic group has contributed to the theatre's history: white people, black people, Latino, Asian, Indian.'[7]

The Apollo Theater was built in 1914 at 253 West 125th Street, Harlem, Manhattan, New York City. It was designed by George Keister, an experienced theatre designer who had also designed New York's Colonial Theater (1905), Loew's Yorkville Theater (1906), George M. Cohen Theater (1911) and the Bronx Opera House (1912). After the Apollo, he would go on to design at least seven more theatres, as well as offices, apartment houses, hotels and a church. Keister had no set architectural style, producing sometimes eccentric designs rifling through patterns from across the centuries: neo-medieval, neo-Renaissance and neoclassical; however, his designs were also patently rational in form and up-to-date in terms of functional operation. For example the multi-use Fitzgerald Building (1911) was an eleven-storey-high 'skyscraper' complex with shops on the lower floors, a theatre and offices above. The design for Hurtig and Seaman's New Burlesque Theatre (as the Apollo was first called) was neoclassical, the façade featuring limestone and granite bases for the ionic pilasters with primarily terracotta detailing above. Inside, the theatre had space for an audience of just over 1,500, seated in ground-floor stalls and two large raked balconies above. Passing through a foyer with plasterwork pilasters and a coffered ceiling, the main auditorium was decorated with plasterwork reliefs in a vaguely eighteenth-century neoclassical style with gilded urns, garlands and medallions – all of this built for $600,000 (about $16 million today). Operating under a strictly whites-only regime, the theatre stayed in continuous operation until 1928, when, after a brief closure, it was reopened under new management but with similar policies – burlesque shows with plenty of dancing girls, comedy and popular music for a white audience. Like many theatres, it closed again during the depressed early 1930s, until it was purchased by Sidney Cohen, an experienced theatre operator, who dedicated his new operation specifically to local African American clientele. After a substantial refurbishment, the Apollo opened its doors on 16 January 1934. The theatre established a reputation for high-quality shows beginning with jazz singer and Broadway star Adelaide Hall, who appeared within a month of the opening, and after Cohen died and ownership passed to Frank Schiffman, another operator who also owned some of the Apollo's main rivals, it continued to do well, initially featuring vaudeville-type shows with music, dancing, comedians and a chorus line, but gradually shifting more towards a focus on popular music performance.

In the 1930s and 40s, the Apollo regularly featured major jazz artists like Duke Ellington, Dizzy Gillespie, Cab Calloway and Count Basie. Later, modern jazz shows by artists such as Art Blakey and Horace Silver took place at the Apollo as well as gospel acts like Mahalia Jackson, Sister Rosetta Tharpe and Sam Cooke. White musicians also played in the Apollo during the 1950s, including swing bands led by Harry James and Woody Herman, and later, jazz artists such as Dave Brubeck, Stan Getz and Anita O'Day. Mainstream pop music was also included with Buddy Holly and Duane Eddy, and later on Stevie Wonder, Diana Ross, Paul McCartney and a long list of artists from almost every strand of popular music either played in the venue or had it on their list to visit for its illustrious history and its special atmosphere. James Brown, legendary soul and funk artist, was a regular from his first appearance in 1959. Performer and audience member Leslie Uggams particularly recalled his shows: 'When he sang "Please, Please, Please" we would all faint… Then he'd drop to his knees and put that cape over his shoulders. You could feel the theatre just pulsate.'[8] A famous feature of the Apollo calendar is the weekly Amateur Night. This started as the 'Harlem Amateur Hour' at Schiffman's other Harlem theatre, the Lafayette. New artists take their chances with the extremely judgemental Apollo audience, first touching a lucky tree stump (belonging to a tree that originally stood outside the Lafayette) at the side of the stage. If they fail to impress the audience, 'the executioner' comes and guides them off stage to ignominy, although it's said to be a rite of passage for performers to go through this and many have nevertheless had success – at a later date. Graduate first prize winners of the Amateur Night range from Ella Fitzgerald (1934) to Jimi Hendrix (1964).

Although the Apollo was very successful throughout the 1960s with a national and international profile, the inner-city problems which Harlem faced during the 1970s, including unemployment, crime and drug use, led to its closure in 1976. However, two television specials featuring artists like James Brown (who played the theatre more times than any other artist) and George Clinton drew attention to its plight and it soon reopened. In 1983 it was purchased by African American businessman and former president of the borough of Manhattan, Percy Ellis Sutton, who led the drive to get the building recognized as both a New York City Landmark and placed on the US National Register of Historic Places. In 1991, the theatre was sold to the City of New York and a non-profit organization was established to run it on a lease costing $1 per year. In 2001 the theatre began a lengthy restoration process under the guidance of New York architects Beyer, Blinder and Belle, organized in gradual phases as the foundation raised funds from government and private grants. Over the years, many of the theatre's original features had been destroyed and much that was left was in poor condition. Careful investigation uncovered information on the form and character of the building, and these features were renewed or replaced by modern equivalents that met current codes (Kahn 2017).[9] For example a broken light controller enabled contractors to reconstruct the original flashing light patterns on the underside of the marquee, now featuring modern, easy-to-replace, long-lasting LED (light emitting diode) fittings. Inside, all the seats have been replaced with examples matched to the period, and new safety features have been introduced including stairways and light fittings. Although not original, the vertical 'blade' Apollo sign (which had been introduced in the 1940s) was so much a part of the building's character that this was carefully reproduced in new materials and replaced.

Although always an important place for popular music culture, the saving of the Apollo Theater became, as New York Mayor Michael Bloomberg declared at the opening of Phase I of the restoration in 2005, 'a symbol of Harlem's new renaissance'.[10] Theatre venues like this make an important

FIGURE 8.3 *The Apollo Theatre marquee, New York, N.Y. (photo: c. 1946–1948, William P. Gottlieb). Source: Public domain.*

contribution to city life because they are usually situated in the heart of our cities – they are an integral part of the urban fabric. In economic terms they are important because the thousand-plus crowds that flock to an inner-city venue of this size feed other night-time businesses in the surrounding area: bars, restaurants – and to a certain extent – hotels and other attractions that overnight visitors will visit during their trip (Plate 10). But they are important in other, more fundamental ways. These older buildings are a part of the continuity of the city environment, contributing to the richness and complexity of the urban scene. Their eclectic, rich façades and elaborate interiors are enjoyable historical artefacts that deserve to be retained as signs of the achievements of our society. They also make for highly atmospheric places in which to enjoy lively entertainment, adding to the atmosphere of the gig experience. It is not hyperbole to describe the Apollo as a 'symbol of Harlem's new renaissance' because it is a real achievement of the society that has brought about its preservation and continued operation. Its physical presence indicates confidence in that society's pride in its past and ambitions for its future. Buildings are the most physical representation of what matters in civic life – the Apollo Theater and the other venues of its type – large, ebullient, unmissable structures in the city centre – are therefore the most physical representation of how popular music can be a positive force in our society. New York City is fortunate in having a history of auditoria that have had a significant impact on popular music such as for example Radio City Music Hall (constructed 1931–32 and still in operation today with a mixed-entertainment popular programme). However, many do not survive, even those that may also have important historic value, such as Fillmore East (constructed in 1925–56 as the Commodore, a Yiddish Theatre, and run as a rock venue by Bill Graham from 1968 for two important and influential years). The Apollo, despite being situated in a city neighbourhood that has more than its share of problems, is an important popular music success story.

Rainbow Theatre, London

Although it existed for a shorter period than the Apollo, the Rainbow was one of England's most important large popular music venues, and unusually for buildings of this type, it was also located in one of London's most memorable pieces of architecture. Like the Apollo, the Rainbow was situated in a theatre designed for a quite different sort of performance, in this case – cinema. By the end of the 1920s, cinema was a well-established, hugely popular mass entertainment in Great Britain, and investment in new buildings that would attract even larger audiences was at its peak. Islington is a densely populated part of North London, which at that time already had two cinemas (the Electric Vaudeville and the Finsbury Park Cinematograph, both of which opened in 1909); however, the new Finsbury Park Astoria (which would later become the Rainbow Theatre) would benefit from the intervening twenty years of design development to become an ambitious advance in cinema design. Created for the Picture House Trust, a business underwritten by the American Paramount Corporation and run by Arthur Segal, the cinema was designed by the in-house architect Edward A. Stone, who was also the designer for three other Astoria cinemas in London in Brixton, Streatham and the Old Kent Road.

The new cinema's site was on a corner at 228/269 Seven Sisters Road, and although awkward in layout being split almost in two with the larger part towards the rear, Stone made the most of it. The smaller corner part facing the site's busiest junction has the entrance, a symmetrical wedge-shaped building with an austere white faience façade relieved by green faience dressings. A marquee spans the entrance, and once inside, the visitor begins to get a hint of the luxurious interior, with an octagonal foyer featuring a geometric central fountain and highly decorated red, white and gold art deco patterns in the columns and the walls. A balcony above was originally the cinema's tea room. The octagonal plan of this area is a clever way to maintain the symmetrical layout but still usher people through to the auditorium, which is situated to the left-hand side. This much larger part of the building is clad in simple brick; however, the interior is spectacular: 'a Hispano-Moresque fantasy' hinted at by its entrance hall, which has a mock tile roof running all around reminiscent of a Spanish courtyard.[11] But nothing can prepare you for the auditorium – a vast space that originally sat 4,000 people (just over 3,000 when it was the Rainbow), which was intended to induce the audience

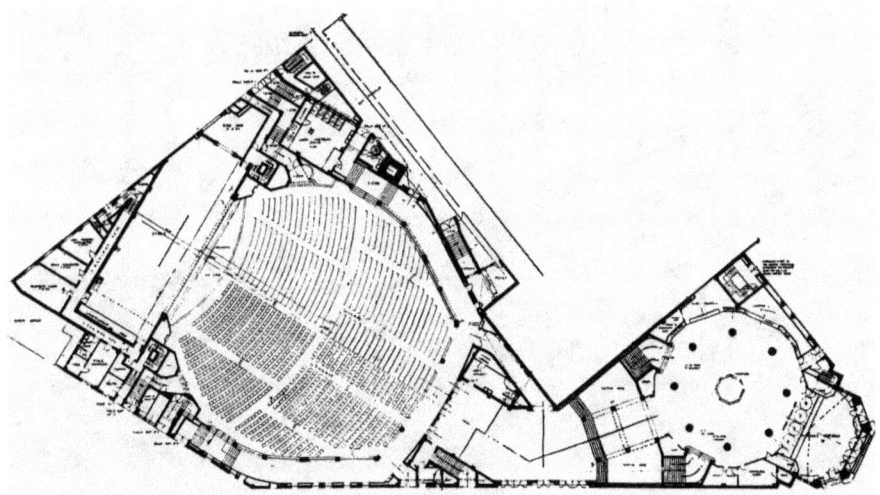

FIGURE 8.4 *Finsbury Park Astoria, original layout plan. Source: Islington Local History Centre/Islington History Services.*

into the illusion that they were seated in the open air near a Mediterranean village. There are sparkling stars above (pin point lights set into the deep-blue painted ceiling) and a castle archway forming the proscenium above the 19-metre (64 feet)-wide stage. Mock villa façades rise up the walls alongside the stairs to the upper floors. Designed by Somerford and Barr, the interior was as luxurious as it was exotic – even the safety screen was painted with an oriental garden seen in perspective, reinforcing the 'outdoor' ambience when the lights went up in-between performances.

Although the Astoria was a cinema, its stage was intended as more than just a backdrop for film projection – a ticket here bought a full night out as the evening's entertainment included a stage show with live popular music, dancing girls and comedians. The theatre's facilities provided for this with a 10.5-metre (35 feet)-deep stage, twelve dressing rooms and a performance team of up to 200 people. The opening night included opera singers from Covent Garden, the Astoria Girls dance troupe, Clarkson Rose and Olive Fox ('Womanly Wit and Manly Comedy') as well as Teddy Brown and his Xylophone, all preceded by the United Artists film *Condemned To Devils' Island* (Wesley Ruggles, 1930) starring Ronald Colman.[12] Although this

FIGURE 8.5 *Finsbury Park Astoria shortly after its opening in 1930. Stage with the safety curtain down. Source: Islington Local History Centre/Islington History Services.*

was undoubtedly a special occasion, the Astoria relied on its accompanying stage shows to sell thousands of tickets every night through the depression years. By 1939, with the onset of wartime austerity, the live shows were, however, no longer viable, and Paramount gave up the Astoria's operation to the Odeon cinema chain. The number of film screenings increased to up the takings, and the cinema was consequently able to survive both the economic situation and the Nazi bombs that obliterated great parts of London, including parts of Seven Sisters Road.

By 1955 the cinema had been in business for twenty-five years, and although the stage shows were now in the past, live music from the Wurlitzer organ was still a regular part of the show. However, other forms of popular music were now drawing large audiences throughout the capital, in particular rock 'n' roll. While the latest films now went first to other Odeon cinemas, big crowds still came to the Astoria to see live performances such as the one by Eddie Cochran, Gene Vincent and The Wild Cats in April 1960 – Cochran would die in a car crash just two weeks later. The Astoria became a major venue in the 1960s with a wide range of mainstream popular music performances from Frank Sinatra, Ray Charles and Nat 'King' Cole, to Cliff Richard, the Beach Boys and the Rolling Stones. The Beatles performed many times at the former cinema – firstly in a stint of thirty back-to-back performances in *The Beatles' Christmas Show* between 24 December 1963 and 11 January 1964, selling over 100,000 tickets. The group also performed on 1 November 1964 and 11 December 1965, although both Ringo Starr and Paul McCartney would return separately in the 1970s (Starr in Pete Townsend's rock opera *Tommy* and McCartney with Wings). Jimi Hendrix played in the Astoria in support of the Walker Brothers tour on 31 March 1967, this show reputedly being the first time he would burn his Fender Stratocaster guitar on stage. On 8 November 1970 the cinema/venue was renamed the Odeon; however, the challenge of television had deeply affected the viability of the cinema entertainment everywhere and it closed in September 1971, the last music performance by The Byrds taking place on 14 August. Nevertheless, this closure turned out to be a new beginning.

John Morris was an experienced live music promoter who had helped stage manage Woodstock and co-founded, with Bill Graham, New York's recently closed Fillmore East live music venue, which was also based in a former theatre/cinema. Morris oversaw the re-creation of the Astoria/Odeon for the Sundancer Theatre Company, naming it the Rainbow. The new venue reopened on 4 November 1971, now showing only live popular music, with a performance from The Who (who had previously played there five years earlier): 'A chorus line of dancers precedes the show and Keith goes into the audience to yell for The Who to come on. Pete wears a silver lamé jump suit with the Rainbow Theatre logo on the back. At the end of the show the chorus line comes back out and The Who join them for a few high kicks.'[13] The ambition was to make the Rainbow a major rock venue, and Morris began by booking major US and British acts over the next few months including Alice Cooper, Wishbone Ash, Mott the Hoople and Family. An unhappy gig for Frank Zappa on 10 December 1971 ended with him being pushed from the stage by an audience member; Zappa spent the next six weeks in hospital and nine months in a wheelchair – his attacker spent three months in jail. Bringing the old building up to modern safety standards had cost £150,000 (equal to £1.9 million in 2018), and consequently economic problems set in. Despite filling seats with Chipperfield's Circus over the Christmas and New Year period in 1971–72, the Rainbow was in financial trouble from the outset, which even a four-night stand by Pink Floyd playing early versions of *Dark Side of the Moon* could not solve. On 12 March, after just four months in operation, it closed again, although not for long.

Chrysalis Records was a London-based record label formed in 1968 by Chris Wright and Terry Ellis. Seeing the Rainbow as an opportunity to feature their artists, which included Black Sabbath, Jethro Tull, Procol Harum and Ten Years After, they stepped up and formed a new team to take over the venue. Over the next ten years, every major rock act would play at the Rainbow, often with shows that have since become seminal moments in popular music history. In 1972 David Bowie rehearsed the innovative theatrical show for his Ziggy Stardust tour at the Rainbow for three days prior to the first performance, and returned on 19, 20 and 30 August for concerts, although the film of this show, *Ziggy Stardust and the Spiders from Mars* (D. D. Pennebacker, 1973), was filmed at the Hammersmith Odeon. However, many other concerts were recorded or filmed at the Rainbow, including performances by Yes (*Yessongs*, 1975), Genesis (*Live at the Rainbow*, 1973), Queen (*Live at the Rainbow*, 1974), Bob Marley (*Bob Marley and the Wailers: Live! at the Rainbow*, 1977 and 1991), Thin Lizzy (*Live and Dangerous*, 1977) and Iron Maiden (*Live at the Rainbow Theatre*, 1981). Cult comedy group Monty Python's Flying Circus used the Rainbow for rehearsals for their live performance tour in 1973. Michael Palin recorded in his diary for 23 April:

> Rehearsals start at 9.30 at The Rainbow Theatre in Finsbury Park. It's a mammoth 3,500-seater theatre, with twinkling stars and above the proscenium and alongside walls are passageways, alcoves, balconies, in a Spanish-Oriental style, with lights in it for the start of a massive Shakespearian production. It's a magnificent folly – and it seems an obvious target for redevelopers. However, it continues in being used as a rock theatre – probably helped by the decision of the Albert Hall not to stage any more rock concerts.[14]

In 1974 the building's architectural and historical status was formally recognized with Grade II (later raised to II*) listing by English Heritage (now Historic England); however, this also put obligations on the owners to maintain it properly and preserve its historic features, which were under threat after years of the rock 'n' roll lifestyle. The leaseholders who put on the concerts found it difficult to afford this and building owners Rank were unwilling to, so the place closed again in March 1975. This time new operators were not so quickly in place; however, by the end of 1976, Strutworth Ltd. started promoting concerts again and the Rainbow reopened with three concerts by Genesis on 1, 2 and 3 January 1977, the first of their world tour. Although rock was still Rainbow's mainstay, punk also now got a look in with bands like The Stranglers, Eddie and the Hot Rods, and The Clash getting gigs (although Dolly Parton and Donna Summer would also pull in a crowd). The Clash's White Riot Tour gig on 9 May 1977 was the biggest punk event to date, supported by The Jam (who later pulled out of the tour), The Buzzcocks, Subway Sect and The Prefects, the event getting lots of publicity due to the destruction of some seats during the four-hour show, which the Rainbow's director Allan Schaverien put down to 'natural exuberance' and not 'malicious damage ... arrangements were made to cover the cost of it ... we shall have more punk concerts soon', which happened as predicted as The Clash returned before the end of the year, and there were other concerts by Siouxsie and the Banshees, Sham 69, The Ramones and Generation X.[15] On 29 September 1980 a concert by Elvis Costello and the Attractions celebrated the venue's 50th year of operation; however, a little over a year later, he was also to play the last live show before it closed for good as a live performance venue.

FIGURE 8.6 *The Rainbow Theatre in 1986 five years after its closure.*
Source: Dusashenka.

The Rainbow's lease was put up for sale, which, with other high costs including building repairs and a twelve-fold increase in the cost of the music licence (£500 increasing to £6000, which is equal to £25,000 in 2018), made its operation as a venue unviable. Rank proposed to turn it into a Bingo Hall, like many former music entertainment venues across the UK; however, this also fell through. For many years the Rainbow remained mostly unused. In 1995 the Universal Church of the Kingdom of God acquired the tenancy to the building and began to worship there while commissioning Farrington Dennys Fisher architects to oversee the restoration of the auditorium and foyer. By 2004 this was mostly complete, thereby saving a wonderful building, although in a very different use from that for which it had become famous.

Theatre venue survival

London is a capital city with 8 million residents and 19 million tourist visitors annually, many of whom still want to see live music. Because of this, there is a legacy of older auditoria that have been repurposed to this function. The Brixton Astoria cinema (opened in 1929) was also designed by Edward A. Stone with an interior by Thomas Somerford who helped design Finsbury Park. After a precarious few years in the 1970s and 80s, it became the Brixton Academy, a long-running popular music venue still in operation and now sponsored by telecommunications company O2. O2 also sponsors the former Astoria cinema in Kentish Town, London, built in 1932. It became a live music venue called The Town and Country Club in the mid-1980s, changing its name to the London Forum in 1993 when new owners Mean Fiddler took over. The Hammersmith Eventim Apollo was opened as the Gaumont Palace in 1932, an art deco 3,500-seat cinema designed by Robert Cromie, becoming the Hammersmith Apollo in 1962, a name most audiences still know it by. Beginning in the 1950s, popular music concerts were also held there, and many of the bands and artists who performed at the Rainbow also appeared at the Apollo, its future becoming more assured after its competitor in the north of the city closed down. After a £5 million restoration in 2013, it is now the most important popular music and theatre auditorium venue in London.

With the stalls seats removed, it can hold a 5,000-capacity audience, and besides pop concerts, it is frequently used for major live television events such as Eurovision and the Royal Variety Performance. A run of concerts that were received more like a major cultural event than a pop music gig was the *Before the Dawn* shows performed by Kate Bush between 26 August and 1 October 2014 in her first return to live performance since 1979. The twenty-two shows featured many theatrical effects, dance, spoken word and special effects, coordinated with the live music selected from several of Bush's record albums, eight of which re-entered the UK Top 40 charts during the first week's shows.

FIGURE 8.7 *Hammersmith Eventim Apollo in 2013. Source: Enmanuelcueva.*

FIGURE 8.8 *Fans in the Hammersmith Apollo auditorium waiting for Kate Bush's* Before the Dawn *show to start, 20 September 2014. Source: Mark McLellan.*

If there was any doubt, events like this that draw national and international attention indicate that buildings like this still have huge relevance in popular music culture. Although the examples here are in North America and Great Britain, theatre venues can be found in many cities of the world. The Paris equivalent of the Rainbow is the Bataclan; built in 1864 as the Grand Café Chinois for café concert performances, it has been a 1,500-capacity popular music venue since the 1970s. The Bataclan was the scene of a horrific terrorist attack on 13 November 2015 in which ninety people were killed and 200 wounded during a concert by US rock band Eagles of Death Metal (see Chapter 12). However, after renovation, the venue reopened a year later with a special tribute concert by Sting for the victims, many of whom were represented in the audience by their families.

However, the fate of the Astoria/Rainbow is also a very typical one for venues of this size. Despite their crucial contribution to both popular music history and development, they are difficult to run successfully, not only because of the economics of balancing ticket prices and sales, but because of other external pressures outside the control of promoters and operators. The Finsbury Park venue was not the only Astoria theatre to have a second life as a popular music venue. The London Astoria on Charing Cross Road (which opened in 1927 and also designed by Edward A. Stone) became first a theatre in 1977 and then a 2,000-capacity music venue in 1985; however, it closed in 2009 to be replaced by a new underground railway station ticket hall, a development which also closed two other music clubs, the LA2 run by the same team and the Metro, a typical cellar club that nevertheless had hosted memorable gigs by up and coming bands like Kings of Leon, Kaiser Chiefs and the Killers.[16] New development threatens the sites on which these buildings sit, often in the centre of cities in areas that have changed economically. Their large footprint makes them tempting commercial opportunities for developers who have scant interest in the history they represent, or the continuing cultural activity they enable. Pressure also comes from local councils who wish to maximize income and therefore raise business rates/tax for venues until the point they become unviable. Improved safety and hygiene standards, which all businesses must meet, impact these older buildings more severely in terms of running and improvement costs. Development away from their immediate location is also a threat to older venues. Newer places, in particular the dedicated arena, which with its large seating capacity of 10,000 or more, very flexible staging options and edge-of-city location, has many advantages for the major touring acts who want to stage expensive complex shows that necessitate a large, per-performance income. Mid-size theatres therefore become less profitable and fall off the booking lists as new larger replacements become available.

Many of the old urban theatre venues that have survived (like the Liverpool Empire and the Hammersmith Apollo) have become more adaptable in terms of the sort of performances they support. As well as contemporary pop music, they will host nostalgia shows (a number of artists touring together to evoke a particular period in musical history, e.g. the 1960s, the 1970s or the 1980s). In the UK, Christmas time will see a pantomime production spiced up with chart hits and a singing star from pop music or a TV soap opera. One-night stands and short runs by popular comedians, touring musicals, opera and ballet, even a fortune teller or boxing match also take place. This also means that to host these family audience events, venues will rely more on subsidies from sources such as the Arts Council, smarten up their appearance and shun the edgier rock, punk and hip-hop in favour of safer audiences. Venues like the Rainbow, where they still operate, are usually situated away from prime city centre locations, in not yet fashionable zones where commercial pressures have yet to impact too severely. The Apollo in New York thrives in Harlem, and its less well-known namesake, the UK's O2 Apollo Manchester (previously the Manchester Apollo and Carling Apollo), continues as a live music venue on the edge of the city centre in Ardwick Green. Built in 1938 as a cinema, but a popular music concert venue since the 1960s, it is a bit run-down, the stall seats sometimes removed, the bar area painted black or some weird colour. You won't see the very big ticket acts here, but they are more than capable of providing a suitable place in which to catch an old favourite still able to fill the same hall they played thirty years earlier, or experience for the first time a stellar performance by the next big thing along with a couple of thousand people who will later say, 'I was there when'. The ticket prices are cheaper, the crowds just as enthusiastic and they provide a mid-point entry for artists with a large following who cannot fill an expensive hall, or don't want to go that way.

CHAPTER NINE

Festival Stages and Travelling Sets

I'm standing at the side of the stage behind the edges of the as-yet incomplete 'wall' when Roger Waters leads out the local school children to rehearse their part in tonight's show. He smiles and jokes with them for a moment and then arranges them in a group and stands before them like a choirmaster and they start to sing: 'We don't need no education'. The rehearsal doesn't last long – they have been practising beforehand – and so they are soon walking back to the green room in the bowels of the Manchester Evening News Arena to wait for their cue. Meanwhile I continue my tour of the complex stage set, which forms the centrepiece of tonight's show *The Wall Live*, with its designer Mark Fisher. For two hours we crawl over and under the structure on which the stage is built, primarily to carry the eponymous 'wall', 10.8 metres (35 feet) high by 73 metres (240 feet) wide, which will be built during the show by eighteen stage hands and then demolished at its climax.

The entire touring team is ninety strong, because as well as the 'wall', there are many more special effects, including giant inflatable puppets, a crashing Second World War aircraft and a continuous complex projection system that uses the 'wall' as a screen. And of course, there is also the stage lighting, musical instruments and amplification system, controlled from the technicians' station on the arena floor, a 100 metres from the stage. Later on, that's my vantage point for the show, perched on a flight case – perhaps the best seat in the house. The twelve-strong band play the lengthy show's music well, although I suspect I am not alone in often being distracted by the complex animations and films, now rendered crystal clear through a digital projection system, computer controlled to be perfectly in time with the sound. Everyone waits for the familiar theatrical set pieces, known by

FIGURE 9.1 *Behind the scenes setting up for* The Wall Live *at Manchester MEN Arena in 2010. The rehearsing school children are on the stage, and the stacked-up 'bricks' can be seen to the right, ready to construct the wall as the show proceeds. Source: Robert Kronenburg.*

reputation even if (like me) they have not seen the show before: a crashing plane early on, a horrific giant school teacher (designed by the satirical cartoonist Gerald Scarfe) and of course the destruction of the 'wall'. Even if you are not a fan of the rock opera, if there was ever an opportunity to appreciate the sophistication that a travelling show can reach with today's technology, it is by experiencing this music's emotive story and its associated powerful imagery, communicated live.

Popular music moved out of the halls and theatres primarily for a commercial reason – to meet audience demand and consequently make more money. If an artist was so hugely popular that all his or her shows sold out and there were still thousands of people still wanting to attend, there were only two ways to go: either do far more shows, which are both tiring and repetitive for the artist, or find a bigger venue. The travelling rock and pop show has sometimes been likened to a circus, moving tons of equipment from place to place, setting up temporarily in some urban building or space, the razzmatazz of the event followed by the dismantling and moving on. But the connection is real; Colonel Tom Parker (who had spent time working in travelling circuses and carnivals in the 1930s) managed Elvis Presley from 1955, and sent the singer out on gruelling tours, initially of high school halls and small auditoriums, but as his popularity grew, to larger venues, stadiums and fairgrounds. In these large open-air spaces, Presley would sometimes perform on the back of a flat-bed trailer without any dedicated equipment except for some primitive amplifiers.[1] Although Elvis had played to 26,500 fans at the Dallas Cotton Bowl almost ten years earlier in 1956, The Beatles's first performance at Shea Stadium on 15 August 1965 heralded the dramatically expanding possibilities for popular music concerts with an audience of more than 55,000; however, it also clearly identified the problems to be faced in creating successful performances for such large audiences.

It was not only the lack of volume from the onstage equipment (although comparatively large 100-watt amplifiers had been specially provided by Vox for the tour) and the quality of sound relayed through the stadium's public address system, but also the distance between audience and performer, and

FIGURE 9.2 *The Beatles live at Shea Stadium, New York, during their second North American tour in 1966. The stadium held 44,600 fans for the concert.*
Source: Tony Griffin.

the lack of staging and stage lighting: 'The Shea experience was a turning point. It encouraged the evolution of larger, more powerful PA systems designed to deliver faithful, controlled sound to larger audiences.'[2]

Festival stages: Popular music performance as a large-scale event

Although at this time only a very few individual artists with massive appeal, such as Elvis and The Beatles, could draw such large crowds, another popular music phenomenon accentuated the urgent need for improved performance technology at large events – the pop festival. Although there were many earlier jazz, pop and rock music festivals (the Newport Jazz Festival, Rhode Island, USA, began in 1954, the Beaulieu Jazz Festival, Hampshire, UK, ran from 1956 to 1961, and the Monterey International Pop Festival, California, USA, was held in 1967), the Woodstock Music and Art Fair is not only the greatest of the early festivals but also one of the most defining musical events in the development of popular music culture. Situated on Max Yasgur's 600-acre farm in the Catskill Mountains, New York State, USA, northwest of New York City, the festival took place on 15–18 August 1969. Originally intended as a paid event for an audience of up to 50,000, problems with finalizing the site meant that too little time was left to erect a continuous fence and the organizers therefore decided to focus in the time available on erecting the stage, sound system and supporting facilities rather than having to deal with tens of thousands of unhappy people. In the event, 186,000 tickets were sold but more than 400,000 people turned up to watch the 32 acts perform. Although the festival bankrupted the organizers at the time, the decision to film and record it meant that they eventually made back what they had spent, these recordings also vastly increasing the event's influence.

The Woodstock stage was carefully situated at the focus of a natural bowl in the landscape, with a design brief that it should be both 'rustic and practical', the former to reflect the nature of the rural site and the latter to ensure it worked efficiently, simultaneously holding the full equipment of two bands to allow quick changeovers.[3] After a competitive submission by three different teams of designers, the design by Steve Cohen and Chip Monck was approved. Monck worked for Bill Graham at the New York's concert venue Fillmore East and had already transformed 'the expectations of rock show lighting', his staging making concerts 'a theatrical experience, loaded with mood and atmosphere'.[4] Their concept was for a 30-metre (100-foot)-diameter turntable constructed of two wooden semicircles allowing bands to set up independently and then at the flick of a switch be turned around to face the audience (although this feature never really worked in practice). Twenty-one-metre (70-foot)-long telephone poles supported a frame above the performance area from which a canvas weather awning and lighting would be suspended. Described as 'the most fantastic outdoor concert stage ever built', the stage and all the other structures needed for the event, such as the fence (where completed), concession stands, toilets, water supply, kitchens, artist and crew facilities, were assembled in the two weeks of August prior to the festival by a 300-strong crew working punishing twenty-four hour shifts.[5] A small group of six workers built the stage, which, because of the slope, stood about 3.5 metres (10 feet) high on the audience side and nearly double that at the rear. Its main platform stood on yellow painted scaffolding frames, which were also used for the giant towers on either side of the stage that supported the sound system, and two further towers in the audience field for lighting rigs. Five roof trusses spanned between two slightly rotten telegraph poles, which were tensioned by guy wires. The stage backed onto a main festival access route, so a long bridge was built from the field behind to allow the artists easy access to the performance area. Steps and an equipment lift also gave access.

Bill Hanley was responsible for designing and installing the sound system, reputedly the most expensive ever assembled up to that date. Hanley was experienced as he had been the sound engineer for the Newport jazz and

FIGURE 9.3 *The stage at the Woodstock Music and Art Fair, New York state, 1969 (still from the film* Woodstock, *1970). Source: Entertainment Pictures/Alamy Stock Photo.*

folk festivals since 1957 (although the crowd for this was no larger than 20,000) and also created the system which operated in Fillmore East. He had arranged that a substantial 440-volt/440-amp three-phase electricity power supply be brought to the site, something that normally fed industrial complexes. With a team of twelve engineers who knew what the performing acts required, he set up sixteen loudspeaker arrays on the two towers as well as monitor speakers on the stage, all linked to specially designed mixer boards.

Finally, just an hour behind schedule, the great show started at 5.07 pm on Friday 15 August 1969 with Richie Havens taking the stage. As it became dark, a large screen behind the stage was temporarily used during the Incredible String Band's set for projecting psychedelic colour patterns; however, this lasted just a few minutes, never to reappear during the rest of the weekend. There was heavy rain during the festival, a problem that the canvas cover did nothing to mitigate, so when the storms happened a large plastic sheet was rolled out to cover the amplification. On the Sunday, a huge storm not only deluged the site with rain but also brought in high winds that swayed the sound and lighting stacks back and forth and weakened the stage foundations, which started to slide down the hill. However, the storm lasted just twenty minutes, the towers stopped swaying and the stage's downward movement was restrained by stakes driven into the ground. By this time, accumulated delays had affected the programme badly and the Sunday was a catch-up affair with acts taking to the stage all through the night – some of the audience began to leave from midnight on. By the time the last act, Jimi Hendrix, took the stage at 8.30 am on Monday 18 August, 'only' 30,000 were left.

Although there had been substantial issues during the operation of the festival and its aftermath (not least the financial losses of $1.6 million, equal to $11.1 million in 2018), there were also some powerful positive messages that became clearer as time passed. The *Woodstock* moving picture released in 1970 had amassed a worldwide gross income of $50,000,000 by 1979 (equal to $182 billion in 2018) and has since gathered much more in theatre rereleases, television screenings, video, DVD and Blu-ray sales – live popular music performance had proven to be not just about revenue delivered at the event itself but what could also be gained subsequently from a remote audience who weren't there. However, as Max Yasgur, whose farmland had been devastated by the storms and the impact of 400,000 pairs of feet, stated a few days afterwards, the event also exemplified a vision of peace and unity delivered by young people in a situation that could easily have broken down into anarchy. It instead became 'three days of music and peace' and led him to optimistically believe 'there is hope, that if we join with them, we can turn those adversities that are the problems of America today into a hope for a brighter and more peaceful future'.[6] In practical terms, Woodstock was proof that such large-scale music events could be staged, and even though the size of the audience was unprecedented, one of the event's promoters Michael Lang could state mostly truthfully that: 'Everyone could hear, nothing blew up, and it all hung together perfectly.'[7]

The following year, one of the world's longest running and best known popular music festivals was held for the first time. Held on dairy producer Michael Eavis' Worthy Farm, in Somerset, England, in its first year it was called the Pilton Pop, Blues and Folk Festival but since 1971 it has been called Glastonbury. The 1971 event was intended as a one-off; however, it was accidentally rekindled in 1978 after police redirected some 'hippy' vehicles to Eavis' farm and an impromptu festival took place. From 1979 Glastonbury became an annual event apart from periodic fallow years to allow the farm to recover. The festival now attracts an audience of 135,000 each June in the years that it operates, although such is its fame that it is always oversubscribed even before performers are announced. Glastonbury is special in several ways. As well as popular music, the festival features many other creative and performing arts, caters for children and appeals to adults of all ages. Apart from a small salary for himself, his daughter Emily who co-organizes the event and his staff, Eavis runs Glastonbury on a non-profit basis, making large contributions to international charities such as Oxfam, Greenpeace and WaterAid. Unlike most pop festivals, the continuity and assured popularity of Glastonbury have also meant that considerable investment has been made into permanent infrastructure, which not only makes the setup and operation easier but also significantly reduces the environmental impact of creating an instant temporary town in the centre of the countryside. This includes access roads, water reservoirs and pipes, tanks for human waste and electricity cables with power provided by 250 temporary biodiesel fuel generators, comparable to the supply for the nearby city of Bath.

To attend Glastonbury means to be faced with many entertainment choices as there are multiple stages and venues set up across the site. At the 2017 festival there were more than fifty separate stages featuring music performances as well as many more venues featuring comedy, theatre, film, circus acts, speakers and debates. Working throughout the year, a small team of permanent festival staff fine-tune the site layout and order in about 330 separate mobile buildings, primarily tents from commercial suppliers. Many more buildings and structures add to this during the final phase of preparation as the concession stands arrive providing food, drink and other items the audience might need or want. Setting-up work begins at the beginning of May about eight weeks before the event takes place on the last weekend in June. Nine kilometres (5.6 miles) of continuous 4.3-metre (14-foot)-high fencing is put in place on a rail system after retrieval from its storage place off-site. At this stage, the site is marked out to ensure all the facilities are placed in the correct locations, along with site signage and lighting. The amplification, lighting and video screen technology associated

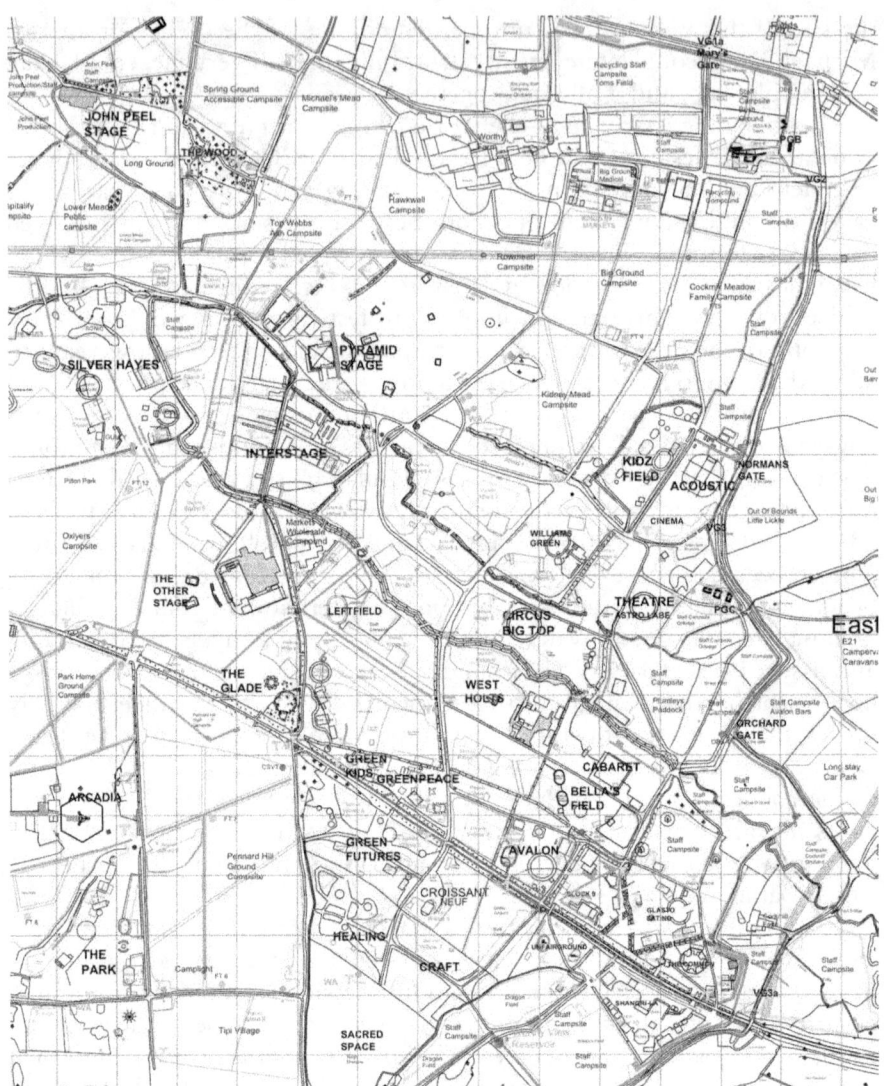

FIGURE 9.4 *Detail of the central part of the site layout plan for Glastonbury 2017 showing the stage areas – as complex as a small city. Source: Glastonbury Festival.*

with performance arrive last of all on the Tuesday and Wednesday before the festival opens on the Thursday. All this construction is managed by the Event Safety Shop with fourteen safety officers and support staff who arrange for licencing and fast response advice as the site swings into operation. Although the vast majority of the stages are commercial items provided by specialist companies (such as Serious Stages, which first started at Glastonbury in the 1980s), there is one special image that distinguishes Glastonbury from other festivals – the Pyramid Stage. First created in 1971, right at the beginning of the festival's history, it is a one-tenth scale replica of the Great Pyramid of Giza erected over the site of a dry spring, although made from a scaffolding structure supporting metal panels and plastic sheets. The current stage has a permanent steel structure, one of several iterations that have been built over the years. Assembled from 4,000 metres (13,123 feet) of steel tubing, the stage is 40 metres (131 feet) wide by 40 metres deep and 30 metres (100 feet) high. Because of its complexity, it is one of the first to be completed during the setup period. The pyramid is fitted with access ramps and extra platforms, then covered with a membrane so that it is transformed into what is essentially an open-side building. Separate structures are constructed on either side for the speaker stacks and video screens, and a front-of-stage control area is built in the audience field.

Glastonbury's ethos of supporting worthy causes and deeply embedded green credentials is a powerful message that ties into the early days of the pop music festival experience as envisaged at Woodstock. In February 2018 it won best festival for the fifth year running at the NME awards, and International Music Festival of the year at the Pollstar Awards.

A very different festival in terms of location is the Coachella Music and Arts Festival, held annually since 1999 near the town of Indio in the

FIGURE 9.5 *The Pyramid Stage and surrounding support facilities at Glastonbury in 2010. Source: Glastonbury Festival and Jackie Slade.*

Coachella valley, part of the Colorado Desert, USA. Rather than rain and mud, the problem in this location is great temperature variation – as low as 6°C (43°F) at night to 41°C (106°F) in the daytime. For this reason, the audience areas must be covered as well as the stage. The largest of these is a temporary structure that has become known as the Sahara Tent, although its form is not a tension structure as found in traditional Berber tents, but a massive prefabricated arched vault (Plate 11). This modular mobile building is constructed by AG Light and Sound, a specialist event structure company owned and operated by Andrew Gumper, and although it has perhaps its most dramatic form in this desert festival, it is actually used for many different outdoor functions. Gumper describes how he created the 'mega-structure' mobile building:

> We had looked at self-climbing structures and the engineering required to create them, and the safety standards were always that, if you knew bad weather was coming, you lowered the structure. This didn't take into account *not knowing* if wind was coming, and this was right around the stage collapse at the Indiana State Fair [on 13 August 2011, during which the roof covering the concert stage collapsed in high winds killing seven people and injuring 58 more]. My engineer and I started from scratch and designed a new system that took into account safety, efficient transport, super strength, and capacity, and would, of course, address wind loads.[8]

The system uses modular components to enable fast and safe erection and can be assembled in multiple formats depending on event requirements. One side of the parabolic vault is assembled and fixed together at ground level and then sections, complete with external cladding, are added one row at a time, gradually pushing the growing roof to its full height. The structure is designed to accommodate the load of lighting, amplification, video screens and other services and can be fully enclosed or, like at Coachella, left open at the sides to allow audiences to pass through freely. AG Light and Sound provides a full setup service including all the show elements as well as the basic structure and its cladding – this is a massive mobile concert hall up to 111 metres (365 feet) wide and 43 metres (140 feet) tall that can be set up in days, and taken down again and be in use at a different site, in a different form, for a different function the following weekend.

Although popular music festivals may follow a similar pattern of organization, they can present quite varied experiences for audiences. The Glastonbury experience is special not only because of the world-class artists on the main stage but also because of the massive range of other activities on offer, with opportunities for learning and personal growth as well as fun and excitement. Because of the diverse range of stages, there are many crossovers between music genres and valuable opportunities for new and emerging artists. This musical showcase element extends beyond the actual event as the entire festival is broadcast live on the BBC, free to UK licence payers, with multiple stages available on the streaming site available for weeks afterwards. Coachella has a different ambience, regarded as a fashionable event with trendsetting performers, a focus on electronic and hip-hop music and crowds who dress to be seen. The entire event is streamed live without cost to the viewer on YouTube but nevertheless is financially very profitable, in 2017 earning $114 million over its two weekends in April.[9] Another large US festival, at which music is an important element although not the primary one, is Burning Man, held annually in the Black Rock Desert in North West Nevada since 1987. Audience members are considered to be participants in this event, physically building the various art installations, theme camps and villages, many of which include stages where music performances, both live and based on DJ sets, take place (see Chapter 12). However, there is no main stage as such, although there is a central camp area where acoustic music sets take place. In addition to these out-of-town events, there are city-centre festivals that take place in parks or other urban open spaces (e.g. South by South West in Austin, Texas, and British Summer Time, London, UK). Although less immersive compared to a rural festival, they have advantages for both audiences and the host city. Transportation is easier to an urban location, and visitors can make use of local facilities like hotels and restaurants. They can also get a taste of the city's other attractions: shopping, museums and perhaps local music venues, all of which bring in additional tourist income and accentuate the location's image. When the festival is held on land that is currently redundant, it draws attention to the site as a potential resource. For example the O2 Arena in Greenwich, London, was constructed in 1999 on a parcel of land contaminated by a gas works that had occupied the site since 1885. It was originally created as the Millennium Dome, a temporary exhibition and event space, which was envisaged to be replaced by other sorts of development such as a football stadium or a business park after the year-long celebrations were over. However, its value as a long-term performance space was recognized by AEG, and after conversion it is now primarily used for concerts and other large-scale events and in terms of ticket sales is recognized as one of the most successful venues in the world (see also Chapter 10).[10]

Compared to the bare scaffolding and simple lighting that were created for the 1960s stages at Woodstock and Glastonbury, contemporary festival stages are vastly more complex and audience friendly. Sound quality is undoubtedly better with multiple speaker locations with time-synchronized sound that reduces crossover due to the distance from the stage. Lighting is improved not only in terms of quality, safety and energy consumption but also in terms of adding to the atmosphere with different effects synchronized to the performance. The largest single improvement for large crowds is the availability of live video screens with high illumination levels that are visible even during daylight, enabling everyone to see what is going on at the front and bringing a degree of customization to the set, with the artists' team deciding what goes on the screen placed at the rear of the stage. However, despite all these technical improvements, the actual experience of a festival is remarkably unchanged. Because there are multiple acts appearing, the stage is generic, artists for the most part having to project their talent via their performance and not via the complex theatrical add-ons that are now an intrinsic component in most top-of-the range shows. And the audiences still have to stand and sit out there in the weather, camp out in a field, make the pilgrimage to a remote location just to be in that place at that time, to be part of the experience. Significantly, they are also a part of the festival show's 'cast' as more and more festivals are televised, live streamed and recorded for future consumption. What would these shows be like if the all-suffering, yet visibly happy and excited festival crowd weren't there to make all that noise?

Travelling stage sets: From concert to experience

Although successful popular music artists moved to bigger shows because it was commercially advantageous, for some there were also important creative reasons. These musicians became more ambitious both in the type of music they were writing and performing and in the way it might be staged. In terms of composition, rather than the short simple song upon which popular music was founded, during the 1960s, complex concept albums emerged, and these longer pieces entailed stories that the artist wanted the audience to appreciate. With regard to staging, there were ready-made precedents in theatre and opera, and film and animation also fired their imagination. To create these more immersive experiences, which were expensive to stage, a bigger audience was needed to pay for the design and manufacture of bespoke stage sets. Festival staging had shown that large, temporary stages were possible and that tens of thousands of people could attend a concert and enjoy the experience, even when simply sitting in a big open field. Reproducing these bigger events in an urban setting meant (at least at first) finding and repurposing the spaces and structures that were available in large cities from which these big audiences could be drawn. The large public event spaces in cities (capable of holding upwards of 10,000 people) were public parks, sports arenas and sports stadia. Instead of performing at a city theatre holding 2,000 to 3,000 people, a stadium show meant that a top artist could come face to face with all their local fans in one go, which might in the past have taken ten or even twenty separate performances. This was a 'reconfiguring of the musical landscape, and concomitant with that new forms and genres of media' associated with the show itself but also its associated elements such as concert films, television and social media.[11]

The earliest popular music stadium events were the rock 'n' roll revival concerts featuring legendary performers from the 1950s such as Chuck Berry, Bo Diddley, Bill Haley and His Comets, Jerry Lee Lewis, Little Richard and Gene Vincent. The first was held at Toronto's Varsity Stadium, Canada, to a crowd of 20,000 on 13 September 1969 (also featuring John Lennon's Plastic Ono Band, Alice Cooper and The Doors on the bill). With a temporary stage set up at one end of the field with an open-ended tent marquee over it for protection from the elements, staging was primitive; however, great performances and a documentary film made by D. A. Pennebacker (*Sweet Toronto*, 1971) ensured its influence. However, there were gestation problems in developing this new approach. Although stage set design was a well-established area of expertise, on the whole it was based around theatres, which had a whole set of permanent support facilities in place such as lighting rigs, stage services, flies for scenery and even workshops to manufacture and repair equipment when it suffered from wear and tear. Moreover, this form of large performance event design was primarily based on repetitive shows in the same place, not on a travelling show that must move from place to place, usually overnight. What was needed for the travelling pop music show was a whole new area of technological development and the expertise to operate it on the road. Progressive rock musicians were ambitious in this way: bands such as Yes, Genesis, and Emerson, Lake and Palmer (ELP) pitched virtuoso musicianship, complex 'symphony'-length compositions that filled one, two or even four sides of a long-playing record. Although they might be mocked in years to come (most memorably, and hilariously, in Rob Reiner's mockumentary movie *This Is Spinal Tap*, 1984), this music had a legion of fans who still remain loyal. In fact, this was just the latest generation of musicians who wanted to 'experiment with long songs, big concepts, complex structures, and fantastical lyrics', which continue in the music of artists like Kate Bush, Radiohead and Opeth.[12]

Pink Floyd are an exceptionally well-placed act through which to relate the history of the development of the touring show from the 1960s to the present day, because they were at the forefront of those musicians who wanted to expand the live concert experience and continued creating new live shows as large touring stage techniques matured. In the mid-1960s, the band had provided musical accompaniment for the exotic light shows devised by architect Mike Leonard (who had been Roger Waters' and Nick Mason's landlord since 1964) and therefore had experience of performing as part of a greater immersive visual experience. They therefore began to incorporate projected light shows into their performances – initially just coloured slides shown through a projector, then via improvised home-built systems using domestic spotlights. Although 'hopelessly primitive by today's standards', at the time it gave Pink Floyd a 'distinct visual edge over their competitors'.[13] In 1966 Peter Wynne-Wilson, who was a theatre lighting technician, began to work with the group, and he brought in primitive though effective innovations (such as dripping oil paint onto stretched condoms in front of the projector) that visually transformed their live music into a 'psychedelic' experience. On 12 May 1967 Pink Floyd played at the Queen Elizabeth Hall in London, creating a show that went far beyond the contemporary concert experience. As well as specially recorded sounds from nature (which they would shortly introduce into their recordings), they also experimented with a primitive quadrophonic system in which sound could be rotated around the room by directing a joystick. Visual effects included light projections and bubbles, and theatrical effects were performed by the band and costumed actors in the audience. As the band became more successful, playing in larger halls, they continued to use projection, often with specially commissioned films related to the content of the music. Pink Floyd's stage sets became even more ambitious with the success of their record *Dark Side of the Moon* (1973) as they shifted from playing in theatre auditoriums to large arenas like Earls Court (see Chapter 10) and stadiums. Playing the album before its release on their 14-date tour of North America, one date was at the Hollywood Bowl on 22 September 1972. For this, a spectacular spatial effect was created by hiring four searchlights and setting them up so that a giant pyramid appeared above the stage. Using a 12-metre (40-foot) circular screen suspended above the band, the show featured work designed by a number of gifted artists and animators including Gerald Scarfe, Anthony Stern and Storm Thorgeson and Aubrey Powell from Hipgnosis, the designers who created their album sleeves and tour programmes. These increasingly complex shows with films and slide projections, sound loops and taped excerpts, smoke, dry ice and on occasion inflatable objects (such as the giant 'octopus' they installed in the lake for the Crystal Palace Garden Party in 1971) suffered from numerous failings. Technically ambitious, their concerts were regularly compromised when elements failed to start on cue or even start at all. Keyboard player Rick Wright recalls: 'The equipment was pretty unreliable. The film would break, or the projector would break. There were a lot of missing cues and trying to get back in time. We were always getting snappy with the technicians ... [we were] in danger of becoming slaves to our equipment.'[14] Roger Waters also worried that that the larger shows separated the band from their audience: 'In the Old Days, pre-Dark Side of the Moon, Pink Floyd played to audiences which, by virtue of their size allowed an intimacy of connection that was magical. However, success overtook us and by 1977 we were playing in football stadiums. The magic was crushed beneath the weight of numbers'.[15] Pink Floyd suffered all the problems of innovators in a new aspect of the live performance business, which was driven by the increased commercial power of popular music. As more people wanted to see them perform live, they had made the shift to bigger and bigger audiences. This had consequently driven them to create a bigger show experience in order that those members of the audience remote from the stage felt engaged with and appreciated the meaning of the music.

The financial heft to create these more ambitious shows was there, but the technical side was still catching up.

The Wall, originally released in 1979, was Pink Floyd's eleventh studio album, and although, in comparison to *Dark Side of the Moon*, not universally applauded by the band's fans, it has achieved remarkable longevity in the public's consciousness. The semi-autobiographical story that underpins the music was first visualized in a hugely ambitious touring show, *The Wall Tour*, opening at the Los Angeles Memorial Sports Arena on 7 February 1980. This version of the show had thirty-one performances but only four venues: Los Angeles, the Nassau Coliseum in New York, Earls Court in London and Westfalenhallen in Dortmund, West Germany. The new touring set industry was now beginning to benefit from dedicated expertise in both design and production. *The Wall Tour* was designed by architect Mark Fisher and engineer Jonathan Park who first worked with Pink Floyd on the design and manufacture of giant inflatable figures for the band's 1977 *Animals* tour. Fisher had been designing and manufacturing large inflatable structures since 1969, inspired by experimental architecture proposed by design groups like Archigram in the UK and Ant Farm in the United States. Other lightweight and mobile structures such as geodesic domes and lattice shells were an inspiration to Jonathan Park who constructed experimental forms of this type at the Architectural Association school in London where he first met Fisher. *The Wall Tour* would feature many complex inflatable structures, some operated as puppets with electric winches. The 'wall' itself posed a particular problem as there could be no scaffolding to support it as when it fell it had to leave a clear space behind. The designers solved the problem by creating an interlocking cardboard 'brick' transported flat on pallets, which had removable sides that formed platforms with safety railings for the riggers as they worked.

This was the first large touring stage set of such complexity, and dry-run load-ins and load-outs, setups and dismantling were held in Culver City and the Los Angeles venue where the tour would start. Although many problems were found and resolved, operating this stage set was never going to be easy. Although the 1980 stage was about the same physical size as the 2010 one, it was far more complex to set up and bulkier to transport. The tour consequently lost money and Waters stated the show would not be revisited partly because 'it's too expensive. And, as its partly an attack on the inherently greedy nature of stadium rock shows, it would be wrong to do it in stadiums'.[16] However, when history was made with the destruction of the Berlin Wall that had divided the city in post-war Germany, he started to work on a one-off version of the show, which would be staged on the derelict site that had once been no-man's land around Berlin's Potsdamer Platz, close to the Brandenburg Gate. For this show the Wall set was even bigger: 25 metres (82 feet) high by 180 metres (590 feet) wide. This time cardboard would not be strong enough, so the interlocking bricks were made from polystyrene foam, which could be recycled as building insulation after the show. Triangulated steel towers that were used as builders' hoists were temporarily repurposed to brace the huge temporary structure. The other past-members of Pink Floyd were not involved as Waters used a mixture of hired musicians and special guests, including the East Berlin Rundfunk Symphony Orchestra and the 150-person East Berlin Radio Choir, all fitting onto a giant tiered stage. Scaffolding supported a 15-metre (50-foot)-diameter circular projection screen, which was served by a 70-mm projector located behind the stage. Front projection onto the 'wall' was made from five 19-metre (62-foot)-high towers positioned out in the audience area.

This entire show had been created in two and a half months, and access to the site was limited to the last four weeks. Although Fisher Park designed the set, the realization of such a massively complex event was achieved by teamwork with sound and lighting designers, graphics and animation designers, film-makers and television producers, choreographers, pyrotechnics contractors, builders, scaffolders, electricians etc. – proof that 'rock "n" roll design is a team business, an integration of creative activity from many different sources'.[17] A total of 350,000 tickets were sold for the concert, which took place on 21 July 1990, eight months after the Berlin Wall fell, although it is thought that the audience might have been closer to half a million as at least 100,000 were let in for free. The show was televised live in fifty-two countries, and subsequently a live CD, Laserdisc and VHS videotape were released. Despite all this, the show was so expensive to

FIGURE 9.6 The Wall *live performance at Potsdamer Platz, Berlin, 21 July 1990.*
Source: *Photograph Reproduced Courtesy of Stufish.*

stage that the trading arm of the charity that was supposed to benefit from the event lost money, although Waters, who had partly funded it himself, eventually made back his expenses from sales of the recordings.

Despite his earlier misgivings regarding stadium shows, Waters decided to tour *The Wall* again in 2010, once more recruiting Mark Fisher (now operating with his design studio Stufish) to recreate the travelling stage show, now called *The Wall Live* in this third iteration. In the thirty intervening years since its first incarnation, touring technology had improved dramatically with the development of specialized equipment dedicated to mobility and speedy erection. Much of the basic gear that enables a contemporary touring show to happen is adaptable and standardized, even for a show as visually unique as *The Wall Live*. This means that much of the behind-the-scenes equipment is hired, and that its principles of operation are well known to the riggers who will operate it on a nightly basis. It also means that if something breaks, it can be replaced at short notice – an essential aspect of the philosophy 'the show must go on'. Another benefit of modern equipment is that it is lighter and more compact, with miniaturized electronic control systems that enable remote operation once it is in place, good news in terms of reliability when you are trying to replicate a complex performance time after time, but also safer as operation can be controlled from ground level rather than suspended high above the stage or the crowd.

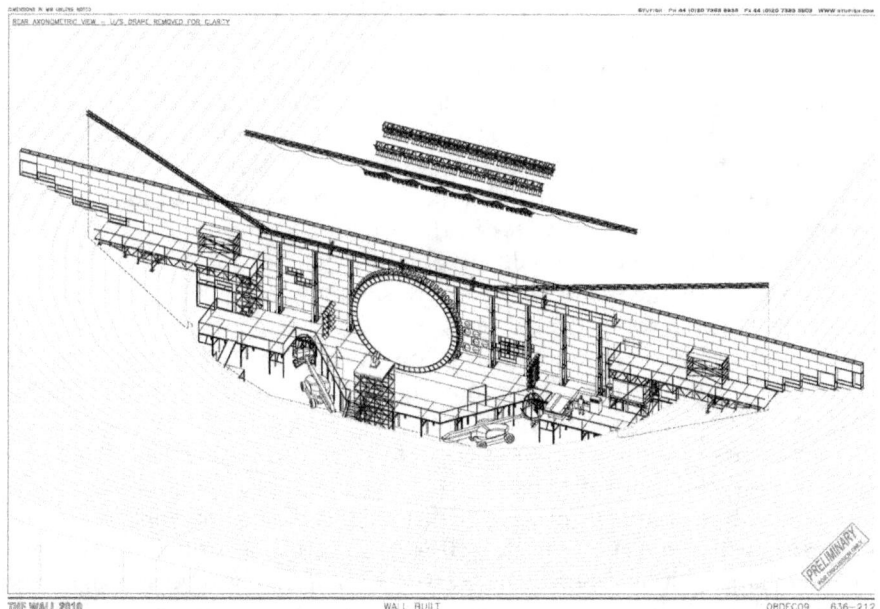

FIGURE 9.7 *Preliminary layout drawing for* The Wall Live *tour, 2019, showing the stage with wall assembly structure from behind. Source: Reproduced Courtesy of Stufish.*

Compact equipment is also easier and cheaper to transport in smaller vehicles. Although still incredibly ambitious, these innovations meant that a stadium tour for *The Wall Live* was now feasible, and eventually a total of 218 shows between 15 September 2010 and 21 September 2013 would take place. As with the first tour in 1980, multiple shows still happened in the same venue in the larger cities; however, such was the flexibility of the new set that many were also one-night stands, sometimes with less than twenty-four hours between shows. By the end of the tour, *The Wall* had visited South America, Australia and New Zealand, and North America and Europe twice each.

Mark Fisher (1947–2013) designed sets for Stevie Wonder, the Rolling Stones, Madonna, Black Sabbath, AC/DC, Robbie Williams, Queen and U2, and the company that is his legacy, Stufish, is one of an elite group of top mobile stage designers who work with the world's leading artists. The team has designed shows that have toured for years (U2 *360°* tour, 2009–11) and lasted for just fourteen minutes (the usual length of half-time Superbowl show). Their work is not restricted to popular music acts, as the same sort of experience is now applied in other large-scale entertainment events including sports (Beijing Olympics opening and closing ceremonies 2008, Asian Games 2010), creative arts (BBC Diamond Jubilee show 2012, British Council Fashion Awards 2017) and family entertainment (Just Dance Live 2018, Holiday On Ice 2017). As well as Stufish, the industry has grown so that there are other specialist designers such as North American team Atomic that has worked with Madonna and Nickelback, as well as music festival and showcase events, and British designer Es Devlin who has designed staging projects for Beyoncé, Jay Z, Adele and Kanye West. Another British designer is Rudi Enos, an engineer who specializes in creating mobile tenting systems that can be used as vast shelters for performance events that are often used at festivals and for one-off and travelling shows. His designs are used at music festivals around the world. In 2000, Radiohead took the circus idea to heart by playing twenty-one UK dates in three rented twelve-pole Kayam tents he designed. The concert would be played in one of the 10,000-capacity mobile venues, while the other two were simultaneously being erected and dismantled. These sophisticated tents provided a temporary 4,600-square-metre enclosed space that could be erected in two days by a crew of eight riggers. Mock Victorian-style promotion material linked the tour's concept to the travelling circuses and freak shows of the past.

Equally important to the designers in the creation of these shows are the specialist staging companies that have developed new techniques, products and assembly methods in order to deliver the sets on time and on budget. Companies like StageCo and Tait Towers are able to utilize a catalogue of interchangeable components to assemble extremely diverse stage sets, which, although they may look completely novel and very different from each other, are actually mostly made from the same reusable components. This has numerous advantages: the products are recyclable into future projects, therefore bringing down cost and wastage; the riggers work with familiar systems, thereby decreasing setup and dismantling time; and many parts are universal, meaning spare parts can be carried in case of failure or damage. As well as the stage structure, these companies are also directly involved in the development of the shows' technical delivery via sound and light systems. This means they are responsible for innovations in projection, display, amplification, computer control systems and, increasingly, software development.[18]

Both Stage Co and Tait Towers were started in the 1970s by founders who started out at the practical end of show production, unsatisfied with the poor standard of equipment that was available at the time to stage their concert events. StageCo began in Belgium in 1975 when its founder Hedwig de Meyer was organizing a local music event that became the Rock Werchter Festival. Building his own superior stage setup, De Meyer's system was recognized by other event organizers, thereby creating the demand for his developing business. By 1986, StageCo was operating a world tour for English rock band Genesis, utilizing the company's own tour system. It now operates worldwide with bases in the United States, the Netherlands, Germany, Belgium and France. Tait Towers was started by Australian Michael Tait after fifteen years as tour manager for the progressive rock group Yes. He set up the company in 1978, in Lititz, Pennsylvania, USA, to be close to his partners Roy and Gene Clair who had been designing and manufacturing amplification equipment since 1966, and whose equipment had been used by Elvis Presley on his large-scale shows.[19] The company is named after the lighting tower Tait designed; however, it now constructs and delivers every aspect of the live performance stage set. Both StageCo and Tait Towers have built and operated sets for Stufish and many other designers. For an example of how embedded the production companies are in the design of the artists' vision, Ric Lipson of Stufish recounts how Bono of U2 envisioned a new stage set for their 2017/18 *The Joshua Tree* anniversary tour that would be a giant screen with the desert cactus emerging from its top. This would mean at least three world firsts in show production: the largest and highest carbon-fibre LED 8k video screen ever built at 61 metres (200 foot) by 14 metres (46 foot); a video-controlled spotlight system that would follow performers automatically, so they could be seen in front of the screen; and an ultra-lightweight sixteen speaker system that could fill the entire stadium with sound.

Lipson states, 'At that point, we didn't know what the kit would be, beyond the hope that technology just on the cusp of being possible would be invented in time for the start of the tour in May [the following year].' Work began with Tait immediately after the December 2017 meeting and the show, of course, went on the road on time: 'rock stars don't want to hear problems and our job is not to say, "That's impossible" – our job is to say, "Yes, of course"'.[20]

FIGURE 9.8 The Joshua Tree *anniversary tour stage at Century Link Field, Seattle, US, designed by Stufish and engineered by Tait Towers. Source: Photograph Reproduced Courtesy of Stufish.*

In the age of music streaming, being on the road is the only way to make money from popular music. Live free streaming of performances (such as those at Glastonbury and Coachella) reinforces this shift. Sites like Spotify and YouTube pay negligible royalties to music writers and performers for screening their music (around $0.00397 per stream for the former, and YouTube's payments rates vary depending on the type of advertisement they attract but average about $0.00074), although some sites such as Amazon ($0.0074) and Apple Music ($0.00783) pay more.[21] Sales of recordings via download cd and vinyl are nowhere near what they were before music became so easily available via the internet. Recorded music sales in the United States fell from $20.6 billion in 1999 to $15 billion in 2015 *including* streaming sales. During this period live US concert ticket sales tripled in the ten years between 1999 and 2009, with live music taking $25 billion in 2016 to which can be added $5 billion in tour sponsorship.[22] Playing live to large audiences willing to pay and see (thanks to video technology) their heroes is where the income is. For example U2's 2011–13 *360°* tour brought in a record-breaking $736 million (equal to $790 million in 2018), a successful outcome for an operation that Willie Williams, show director for U2, calls 'a competitive relationship between art, commerce and logistics'.[23] Taylor Swift's *Reputation* tour is set to be even more profitable on a per-show basis.

This is her fifth concert tour and is scheduled to visit 53 stadiums between May and November 2018. With a target audience of 50,000 to 60,000 per show, she will play to 3,000,000 people in total. With a gross ticket income of c. $7.5 million per show, the tour will gross about $400 million by its end (Plate 12).

These large shows are a phenomenon that has emerged in the last few decades, and a whole industry has been revolutionized to make them possible. As well as the sets and the touring technology that makes them work as an experience accessible to every person in the house (or stadium, or field), in the last two decades there has been the creation of dedicated venues that cater specifically to their needs – the arenas (see Chapter 10). But why are these shows so popular? Clearly the scale of the event is capable of providing an amazing show, unlike that seen in any other forum. The pop concert of this type has become a spectacle: 'a highly developed form of rock theatre, calling on inspiration and influence from a vast range of media, from fine art to advertising by way of cinema and opera'.[24] The phenomenon has also been criticized as 'technological, mediated, materialized and dominantly superficial', created from a complex mishmash of pre-prepared recordings, visual effects and carefully scripted moments carefully arranged to stimulate a reaction from the audience.[25] Indeed, these shows are undoubtedly stimulating events; however, the memories they create in audiences are not transient – fan forums are full of affectionate and enthusiastic recollections not only of the entire concert but also of specific key incidents. It may also be that in an age where digital, media-based, interaction has become the norm, these concerts and festivals, made possible by sophisticated, planned audio-visual effects as they are, are still plenty live enough to provide an important opportunity for 'the intense experience of face-to-face (musical/cultural) community ... as a compensation for its lack in the everyday life of social media'.[26]

CHAPTER TEN

Arenas

In 1978, Bob Dylan toured the world beginning in Japan and ending in the United States – giving 114 concerts in all.[1] These were all big shows in stadiums and arenas, played with a large twelve-piece band presenting much of his back catalogue in new arrangements. When he landed at London's Earls Court for six shows in June 1978, I was there. The Earls Court Exhibition Centre was built in 1937, although the site had been used as a showground since the 1880s. The building was designed by American architect C. Howard Crane as a large multifunctional space, essentially a 40,000-square-metre shed with an *art moderne* façade at the entrance. Everything from motor shows to military tattoos were held there, and the building even hosted events at two Olympic games in 1948 (boxing, gymnastics, wrestling, weightlifting) and 2012 (volleyball). From the early 1970s, the building was used as a popular music performance venue and it became by default the largest music arena in the UK. Up to 19,000 fans could fit into the rectangular building, which had movable raked seating on four sides surrounding a flat floor.

Dylan's show in 1978 was my first arena event, and my overwhelming feeling was remoteness from the stage. Sitting on the floor three quarters of the way back, Dylan and his band were just dots in the distance. The music was loud enough but muddy to say the least. During a break I walked up to the front just so I could see what the stage area looked like. The circus performers doing their thing in the entrance hall didn't make up for my general disappointment. In the early days of these large arena shows, many in the audience must have felt like me. The music that had been created in the intimate circumstances of small clubs and studios could just about transfer to a theatre which was designed to project the actions and sounds of a human being to an audience – but early arenas were giant amorphous spaces built without stage sightlines or acoustics in mind. Setting up seating and a stage within a giant shed didn't make the artist come any nearer or

FIGURE 10.1 *Earls Court Exhibition Centre. Source: Damien Everett.*

improve the acoustics. It is hard not to think that the whole thing had been a mistake for an artist like Dylan, and indeed he later admitted the tour's ambition had been to make money (it grossed over $20 million, equal to $79.4 million in 2018) as he had debts arising from his divorce and his movie project *Renaldo and Clara* (1978).[2] The first concerts on the tour had been at the Nippon Budokan Hall in Tokyo in February and March, and these were released the following year as a live album. I bought it to see what I had missed on the night.

Although my experience was not unusual for an arena concert at the time, this new setting was, however, recognized by some music performers as an opportunity that went beyond the simple possibility of selling more tickets per performance. For all its limitations, Earls Court did show how the popular music arena event might be more successful, particularly as staging, sound and projection technology developed (see Chapter 9). Large complex, theatrical shows coupled with an attention to sound quality could fill the space visually and acoustically. Well-designed large-scale visual effects might be appreciated from every seat. The partnership of stage set, sound and video, designed to enhance and communicate the performance, meant that big audiences could experience something special that was simply not economically or artistically possible in a smaller venue. Earls Court therefore had a long operating life, remaining the largest arena in Great Britain for many years, including concerts from Pink Floyd, Queen,

U2, Led Zeppelin, David Bowie, the Spice Girls and Arctic Monkeys, as well as the annual British Phonographic Industry Awards and the Brit Awards. However, competition from the refurbished Wembley Arena (see below) and the O2 Arena, Greenwich, helped determine its closure in 2014 to be replaced by 8,000 flats and a retail development. The last show was on 13 December 2014 when Bombay Bicycle Club headlined, although they were joined on stage by Pink Floyd's David Gilmour for two numbers, including Wish You Were Here.

Sports stadia and arenas

Large entertainment and performance buildings that stand apart from the conventional theatre or concert hall existed in the nineteenth century. Buildings such as Castle Garden, New York (1824, although built on an earlier military fort from 1811), the Royal Albert Hall of Arts and Sciences, London (1871), and the Alexandra Palace, London (1873, rebuilt 1875), were ambitious multipurpose structures intended for multiple uses – concerts and shows but also exhibitions, meetings and other events. However, the architectural character of these large enclosed spaces differs significantly from the modern arena, which has an alternative ancestry. Its contemporary architectural form arises from the mid-twentieth-century design brief as a container for large sports events, and its progenitor is therefore the open-air stadium with its all-encompassing seating, raked stands and multiple points of entry for both the viewed and the viewers. A sports stadium is defined as a home for field events, for usually being open to the air and for its large size, capable of holding crowds of up to 100,000. Most are roofless because of the requirements of the sports they support but also because of the constructional problems inherent in lightweight, wide-span roofs. A roof with intermediate columns would interfere with audience sight lines, a problem that is exacerbated when covering a field of play that cannot be obstructed. Today's lightweight structural technology does, however, mean that fully enclosed (e.g. Tokyo Dome (baseball), Japan, 1988, 55,000 capacity) or opening rooves (e.g. Wembley Stadium (soccer), London, UK, 2007, 105,000 capacity) are technically possible for large-span structures. Popular music concerts are possible in both indoor and outdoor stadiums because of the sophisticated stage sets described in the previous chapter; however, despite the huge technical advances in this area, their operation in this way is frequently compromised by building designs that have been created as sporting facilities, not as entertainment venues.

The sports arena is a smaller structure than a stadium, usually up to 20,000 capacity and always enclosed. Emerging as a distinctive building type in the first half of the twentieth century, their size was set as a consequence of structural restrictions, the building layout and capacity determined by the technical and economic limits of building large open-span roof structures. Early modern-day arenas, such as the Antwerp Sportspaleis, Belgium (1933), a cycling venue, and the third Madison Square Garden, New York (the earliest venue on this site that can be classed as an arena, 1925–66), built for boxing, were usually primarily dedicated to one sport. However, it soon became recognized that the spatial arrangement of arenas had benefits in terms of flexibility.[3] The large flat floor area (for the sports activity) could be used for many different events, sporting and otherwise. The fully enclosed space allowed setup and use independent of the weather and, if blacked out, full control over artificial lighting, providing staging opportunities not available in open-air venues. All this encouraged entrepreneurial operators to seek alternative ways to use the building – for exhibitions, meetings, conference events and popular entertainments. If the acoustics and internal environment in terms of air quality, temperature and character were lacking because of the shed-like qualities of the building, the ability to host multiple different events combined with a quick turnaround still made the development of new buildings commercially viable. As has been stated, although it became technically possible to enclose stadium-sized structures in the early 1980s, arenas still continued to be designed and built, primarily as sports facilities but also now with the potential to host family entertainment, exhibition and conference events. Despite being used for popular music concerts from the 1960s on, very little was done by arena designers in this period to improve the inherent problems that these very large internal spaces provided for a live music event. Poor acoustics, great distance to the stage, lack of comfort and other 'hassles' were perceived as 'inevitable'. They came with the territory – the higher quality of sound, vision and comfort expected as the norm in other entertainment industries was at first absent in the big sports arena rock show.

In North America, sports such as basketball and ice hockey meant that there was already a legacy of suitable spaces that could be adopted for the big rock show, and venues like Madison Square Garden (1968) in New York and the Los Angeles Memorial Sports Arena (1959) in California became well-known 'arena rock' venues. Bruce Springsteen played the last three concerts in the Memorial Arena in March 2016, announcing his song Wrecking Ball as a tribute to the venue: 'We're gonna miss this place, it's a great place to play rock 'n' roll'.[4] However, in the UK the most popular sports (soccer, rugby football and cricket) were all played outdoors in stadia (although smaller indoor sports buildings featured wrestling and boxing). However, some arenas were built to fulfil the requirements of a special sporting event, with the permanent building identified as 'legacy'. For example the Empire Pool and Sports Arena was built in Wembley, London, in 1934 as a swimming pool used for the British Empire games of that year. The reinforced concrete building designed by engineer Owen Williams spanned 72 metres (236 feet) across both the pool and the raked seating for 4,000 spectators on either side. This was an innovative structure for the 1930s, providing the building with the long-lasting flexibility of a column-free space. In the mid-1960s the arena was the venue for the *New Musical Express* awards events at which The Beatles, The Rolling Stones, the Beach Boys and many others played live in shows that were filmed and then broadcast on television. For these events, a stage was set on the floor towards one end of the arena with the audience on the floor in front, and in the surrounding raked seating, a semi-in-the-round performance, although those behind the stage must have had both a poor listening and seeing experience. The Beatles played in the arena three times, and it was the venue for their last live scheduled show in the UK on 1 May 1966 (although they subsequently performed unannounced on the Abbey Road studios rooftop in 1969).

Such well-publicized events provided an identity for the Wembley Arena (as it was now called) as the largest-capacity music space in London, and although its primary role remained in hosting family entertainment and sports such as tennis, wrestling, ice-skating and the Horse of the Year show, throughout the 1970s, 80s and 90s top music acts filled the former swimming pool with big audiences despite its typical echoing shed-like environment. In 2006, it benefited from a major £35 million refurbishment as part of an urban redevelopment plan led by Brent Council that included building a new Wembley Stadium, shopping and commercial centres and

FIGURE 10.2 *The Beatles play at the Empire Pool, Wembley, during the New Musical Express Awards concert, 11 April 1965. Source: Trinity Mirror/Mirrorpix/ Alamy Stock Photo.*

FIGURE 10.3 *SSE Arena (formerly Wembley Arena) London (photo: 2007). Source: ©Peter Stevens Photography.*

over 11,000 homes. Architects Tooley and Foster relocated the main stage to the opposite end of the building with a new main entrance and service yard. Concourses containing merchandising and catering kiosks were introduced, and the building's roofs, walls, windows and doors were renewed. Wembley Arena (12,500 capacity) is the second largest venue of its type in London after the opening of the O2 Greenwich Arena in 2007 (20,000 capacity); however, with the improved facilities, it has continued to be successful. In April 2014, AEG signed a fifteen-year contract to run the facility and announced it would now be known as the SSE Arena, its new operators showing confidence in its long-term viability. The 2006 regeneration at Wembley is a familiar pattern in arena development – part of a trend in new building and refurbishment that has taken place across the British Isles in the last fifteen years.

Multipurpose arenas

One of the first arena venues to be designed with both sport and popular music shows as an integrated brief was the Spectrum, Philadelphia, USA, which opened in September 1967. Designed by architects Skidmore Owings and Merrill, the 18,000-capacity arena was initially home to both a basketball team (Philadelphia 76ers) and an ice hockey team (Philadelphia Flyers); however, its flexibility as a venue for a wide range of other popular entertainment events was also important. The facility was named by

Lou Scheinfeld, former President of the Spectrum, ostensibly as an acronym: SP for sports and South Philadelphia, E for entertainment, C for circus, T for theatricals, R for recreation and UM for 'um, what a nice building',

FIGURE 10.4 *Spectrum Arena, Philadelphia, USA, showing its typical sports-style-encompassing seating layout. Photograph taken during the 'last stroll' around the building to allow fans to say goodbye, October 2011. Source: Doug Kerr.*

although another story is that 'spectrum' sounded similar to other words like spectacular and splendid and its reference to a variety of colours and types fitted with the developers' vision.[5] The first-ever event held in the arena was a musical one, the Quaker City Jazz Festival, which sold out; the second was a boxing match.

The promoter for rock concerts at the Spectrum was Larry Magid, co-founder of Electric Factory Concerts, who recalls:

> What happened with the concerts was that we started looking at the Spectrum as really just a big club. What if we didn't have seats on the floor? We said, we'll call them dance concerts. We'll keep the ticket prices low and try to build exciting shows, rather than waiting for the headliners or the Johnny Cashes or the Ray Charleses of the world, which was the standard. Let's break out of this mold, and let's go into the Spectrum with rock shows.[6]

For four decades the Spectrum provided the venue for virtually every major rock act that toured the United States, some artists returning many times. The Grateful Dead played at the Spectrum fifty-three times and recorded three live albums there. British progressive rock group Yes played there thirty-two times. Magid recalls: 'A lot of it becomes a blur, because there were so many. Dylan coming back and playing with the Band, that was a big deal. The Rolling Stones in '69. Elvis in '71. We did a show with Led Zeppelin ... Springsteen's first show there – he opened for Chicago and got booed.'[7] One of the first rock shows at the Spectrum was on 1 November 1968, the fourth from last date on British power rock trio Cream's farewell tour. The stage was set in the centre of the arena and slowly revolved. Yes also used an in-the-round stage, which rotated for their 1979 tour (the concert was released on record, *Live in Philadelphia*, 1979); however, most music performances were from a fixed stage positioned at one end of the arena. The Spectrum's last event was a Pearl Jam concert on 31 October 2009, its sport and concert functions now taken over by the larger, 20,000-capacity Wachovia Center (now Wells Fargo Arena), which opened in 1996.

The Spectrum was an immensely popular venue, inspiring great nostalgia among those who saw their favourite acts there. Some talk of its intimacy (compared to its replacement), of the freedom to approach the stage (at least in the 1970s) and of the sense of event that the big concerts had.[8] The sound had all the qualities of an arena show in one of these 'first generation' buildings – for good or ill. A report by W. Mandel on Led Zeppelin's show on 13 June 1972 describes the technical conundrum:

> To fill a hall the size of the Spectrum (which last night held 16,847 persons), huge amplification systems are needed. Every little instrument, even the hi-hat on the drum kit, must have a microphone placed next to

it. What happens then is that a little sound, such as a tambourine being shaken, becomes a mighty apocalyptic noise, louder than if the sky were to fall. Everything, in other words, gets bigger and louder and seemingly more important.[9]

And then there is the recognition of what the performers have to do to reach their immense audience: 'The histrionics of the band members, the awesome pretension of their loudness and stage antics, made it clear that several elements go into "superstar" concerts.' Mandel had identified that the arena concert adds up to something more than a music experience, is more than the sound and the sight of musicians – it becomes an event in which the venue becomes an integral component: 'the ambience of the hall and the people in it is important. With about 17,000 people on hand, rock-festival-like hassles are inevitable. That sense of hearing the concert, "in spite of" the surroundings make everything seem that much more delicious.'[10]

The commercial model for arena development in the UK was significantly influenced by the Manchester Arena although the building was originally commissioned as an athletics venue as part of the city's unsuccessful bid for the 2000 Olympics.

FIGURE 10.5 *Waiting for the show to begin – Arcade Fire in-the-round performance at Manchester Evening News Arena, 9 April 2018. Source: Robert Kronenburg.*

Designed by DLA Ellerbe Beckett with local architects Austin-Smith: Lord and engineers Ove Arup and Partners, the arena was built in 1993–95 close to the city centre, over the top of Victoria Railway Station. It was the first enclosed arena in Europe to follow the US model of having seating arranged on multiple tiers all around the viewing area, a vast open space made possible by a 105-metre-long (344-foot) steel truss to support the roof. The building's sporting roots were at least partly fulfilled in 2002 when it was used to host the Commonwealth Games, and other sporting events have a regular place in its events programme including basketball, boxing, ice hockey and gymnastics. When it was built, it was anticipated the arena would also hold exhibitions, conferences and family entertainments such as ice shows; however, its largest source of visitors has been as a touring popular music venue. Between 2003 and 2007 more tickets were sold at the Manchester arena than for any other comparable venue around the world, and even in 2016, it sold the fourth-most number of tickets for concerts and shows (851,785) (the O2 Greenwich Arena, London, came top with 1.59 million).[11]

The Manchester arena could not be described as a memorable building, nor does it add to the urban character of the city, graphically described as a 'huge soulless sports and entertainment complex' by the architectural historian Nikolaus Pevsner.[12] It was not designed primarily for staging concerts, and audience experience was in the past routinely described as poor inside its shed-like space with associated acoustics; however, travelling sound systems have improved dramatically since the early 1990s, and a 2015 refurbishment by new operators SMG Europe has undoubtedly improved things. This arena also has some key advantages for promoters. Its location is excellent, close to a major city centre that is itself the centre of a large conurbation, with both good public transport links and substantial on-site and local car parking. Its size is right, able to hold a very large audience at its maximum capacity (floor standing plus tiered seating in-the-round shows). Finally, it is flexible, allowing many different show configurations: side-stage for an 11,000 audience and end-stage for up to 16,000 fully seated or nearly 21,000 in-the-round. With major acts seeking bigger audiences to make touring their large, expensive shows viable, the Manchester Arena with its large, adaptable space and good position at the centre of a large, interested audience catchment has proven to be an inevitable port of call. Although not originally designed specifically for music concerts, the Manchester Arena was pivotal in showing not only how a large-scale arena could be profitable for this form of entertainment, but also how it could also be an important element in generating income and recognition for the city in which it is located. Manchester became a name that promoters recognized as the building was nominated for the International Venue of the Year in the Pollstar awards every year between 2003 and 2009 after winning it in 2002.[13]

Facilities like Manchester Arena provided an important new opportunity in the development of popular music entertainment, and yet these ex-sports and exhibition halls clearly had many shortcomings. Compared to traditional theatres and concert halls, for most of the audience the experience was compromised with poor sight lines, much longer distance to the stage and dreadful acoustics. Servicing facilities for audiences such as catering, toilets, air quality and temperature and accessibility were aimed at sports fans rather than big-ticket concert audiences. Other factors such as speedy and convenient loading for large, complex sets, acoustic separation from neighbours to avoid time curfews and planning restrictions were also not fully resolved. Building owners and developers began to recognize the viability and potential of dedicated new facilities, created around an enhanced commercial model; this concept spawned a spate of new arena building and refurbishments of older exhibition and sports centres in the UK and beyond. Including Wembley Arena and the O2 Arena Greenwich, there are now sixteen arenas in the UK ranging in size from 10,000 to 21,000 seats.

The multipurpose entertainment arena is a global phenomenon. Although in some regions, such as the United States, the primary emphasis remains sport, even here venues such as the Golden1 Center, in Sacramento, California (2016, 19,000 capacity), built as a partnership deal between the city and the Sacramento Kings professional basketball team in order to keep the franchise in the city, opened in its first week with a concert by Paul McCartney on his 2016 *One on One* tour. This 19,000-capacity venue, designed by global design practice AECOM and San Francsico-based architect Mark Dziewulski, is built on a tight downtown site with the aim of reinforcing local businesses (rather than drawing visitors away from the city) and taking advantage of public transportation links (see Chapter 12). As might be expected, the T-Mobile Arena in Las Vegas (2016, 20,000 capacity) has a special emphasis on entertainment because of the city in which it is located (Plate 13). Jointly developed by MGM Resorts International and the Anschutz Entertainment Group (AEG), the building was the result of long-term interest in creating a major arena venue in Vegas by AEG who as well as a sports team owner and events coordinator are second only to Live Nation Entertainment as the world's largest live music promoter. Although the opening-night concert by local band The Killers was on 6 April 2016, the first sporting event (a boxing match) did not take place until May that year, and the Vegas Golden Knights ice hockey team did not play in the arena until 2017. Other North American sports/music arenas include Nashville's Bridgestone Arena and Memphis' FedEx Forum (see Chapter 12).

Each of these arena projects has its own specific local context; however, they share a similarity in brief that can be summarized in three key ambitions: to provide an improved customer experience that will draw audiences regularly and increase the arena's appeal as a destination venue; to provide an improved operating experience that encourages repeat bookings by promoters and major artists; and to provide a focus for development opportunity and urban regeneration in the cities in which they are sited. All these ambitions connect with the commercial importance of creating a new brand. The management companies of arenas that were once named for their location or function now often seek out sponsor partners anxious to connect directly with the thousands who attend events in the building, but also to take advantage of the publicity associated with the promotion of the artists who perform there (e.g. Empire Pool, then named Wembley Arena, now SSE Arena). Branding also has building design implications. The quality of the environment and the experience needs to be high to reinforce the brand; frequently, new buildings or ones that undergo rebuilding are able to attract a new sponsor as the project comes to completion, or the introduction of a new sponsor is directly connected with a subsequent investment in freshening the image and facilities. For example Manchester Arena (which had previously been named the NYNEX Arena and the Manchester Evening News Arena) underwent a comprehensive refurbishment of its interior and exterior as part of a deal between Phones 4u (naming rights sponsors 2013–15) and operators SMG Europe.[14] Competition between venues has stimulated the creation of new or improved facilities across the sector so a stream of new and refurbished arenas, utilizing designs that are enhancements of older specifications, has appeared in a relatively short amount of time, effectively creating a new building typology for large-scale performance spaces.

FIGURE 10.6 *The Dublin Arena in its docklands context (photo: 2010). Source: Tonkie.*

One example of how an existing venue has changed over the years in order to stay competitive is the 3Arena, Dublin (the O2 Arena, until 2014). Originally a Victorian railway goods terminus situated on the banks of the River Liffey in Dublin's docklands, the building was converted into The Point concert venue by local developer Harry Crosbie and promoters Apollo Leisure in 1988. The 8,550-capacity venue was notoriously uncomfortable with poor sound, sightlines, primitive catering and toilets, although it had a long history of memorable performances, which meant that for many fans it was regarded with affection: 'The Point was a kip [Irish slang for a slum] but it was our kip … Imagine what it was like to be there, memories that they will never forget.'[15] By 2007, the Dublin Docklands North Lotts Area in which the building was sited was undergoing regeneration, and the new Dublin light railway (LUAS) improved audience transportation with a stop right outside the venue. Apollo Leisure had also changed, becoming Live Nation Entertainment, the world's largest music promoter, and its Dublin venue was now just one of the many it owned or managed internationally (220 by 2018). The Odyssey Centre in Belfast (100 miles away) had intensified the competition, and so the decision was made by Crosbie and Live Nation to remake the venue into a new arena with much increased capacity, new facilities and a new image.[16]

Much improved bar and restaurant facilities were placed within the elegant nineteenth-century part of the building that faces the river, creating a destination element for the site. The historic façade became an architectural symbol both for the building's reinvention and for the regeneration of the area as a new and fashionable place to visit regardless of whether or not there is a performance. The rest of the building was new – a vast steel frame spanning 50 metres (164 feet), column free so sightlines are not impaired, but also with a 50-tonne load capacity to support flown equipment needed for a variety of shows. Thick skin roof and wall-layered constructions substantially reduce sound transmission, thereby mitigating (if not removing) curfews for performances – a crucial feature for new urban arenas. The ideal acoustic environment for amplified sound is a neutral one so that the desired experience can be created at the desk and reproduced by sophisticated sound systems with speakers set around the performance space. The naturally 'live' acoustic environment of the space should be minimized for good sound quality, although this is not always guaranteed by touring sound systems.

The new arena's floor plan was turned through 90 degrees with the stage now along the long side of the building, and directly behind it, a new internal loading area through which articulated lorries can drive was created, with internal parking for six in total. A flexible flat floor area, coupled with retractable seating, allows for speedy changes with a variety of layouts ranging from 9,500 fully seated to 14,500, utilizing the maximum standing area. Even with this increased capacity, turning the plan around has meant that the furthest seat from the stage is 60 metres (197 feet):

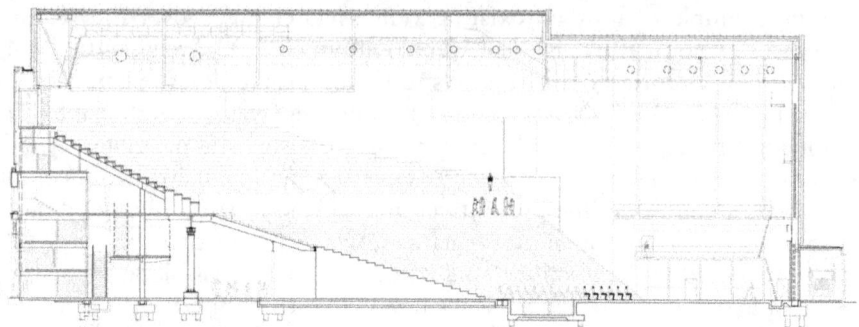

FIGURE 10.7 *The Dublin Arena section through the fan-shaped seating to the performance area (architects Populous). Source: ©Populous.*

20 metres (66 feet) closer than it was for The Point. The arena space is not in the round, as with sports-focused arenas, but is fan-shaped – a raked seating area behind which a continuous concourse provides bars, kiosks and access to toilets at two levels. This space to socialize and enjoy the pre-show anticipation is praised by fans but also aids crowd access and escape in an emergency. There was great nostalgia for the old building; however, the new building receives unremitting praise from audiences for views of the stage, speedy entrance and exit, plentiful concessions and easily accessed toilets: 'A far cry from the grotty (and beloved) Point depot. The O2 is a great venue for gigs of any sort, I've been to comedy, theatre and music events here and it works every time.'[17]

The architects for the Dublin arena were Populous (at that time HOKSVE), a global design practice, well experienced in sports and entertainment facility design, and their next arena building, First Direct Arena in Leeds (2013), although a completely new facility, followed the same plan shape and seating layout. This shape provides a compact spatial layout allowing greater control of the performance systems (visual and acoustic) but also the environment in terms of air quality and temperature. Moreover, there is no lost seating to the rear of the stage area for the majority of shows, which are not in the round performances. The sport-focused arenas in the United States (including Las Vegas' T-Mobile Arena, also designed by Populous) have an in-the-round seating layout; however, the new, dedicated entertainment buildings prevalent in the UK focus on flexibility (multiple layouts for different types and sizes of performance), made possible by modern building structures that can span the required volumes while still providing acoustic containment. Whatever the layout, the focus on easy and quick turnaround means that the buildings are in use more often, and less staff are needed to operate them. There is an increase in the size and quality of backstage areas to provide better facilities for performers and crew and to cater to the increased trend towards multiple night runs. Attention to sustainability issues is now important, with buildings not only conserving energy through sophisticated monitoring of environmental equipment, but also making energy through solar panels and recycling rainwater. Another development is in front of house facilities. The O2 Greenwich (also a Populous conversion of the Richard Rogers Partnership-designed Millennium Dome) has led the way in this regard. The venue becomes a centrepiece for the facility but not the only reason for visiting it. Bars, restaurants, shops, VIP and membership lounges and other entertainment facilities providing cinemas, bowling, casinos and shopping provide an entire leisure experience.[18]

It is certain that the demand for new popular music performance-focused arenas is still developing outside the UK, and design firms with expertise in arenas such as AECOM and Populous have recently designed new buildings in Australia and the United States. Populous' largest project in terms of audience capacity is the Philippine Arena, at Ciudad de Victoria, Manila, a 50,000-place indoor venue (its fan-shaped auditorium means it cannot be classed as a stadium), which opened in July 2014 – it is now the largest in the world.

FIGURE 10.8 *O2 Arena Greenwich, London. A purpose-built complex of event spaces and other leisure buildings within the converted Millennium Dome, urban regeneration of derelict land polluted by a former gas works (photo: 2012). Source: Danesman1.*

FIGURE 10.9 *The Philippine Arena, Manila, designed by Populous. This is the world's largest indoor mixed-use arena, a 50,000-capacity enclosed event and performance space. On New Year's Eve 2014, 1,000,000 people celebrated in the arena's grounds. Source: ©Populous.*

Designed to accommodate church services, sports events and popular music concerts, the plan form expands the fan shape into a giant one-sided bowl. The 170-metre (558-feet)-span column-free performance space can be divided with visual and acoustic curtains so that just the lower tier can operate for smaller audiences. However, innovation in large venue design is not just in the capacity to make them cater for ever-increasing audiences but also in the ambition for more and more intense audience experience delivered by new technologies. The most radical concert venue currently proposed is the MSG Sphere, currently under development by the Madison Square Garden Sports and Entertainment company with architects Populous. This new type of venue is proposed for a site in Las Vegas adjacent to the Sands hotel and casino complex (due to open in 2020), with a further site in Stratford, London, also out for public consultation.

The building consists of a 110-metre (360-foot)-diameter truncated spherical dome situated on a rectangular podium, a dramatic building form for sure; however, it is the communications and presentation technologies that are the most innovative. The dome's exterior is to be clad with 5.8 linear kilometres (190,000 feet) of LEDs that will combine to make the entire surface of the building a video screen, which can transform the image of the structure into anything from a giant football to a small planet, but also convey what is going on internally when there is a live event. The same informative façade strategy applies inside, although this time with a high-resolution

FIGURE 10.10 *The planned MSG Sphere proposed for a site in Stratford, London. The Las Vegas version is predicted to open in 2020. Source: ©2018 MSG Sports and Entertainment, LLC.*

screen covering the entire internal surface, immersing the audience in a 360 degree 'IMAX-like' experience. The sound system is unique too – beam-forming audio that projects sound directly to each location within the venue to each individual seat, improving quality without excessive volume, even tuning the content (e.g. language) to the listener's requirements. According to MSG's CEO James Dolan, the 18,000-seat venue's characteristics was inspired by contemporary popular music performance and designed to fulfil the requirements for electronic dance music shows with their highly choreographed visual experience, along with conferences, commercial presentations and other screened entertainment.[19] Buildings such as this make it clear that the arena's beginnings as an adopted sports venue have been firmly left behind as the function, layout and embedded technologies required by twenty-first-century entertainment form a core part of their design – this is now a mature, independent, architectural typology.

Popular music is, however, a business that fluctuates; SMG, operator of both the Manchester and Leeds Arenas and twelve other venues across Europe, found that audience numbers were down in 2012 as the buildings struggled to match the number of events held the previous year.[20] Live Nation Entertainment saw profits drop in 2014 due to falls in concert attendance,[21] although they have since risen again as the company increases the number of concerts and festivals it promotes and the number of tickets it sells year on year.[22] There is still uncertainty in how this business will develop, depending on the changing nature of recorded music distribution and the role of ticket resellers. Nevertheless, the two key factors in the design of the new arenas (that is also present in the older buildings that have been refurbished to extend their viability) are that of flexibility – the capacity to cope with many different types of event and therefore change in the entertainment industry – and the addition of multiple attractions to visit arenas alongside the central event, for example restaurants, clubs, shopping and cinemas.[23] The big businesses, such as Live Nation Entertainment that operates new arenas (and promoting, ticket sales, advertising and artist management), lead to the assertion that these buildings are a prime example, perhaps the ultimate one, of how popular music has been commodified – massive financial investments, underwritten by corporate sponsorship, providing a facility for global artists to sell their product to millions of avid consumers: 'The concert ... becomes the prime generator of revenue itself. Thus the music ... becomes little more than a flyer for the impending, and at times impossibly expensive to attend, arena concert.'[24] However, despite the business uncertainties and the changes in how venues operate, and the complex economics on which they are based, the fundamental existence of live performance as a draw for large audiences is not in doubt – with year-on-year increases in both numbers and income generated identified in music industry surveys (see Chapter 12). It also cannot be doubted that arena architecture has added a new and dramatic element to urban leisure, dramatically expanded the creative limits of the popular music performance experience and it has added a catalytic component to aid in the regeneration of cities.

CHAPTER ELEVEN

Record Scenes

Although up Whitworth Street West there is an animated line of people waiting patiently behind metal railings, we don't have to queue to get in as we are with someone who works at Factory who has put his name on the door. Through a small entrance, with barely a sign of what lies behind, past a hatch in the wall, we pass into the main dance space. I had seen the design before in the architectural journals, although the photographs were taken in full daylight with all the lights on, not like it is now. In print, the building is a remarkable mix of industrial chic and something reminiscent of the Dutch De Stijl style from the 1920s and 30s – plain cool blue and grey walls with contrasting blocks of bold colour and black, steel 'I' columns and roof trusses, zigzag black and yellow hazard stripes around the steps and lower part of the columns. A balcony runs around one side of the space, which has at its centre a natural-wood dance floor – standard industrial elements like bollards, cats-eyes and warning signs are used to dress the space (Plate 14). I had heard there is also a dubious cafeteria, a hairdresser and downstairs another bar away from the dancing. Now, the overwhelming sensation is sound – a loud repetitive, but addictive dance beat, matched with flashing lights and reflections from a retro disco ball. People dance with arms outstretched on and off the dance floor, clutching bottles of water and cigarettes, sometimes shouting in each other's ears – more often just moving with the beat. Without a band to focus on, it's the dancers who take centre stage. We force a way through to the bar, and maybe because the crowd are too busy dancing, or perhaps have their own way of getting high, we get our drinks straight away. Although I have been working in Manchester for a year, this is my first visit to the Haçienda and I can't see why that is.

The Haçienda was a key venue that altered the direction of popular music in the 1980s, and although it was associated with live performance as a place where the artists from the Factory record label could be showcased, it was also operated as a dance venue, pioneering a scene focused on imported and locally recorded house music. For centuries, live music was only delivered by musicians playing their instruments and using their voices; however, in the twentieth century, the development of popular music began to be influenced by the playing of prerecorded music, sometimes associated with newly developed styles of live performance. The places where recorded music has been the dominant soundtrack have therefore also paralleled changes in the development of venues for live music, and it is important in this study to examine some key examples where this influence has been felt.

Disc jockeys, deejays, MCs and rappers

The person who chooses and plays the records in clubs and other venues has a crucial impact on the development of music scenes. Even the selection of specific recordings for a jukebox has importance, attracting particular groups of people to particular places at a particular time, which in turn can instigate the creation of new music from the participants. Before radio and record companies made it possible for individuals to listen to and buy music usually only available in other markets far from where they lived, selecting and transporting recorded music overseas had a profound influence on the development of new music scenes. The 'Cunard yanks', young men employed on the transatlantic shipping lines, were popular people in 1950s Liverpool, not only for their sharp clothes, but also the latest North American records that they selected and brought back to the city. These records, sometimes purchased cheaply as US jukebox castoffs, were popular currency in Liverpool, stimulating the active youth music scene that would develop into Merseybeat. One of these sailors, Bill Harrison, recalls how he brought back an album by soul singer Roy Hamilton, which was passed to Gerry Marsden. Marsden and his band The Pacemakers later had a major hit with the song that Hamilton had covered, taken from Rogers and Hammerstein's show *Carousel*: 'You'll Never Walk Alone'.[1]

DJ and author Dave Haslam relates how in Britain in the early 1960s, 'Pre-recorded music was being heard in a variety of locations with disc jockeys having an increasingly important part to play ... house parties, town hall gatherings and community centres ... Much of this was happening outside the control of the established venues and promoters.'[2] This was for a number of reasons, sometimes because it was cheaper than hiring a large band or orchestra (which was still the main form of dance music), but often also because rhythm 'n' blues and soul (and subsequently ska, blue beat and reggae) was just not available any other way. At this time, record-only nights had an advantage for people who liked this music as instead of a 'rhythmically challenged drummer and a singer with the right trousers but a thin voice murdering songs like "Hound Dog" and "Long Tall Sally" ... DJs could stick with the original versions, the real deal'.[3] These pioneering

DJs (such as Guy Stevens in London and Roger Eagle in Manchester) played music from artists like Chuck Berry, Jimmy Reed, John Lee Hooker and The Coasters, which they sought out at specialist record shops or imported directly from the United States. The music was popular with audiences but also influential among musicians who liked the scene (with its own dancing style and fashions) as well as the sound – this happened with The Beatles in Liverpool via the imported 'Cunard Yanks' records, and with The Who and The Rolling Stones who heard the music at clubs like The Marquee and The Scene in London.

The creation of discotheques such as the Peppermint Lounge in New York (1958–65) and Annabel's in London (1963–date) introduced a primarily recorded music experience, with light shows designed to focus on the dancers as live musicians were not a big part of the scene. This sort of dance club often replaced former ballrooms, dance halls and cabaret clubs as the big bands and dancing styles that went along with them went out of fashion, and although they often focused on distinct musical styles thereby attracting specific crowds, the majority operated on a commercial basis without an ambitious live music agenda (how discotheques developed out of these venues has been discussed in Chapters 5 and 6). They did, however, provide one of the settings for the creative DJ/musician to establish his or her craft, which is now an important part of live performance, a role that has evolved to have equal status with other musicians. DJs were finally accepted as members of the Musician's Union in the UK in the 1990s.[4] A crucial part of this story is the development of the 'sound system', the large powerful amplifier and speaker setup associated with this music, which also describes a specific sort of travelling recorded music experience. Developed in Jamaica in the 1950s, the sound system had a large role in converting the image of the person playing the records into a creative personality, as the Jamaican 'deejay' would not only play the records but also sing or 'toast' to the rhythm.

Although at first focused on playing imported US rhythm 'n' blues music, the need to always have new music unique to their shows led deejays into production, thereby creating the Jamaican ska style. Sound systems first arrived in the UK in the early 1960s with Jamaican immigrants and in the United States in the 1970s. They were important connections with their roots for new immigrants, and because of their portability, they could be played anywhere: homes, clubs and the street. They also introduced vibrant new musical styles like rocksteady, reggae and dub that became internationally popular, leading to live music tours by its most famous stars (such as Desmond Dekker and Bob Marley and The Wailers) and huge record sales.

Another form of popular music that developed out of the manipulation of prerecorded sound that has also risen to global popularity is hip-hop. Beginning in New York City's Bronx in the mid-1970s, the music developed as a result of DJs extending the 'breaks' in music where percussion was

FIGURE 11.1 *A section of the Bass Odyssey Sound System, Tropical Hut, St Mary, Jamaica, 2012. Source: Yaniq Walford.*

the dominant sound, thereby creating new beats and rhythms. To this was added other techniques such as scratching, where the sound from one record is mixed or transposed over another. Rap is an important component of hip-hop: dynamic, rhyming spoken word performed by the MC (emcee) in conjunction with beats and music or on its own. Hip-hop began not in formal venues but at house and street parties and from the beginning was used to express powerful political and social messages, honed in the tough, often-deprived African American neighbourhoods in which it was created. The reputed site of the first hip hop party was the home of eighteen-year-old DJ Kool Herc at 1529 Segwick Avenue, Bronx, who threw a party to raise some funds to buy new clothes.[5] Very quickly hip hop became a popular mainstream music genre, developing in the recording studio as well as on the street, infiltrating music venues that up until that time had focused on other genres. One of these was Bronx venue Disco Fever, its name taken from the currently popular movie *Saturday Night Fever* (1977, John Badham). The venue was opened at Jerome Avenue and 167th Street by Sal Abbatiello's father Albert, who owned two other bars in the area, although originally it catered to an older audience playing top 40 hits. However, after the success of a hip hop night in 1977 that Abbatiello organized featuring one of the innovators of the scene, the then eighteen-year-old Grandmaster Flash, the club turned towards hip hop with long all-night sessions. The venue then developed into an important home for the scene, featuring many different DJs, MCs and rappers including Run-DMC and Kurtis Blow (who featured on the first release from the record label Abbatiello started in 1982). Cleveland rapper M.C. Chill was first signed with a New York record label in the 1980s: 'The Fever was one of the first hip-hop clubs of any note. Any day at The Fever you just met whos who – I met Afrika Bambaataa, Kool Herc, Red Alert, just hangin' out.'[6]

Situated on the first floor of a two-storey commercial building, the ground floor was plastered in crazy-paving style with a yellow plastic awning over the entrance and an illuminated sign pointing to the entrance. The venue could hold up to 600 in its crowded main bar space, although there were also VIP spaces accessed via the cards Abbatiello handed out to many of the now-famous artists who frequented the place. Although drugs, particularly cocaine, were a dark part of this scene, Disco Fever avoided the worst of the violence that often went along with it, mainly because Abbatiello instigated many community charity events benefiting local people in an area where poverty and unemployment were at catastrophic levels (although he did also install a metal detector to stop guns from being brought in).[7] In 1983, according to *People* magazine's Bill Adler, the club was alternatively: 'the rap capital of the Solar System' or 'the hottest spot in New York City'.[8] The club was so famous that in 1985 the hip hop movie *Krush Groove* (Michael Schultz) featuring many of the top artists was filmed in the club, its production unfortunately leading to the club's closure as the producers' application for film permits led to the discovery that Abbatiello had never applied for a cabaret licence and the police closed the place down.

DJs and Northern soul

Manchester's Twisted Wheel was one of the many British clubs that developed from coffee bar roots (another influential one was the Jacaranda in Liverpool, where the Quarrymen and many other Liverpool beat groups performed). Formerly the Left Wing coffee bar, the club was situated in a basement on Brazenose Street, with black and red painted walls, lit by some bare light bulbs and decorated by a random collection of wheels collected by the owners: the five Abadi brothers.

The key feature of the Twisted Wheel was the music choice selected by DJ Roger Eagle – blues, rhythm 'n' blues, blue beat and soul. Opening in 1963, the 300-capacity club had 14,000 members by the following year, and the fact it did not sell alcohol and was a members' club gave it the freedom to have a radical opening policy with all-night sessions every Saturday night. DJs like Eagle 'eschewed the easy option with their music choices and music fans gravitated towards them. They didn't just demonstrate pioneering music taste, but also encouraged it. They both had an influence beyond the four walls of their … basement music venues'.⁹ Although the Twisted Wheel had some great live music, not only local bands such as The Hollies but also US blues artists introduced by Eagle like John Lee Hooker, Screamin' Jay Hawkins and Sonny Boy Williamson, the all-night sessions with rare imported

FIGURE 11.2 *The building that housed the Twisted Wheel in Whitworth Street, Manchester, before demolition in 2013. The venue's sign was in the top part of the central window (blocked up in this photograph) with spoked wheel decorations below. Source: Robert Kronenburg.*

soul records was its legacy. What was happening at the Twisted Wheel was the beginnings of northern soul, a scene that revelled in relatively obscure although high-quality US soul music with its own associated dance and fashion style. Northern soul music became popular in the north of England and the Midlands in other clubs such as the Golden Torch, Stoke-on-Trent, a church that had previously been a skating rink and a cinema, and the rather unlikely setting of a basement disco in a grand nineteenth-century house modelled on a French chateau outside Droitwich in the West Midlands – Chateau Impney. All these clubs had all-nighters featuring continuous dancing to soul music, although the owners also brought in influential musicians such as Edwin Starr and The Drifters. Of all the venues for northern soul, the most famous was, however, undoubtedly Wigan Casino.

The Twisted Wheel moved to a new site on Whitworth Street in 1965, but this closed in 1971, and when the Torch also closed due to its licence being refused in March 1973 (drug use and overcrowding were a problem), DJ Russ Winstanley and the Casino's manager Mike Walker started an all-night event beginning after the venue's other activities closed at 2.00 am. The first northern soul all-nighter began at 2.00 am on Sunday 23 September 1973, keen dancers arriving earlier on Saturday night or travelling across from the Blackpool Mecca, which closed around midnight. The Casino Club (as it was called from 1965) was built as the Empress Hall in 1916, a ballroom with a sprung dance floor, a billiard room and a smaller 'Palais de Dance' space added in 1926.

FIGURE 11.3 *Empress Ballroom postcard c. 1930. Source: Collection of Ron Hunt.*

From the 1950s popular music concerts were held there, including the Rolling Stones in 1964. The ballroom was the main all-nighter dance floor, with the turntables set up on the old orchestra stage at the end of the room. A balcony ran around three sides, providing a good view of the dancing below. There was also a tea room where snacks and hot drinks could be bought, and a second smaller dance floor called Mr M's (named after the club's owner Gerry Marshall) where slightly older 'classics' from the heyday of the Twisted Wheel and Torch were played. Winstanley and the other DJs like Ian Fishwick, Kev Roberts and Richard Searling worked hard at finding unusual, rare records that fit within the genre of hard-driving, powerful, dance tunes. Winstanley ran a record stall, and his discs were imported directly from the United States or were UK re-pressings. Selectadisc, a record store in Nottingham specializing in northern soul, would also supply new records by mail order.[10] Guy Hennigan, a frequent visitor to the Casino, describes the importance of the records: 'The music was spectacular, in the fact that it had drive and vibe, I couldn't tell you what people called a shit record, or a good or bad record at the time. Just the fact that it was played at Wigan was enough then. The whole excitement of it all. You'd never get that anywhere else.'[11]

Regulars to the all-nighters developed their own dance moves, spinning and jumping often on their own rather than with a partner, as well as their own fashions – tight short sleeve sweaters, vests and baggy pants worn by the 2,000 or so customers each Saturday night/Sunday morning.

FIGURE 11.4 *All-nighter at the Wigan Casino c.1980 (photo: Richard Simner). Source: Collection of Pete Smith.*

Dedicated fans came from all over Britain, travelling up by train, in cars and specially hired buses, but it was also a tough place, with drugs a prevalent part of the scene and regular fights, although the latter happened mostly outside during the long wait for the place to open. Wigan casino also featured live performances by famous US musicians such as Edwin Starr, Junior Walker and Jackie Wilson and James Brown was supposed to have visited although he refused to perform. Another regular, Ant Wilson, recalled: 'The first time you went through the doors into the main room of the Casino was something. You were literally propelled by the sound and the atmosphere. You could not help but dance. You felt like you were going to take off.'[12] Each morning ended with the same records played just before 8.00 am – the '3 before 8' – 'Time Will Pass You By' by Tobi Legend, 'Long After Tonight is Over' by Jimmy Radcliffe and 'I'm On My Way' by Dean Parrish. The last dance was held on 6 December 1981 (the building was due to be demolished for a new civic centre, which never went ahead due to lack of funding); however, a reunion takes place each year featuring Russ Winstanley and the other DJs in a record-based scene that 'has maintained itself, with fanzines, continued all-nighters and record compilations'.[13] The Twisted Wheel, however, after years of intermittent operation at several locations, continues in a two-room basement at 105–107 Princess Street, Manchester, with Sunday soul sessions twice a month.

Superclubs and raves

The Haçienda was one of the most famous dance clubs in the world; opening in 1982, it lasted, against the odds many would say, until 1997. It was a venue started with the best creative intentions, and although it was meant to make money for its operators, it failed dramatically in this regard. However, it did leave an enormous legacy of high-quality music, almost unbelievable anecdotes and a haul of entertaining and informative books and films. If a single venue can be said to change the image of a city, the Haçienda is certainly a viable example. Rob Gretton was a deejay and band manager of Joy Division (later New Order) who helped set up Factory Records in 1979. Factory was started by Tony Wilson and Alan Erasmus in 1978, joining with Martin Hannett's local punk label Rabid Records. Factory soon had a catalogue of high-quality alternative artists including Durutti Column, The Fall, and Slaughter and the Dogs. New Order, formed from the remaining members of Joy Division after their lead singer Ian Curtis passed away in 1980, were particularly successful and influential, and became part owners of the club. Factory Records was not a conventional company but run on an idealistic basis that unfortunately was one reason for its early demise; however, its ethos was to embrace multiple

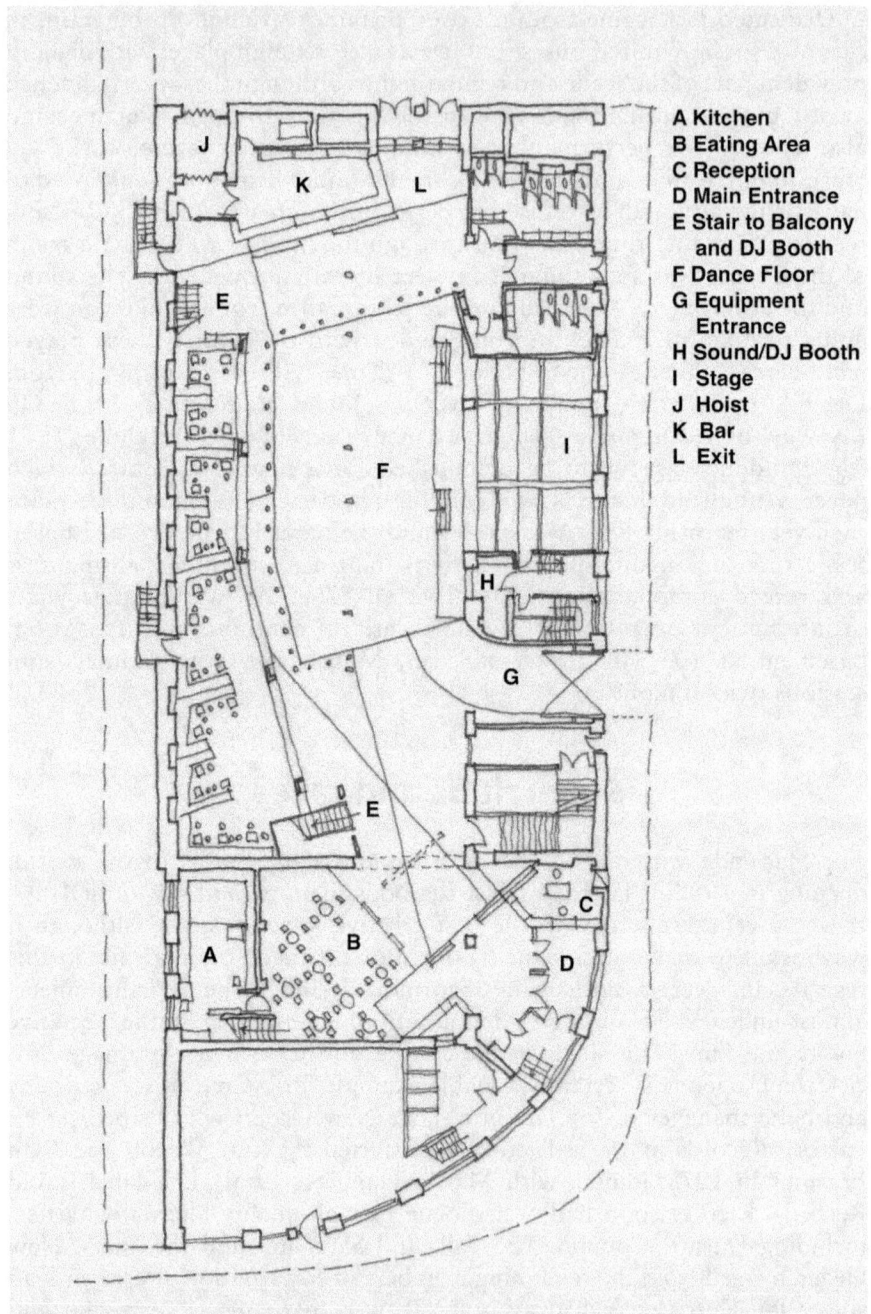

FIGURE 11.5 *The Haçienda ground-floor plan (designer Ben Kelly, 1982). Source: Robert Kronenburg.*

aspects of the music business to create a strong image, and Gretton's idea to open a new venue in the city to showcase their artists and the scene they were creating was one of these.

The club was situated in a former warehouse that had previously been used as a boat showroom, in an area of the city that was just beginning to be revitalized. The Haçienda was named after the socialist revolutionary slogan 'The Hacienda Must Be Built', but also became known as FAC51, as Factory gave a code number to every output of their business. The *cedilla* attached to the letter 'c' in Haçienda was added as it made the letter look like the number '5', and with the 'I' alongside, it became '51'. Design ideas like this were an important part of Factory's output and they employed graphic design Peter Saville to create a look for the label. Saville suggested that the interior designer Ben Kelly be used to create the club's interior, and it remains his most influential work. It was intended to be 'without precedent. Acknowledged as reinventing and reinvigorating the nightclub genre, it was a real-life stage-set built with everyday materials which were used to maximum effect'.[14] Tony Wilson complained in his novelization of the *24 Hour Party People* film (see below) that the opening night was too busy as you couldn't see the design, and yet 'This piece of industrial fantasy street was perfect for parties. Nooks and crannies, a narrative od space, taking you to the balcony via Ben's [Kelly] joke post-modernist arch, up and down the corridor that took you behind the games room to the basement cocktail bar.'[15]

Although this was a nightclub in which recorded music was primary and the deejay was crucial in creating the musical ambience, the Haçienda was also used regularly for live music events. One of the earliest bands to perform there was The Smiths, who played their third ever gig at the club in February 1983 and, although they were not signed by Factory Records, two more later that year. The club was also used on 27 January 1984 for a one-off episode of Channel 4's televised music programme *The Tube*, which included Madonna's first ever UK performance. Factory bands like New Order and The Happy Mondays played at the club throughout its existence. The Haçienda was an influential club that introduced new trends in dance music to the UK. It was one of the first venues to play house music in 1986 by deejays Mike Pickering and Little Martin, helping to alleviate, at least temporarily, its financial losses as these nights were always full. Acid house music appeared in 1988; however, along with this came an increase in drug use, particularly ecstasy, and the first UK death from this drug happened there in 1989, resulting in an increased police presence and eventually the club's temporary closure in 1991. Violence inside and outside the club was probably drug-related and this, with of course its ever-present problematic finances, led to the Haçienda's permanent closure on 28 June 1997.[16] The last live performance was two weeks earlier on 15 June 1997 by psychedelic rock band Spiritualized.

The Haçienda led the way in creating a dance venue that had musical ambitions and cultural relevance. Following on from its local cousin the Twisted Wheel, and the event-based music scenes such as that created for northern soul, this success proved that like live music scenes, recorded music could also represent an exciting and daring alternative outside the mainstream. That daring also extended to unauthorized recorded music dance events. Acid house electronic dance music had emerged in Chicago; however, it quickly became popular in the UK, first in Manchester, where artists like 808 State and Orbital produced local variations of the sound. Beginning in the 1980s, 'rave' events took place in abandoned industrial zones or rural sites near cities, the location usually kept secret until a few hours before the event began. Large mobile sound and light systems were set up clandestinely for DJs to entertain the crowd until dawn (Tucker 2013). The illegality of the events, using private property without permission, and widespread recreational drug use led of course to hostility from the authorities. The UK government passed the Criminal Justice and Public Order Act in 1994 aimed at stopping illegal rave parties and mobile anti-road protests. However, it was noticed that these early rave organizers had made money at their events by charging for 'VIP' tickets and sometimes by providing a bar, so it became clear that there was an audience who wanted them to continue and a potential commercial basis for them to be successful. The now-legal commercial dance music scene included clubs operating from their own venues such as Ministry of Sound (London, 1991) and those that worked out of existing nightclubs like Cream (which was based in Nation in Liverpool from 1993) and Godskitchen (Air in Birmingham and Planet Nightclub in Coventry). By 2000 the scene had largely migrated to activity taking place in nightclubs like Fabric in London (see Chapter 12), Tunnel in New York and Space on the Spanish Mediterranean island of Ibiza. Today, official rave events and festivals are held across Europe, Asia and Australasia.

After the Haçienda closed, the building it had occupied briefly became an art gallery, although two illegal parties shortly after destroyed much of the original Ben Kelly-designed interior. In October 2000, the building was demolished after developers purchased the site in order to build apartments, licencing the name for the new project from New Order's bass player Peter Hook. There was, however, a surprising reprise. In 2002, Michael Winterbottom made the film *24 Hour Party People*, telling the story of Factory Records and the Haçienda from Tony Wilson's perspective, rebuilding a temporary stage set of the club in a Manchester Factory, which then hosted its own club night to be included in the film. The club was one of the first to be identified as a 'superclub', a venue with a reputation that far outstripped local popularity and drew fans from around the UK and beyond. Despite this international presence, it was still an intensely local venue, built and operated by Manchester-based enthusiasts to, at least at first, showcase their music and cultural identity. Although the Haçienda cannot be replaced, Hook opened a new club in the city in 2010 called FAC251, based in what was once Factory Records offices on Princess Street. Once again designed by Ben Kelly, the building has three floors, with a live music venue 'The Bassment' on the ground floor and a dance space on the second, with the top floor left unchanged from its Factory Records days.

Record shops

There are many sorts of buildings that, on occasion, host popular music performance, although they have not been designed or adapted for that purpose (often made possible by the use of mobile stages, see Chapter 9). Pressed into service for a special occasion, or where opportunity and need coincide, musical equipment and musicians are adaptable enough to work with what they are given, and sometimes the uniqueness of the situation adds novelty and creates something memorable. Record shops (or stores in the United States), however, provide a particularly apt setting for live music, and there have been some memorable occasions where bands have played live, to promote either their recordings or the store itself. However, they also provide a focus point for music enthusiasts to meet and tune in to the word-of-mouth activity that an active scene needs: 'Record stores are not merely retail outlets; they are spaces of social interaction and socialization … Customers … learn not just about various artists, records and genres, but also about the local music culture.'[17] Record shops appeared at the end of the nineteenth century, often evolving out of sheet music shops, to market the new gramophone records. As new recorded mediums emerged, they sold those too: tapes, cassettes, CDs, as well as related items including books, videotapes, DVDs, Blu-rays and then most recently back to vinyl again (see below). By the 2000s many independent record shops had closed or were under threat, having been put out of business by competition from large chains (such as HMV in the UK, Sam Goody in the United States), by mass-market music recordings sold in supermarkets and department stores (such as Tesco and Walmart) or by online retailers such as Amazon. Small independent shops do, however, survive by providing a specialized service that may focus on a particular genre of music, the local scene or by adding other products to their inventory, including second-hand records and CDs. Perhaps the oldest record shop in the world exists in Cardiff, Wales. Opened in 1894, Spillers Records started by selling phonograph cylinders and shellac discs but now sells online as well as in-store – internet retailing, although a threat to many aspects of the traditional popular music scene, is a benefit to specialist interest stores who can access non-local customers much more easily.[18] Live sets to launch local record releases also happen in-store on a tiny stage. Although threatened by closure due to a rent rise in 2006, the shop made a successful move to a nearby location in 2010.

FIGURE 11.6 *Easy Street Records, West Seattle. Source: Patrick Tyree.*

Easy Street Records is an independent store in West Seattle, USA, which opened in 1988, although between 2001 and 2013 it also had a larger location in the Queen Anne area of the city. The West Seattle store is located in 'The Junction', an area of the city developed during the 1920s when the street car lines were extended out west. Its store is in the Crescent-Hamm Building, which was designed in 1925 by local architect Victor W. Voorhees and completed the following year. Made from buff brick, dressed with terracotta and blue painted details, the building is a restrained version of the Streamline Moderne design.[19] Designed as a mixed-use commercial building with retail outlets on the ground floor and shops or offices above, this elegant though relatively undistinguished piece of architecture has served exactly the same purpose for nearly a hundred years. Inside the store, which fronts onto the California Avenue end of the building, there are two main spaces – the left-hand side is for records and the right-hand side the café. The record store has blue painted walls and ceilings on two sides and bare concrete on the other. The high ceilings meant that a mezzanine could be added, accessed by a stair along one side – CDs, new vinyl and the counter are on the ground floor and second-hand records are upstairs.

Easy Street has a policy of 'in-store' performances, and the Queen Anne building even had a permanent stage that regularly featured touring artists and local bands. Name acts such as Lou Reed, Elvis Costello and Patti Smith have featured in the more than 500 performances held during Easy Street's existence. Despite these well-known names, the most resonant performances at the store have been by local artists done in recognition of the importance that record stores play in supporting musical activity. Described as 'one of the most memorable days in the history of Easy Street', Pearl Jam played in the West Seattle store on 25 April 2005 as a thank you, not only to Easy Street but to all independent record stores, later releasing a vinyl EP *Live at Easy Street* (2006), which has been the store's biggest selling record to date.[20] On Record Store Day in 2015, local band The Sonics played a rare gig at the store bringing in as guests members of Pearl Jam, Mudhoney, Soundgarden and Screaming Trees among others to create a one-off concert experience for 200 people crammed in among the records and CDs (also recorded and later released as *The Sonics Live at Easy Street*, 2016). In a time when record stores are under threat from online shopping, gigs like this reinforce their relevance, the live music and subsequent recording 'a good reason why cool bricks-and-mortar record shops still matter: seven songs cut live and hot in front of fans and customers ... then released through indie stores and priced to move'.[21]

Recorded music and live performance

Recorded music inevitably has a profound impact on popular music development; however, it is now no longer necessary to go to a venue to experience that, or even to a shop to bring the record home. When asked if the heritage of The Beatles had influenced him as an artist, Harry Chalmers of Merseyside band, Hooton Tennis Club, replied: 'Because of the internet, your influences are no longer about what's in the local record shop – they can be anything that's ever been recorded.'[22] The examples described in this chapter are ones where recorded music was key in generating a scene – a time and place where people gathered with a shared interest in the music (and other cultural aspects such as fashion, dance, even illegal activity such as drug use). The recorded music was important to these scenes because it was new, foreign, innovative or all three.

The instant global availability of almost any type of streamed music for a modest monthly sum means that today the possibility of recorded music instigating a new scene in a specific place at a specific time has been dramatically reduced. However, popular music has the habit of reinventing itself time after time, and new experiences are inevitably in the pipeline. Or perhaps they might be ones that hark back to the past. In the twenty-first century, vinyl has had a dramatic resurgence as a medium, not just from purists who decry the compressed signal available in streaming but also from those who enjoy the whole experience of the larger physical format, the sleeve artwork and the tactile engagement with the medium. Although in 2017 musician Jack White opened the new Third Man Pressing plant in Detroit (he also owns a label and chain of record stores), vinyl's economic performance is still stunted by delays in manufacture due to many plants having been closed, and the outdated forty-year-old equipment in those that remain in operation.

Although the sort of places described in this chapter are not those that have been designed for live performance, music has nevertheless had an important part in the activities that have taken place there, be it as a focus for the gathering of people interested in the same sort of music, fashion or ideas or as an element without which another part of the activity could not take place such as dance. So, although architecturally, these spaces have not been organized around the performance of live music, the question remains have they nevertheless informed the development of the architectural places that do support and promote it? With regard to places where recorded music has been the focus, these certainly have a connection with live music. In the first place, although the music may be recorded, the selection of the recordings as well as how they are combined is in itself a skill. This started with someone knowledgeable about the music playing recordings (usually from their own collection) for an audience – the expertise they bring and the preparation that goes into this activity bring an element of uncertainty and novelty to the juxtaposition of the musical selections, thereby making the playing of them 'live'. The enhancement of the disc jockey's role into someone who engaged more fundamentally with the recordings, toasting, rapping, creating a show through their interventions and the utilization of other elements including lights and projection, and through new music production, developed parts of the recorded music scene into one different from but analogous to the live gig. There are a number of predominantly recorded music venues (e.g. Wigan Casino), which, through the vibrant scenes that they started, became able to sponsor a visit by the musicians they championed. That live music is the root of all recorded music is of course a fact; however, in many circumstances, playing recorded music can generate live performance as well – the relationship is reciprocal, not one way. Although this book is about live music performance, and so discussion of discothèques and other record-based venues has generally been only with regard to the performers who also played there, there can be no doubt of the importance that recorded music has in the story of live popular music venue development.

CHAPTER TWELVE

Conclusion: The Significance and Value of Popular Music Venues

This is more of a pilgrimage than a night out. The outside of the venue is as I have seen it in pictures I have been looking at since the 1970s, fascinated by the roots of my favourite music of the time, in particular Talking Heads, but there were others I liked who also got their start here – The Ramones, Television, Patti Smith and Blondie. Although I had been to New York before I hadn't made the effort to come to this place, too intent on those earlier visits on what was currently happening at clubs like the Blue Note in Greenwich Village, Paris Blues up in Harlem and the Knitting Factory when it was in the Bowery (the club is now in Brooklyn). But somehow, now in 2005, it seems important to go to CBGB, perhaps because it looks likely that the club may soon have to close.

CGBG and OMFUG (famously an acronym for Country, Bluegrass, Blues and Other Music for Uplifting Gormandizers) is an archetypal music venue that was opened by Hilly Kristal in 1973 on the site of his earlier bar Hilly's. Situated in a four-storey brick building, upstairs was the Palace Hotel, a 'flop house' which Hilly described as an advantage as the 'derelict, alcoholic, or drug-addict' residents weren't that bothered about having a rock club beneath where they slept.[1] Kristal's original intention for the club's musical ambitions are obvious from its name; however, it instead became synonymous with the establishment of American punk rock, with many of the key exponents of this new music meeting there, seeing each other play in pre-punk bands and influencing each other as the genre developed – CBGB is the archetypal venue in which a music scene was established and grew. While disco had a hold in many New York clubs and hip hop was getting

FIGURE 12.1 *CBGB and OMFUG location in the Bowery, New York City, 1985 (still from* Burning Down the House: The Story of CBGB, *2009). Source: Everett Collection INc/Alamy Stock Photo.*

started in the Bronx, CBGB was a cheap place in a decaying part of the city that had a policy of 'only original songs, no covers' that brought in new guitar bands. Patti Smith recalls: 'When we started building CBGB as a place to play, it was because there was no [other] place to play for people like us.'[2] On 14 April 1974 Television's first gig took place with Patti Smith in the audience. The Ramones first played there on 16 August 1974 (before Tommy joined) and on 16 August the following year Talking Heads and Blondie featured in the same show, although both bands were regulars by then. The Damned were the first British punk band to feature in April 1977, but others soon followed. Later, the club became home to hardcore rock bands like Green Day, Sum 42 and Guns and Roses (in an acoustic set in CBGB Record Canteen, the storefront next door that Kristal opened for a time in the late 1980s) – all soon to become stadium-filling acts.

In through the entrance, I'm surprised to see a shop selling merchandise – mainly racks of T-shirts in all colours stacked to the ceiling. The club itself is a long room, low lighting, seating on the left and bar on the right. Passing a huge mixing desk, I walk up between these two and it's clear I'm early as the place isn't even half full. I grab a beer and get a chair near the stage where a few people, obviously the first group on, are still adjusting their gear. The place is a mess, intentionally. Every surface is plastered with stickers, posters and random graffiti, the floor is uneven and in some places has holes plated with misshaped pieces of metal (Plate 15). The stage itself, crammed into the end of the room, is at an odd angle to the standing area in front of it, with large speakers on either side and above the stage – they look loud just sitting there, although the current recorded music appears to be coming from something else tiny and tinny. The toilets seem to be carved out of ancient stone and brick, although still plastered with stickers and graffiti. Hilly threatened to take the urinals to Los Vegas after the club closed, where he planned to open a new place. Tonight is a showcase, so for a few dollars I get to see four new-ish bands. I assume at first these will be local, but when the first one starts they immediately announce they are from Philadelphia. Those speakers make a difference and the sound is great – David Byrne put it down to:

> the amount of crap scattered everywhere, the furniture, the bar, the crooked uneven walls and looming ceiling made for both great sound absorption and uneven acoustic reflections – qualities one might spend a fortune to re-create in a recording studio ... Because of the lack of reverberation, one could be fairly certain ... that details of one's music would be heard.[3]

Like me, the band is also on a pilgrimage – to play at CBGB before it closes. They are pretty good, and when they finish the lead singer walks through the thin crowd passing out free sampler CDs – he's obviously still pumped from standing on the stage of his heroes: 'Can't believe we actually did it', he tells me, 'this must be the place'. I recognize the title of the Talking Heads tune, so we have that in common, but then I finally figure out why I am there too.

This must be the place where it happened, where all that music began, where the artists I admire played live to audiences who saw them first and recognized their qualities, who gave them the impetus to carry on and make more music that could communicate its value to people a long way from New York City, including me on the other side of the Atlantic Ocean. Although I didn't get here for another three decades, the bands did travel and I got to see some of them in Liverpool in the late 1970s (Talking Heads, Blondie and The Ramones all played at Eric's) and in some cases continued seeing them live in years to come (including Patti Smith with my two grown-up daughters in 2015). Like many others, my own history is bound up in this music, and to visit the venue where it was originally played is to connect to something physical that somehow makes it real – not the actual musical experience, but still, I'm present in the place that represents its significance. Music is ephemeral – you listen to a song and then its past – a building is something more permanent, although often not completely so. As for the end of CBGB, a long-running lawsuit was lost in 2006, and on 15 October that year the club closed, its last show featuring Patti Smith. At one stage during her performance, she recited all the names of the musicians who had played in the club who had since died, forecasting the description of the club she penned a few years later in her book *Just Kids*, a place where 'the sounds of a scene were emerging. Though no one knew it, the stars were aligning, the angels were calling'.[4] Hilly Kristal passed away the following year. Since then the space has been a fashion store and a photography gallery, although there have been various concerts and one-off events that retain its name and, in an ephemeral way, its ethos.

Although there is undoubtedly an element of nostalgia in fans' affection for the places where the popular music they loved began, these places nevertheless possess real importance as they are sites of cultural development. They are crucial to the dissemination and continuation of their influence on that particular music style and its associated fashions and memes: 'Live performance venues ... act as a social hub of the scene, providing a space where musicians and musical styles can interact and where the scene is made more visible, physical and real.'[5] They are locations in which events take place that shape how the world is today, how people behave and how they think about their life and its meaning. To be part of a music scene that happened at a particular time was to be inside the cult – something eminently desirable, particularly to many young people seeking to forge their own identities away from their parents' influence and family upbringing. The spaces in which those scenes happened are an important part of the resonance that they have at the time they are being generated, but also in individuals' memory and for our shared collective history. The CBGB scene had this quality. Carter Cathcart played with The Laughing Dogs at the club: 'there was room for everybody down there. It was quite an amazing thing ... There was a lot of camaraderie. And I mean, groups that you'd totally expect not to get along because the music was so different [from each other but] everybody got along.'[6] Guy Garvey, lead singer with Manchester band Elbow, was asked about the Tuesday night acoustic sets he helped organize in Manchester in the late 1990s, a scene from which not only his own band sprung but also I Am Kloot, Badly Drawn Boy and Doves emerged as successful acts: 'You don't realise you're on the inside of a scene until afterwards when someone marks it as that ... we were in the middle of something special. We just didn't know it.'[7] But the buildings are often not special at all. Garvey's scene was set in an Australian-themed bar called Down Under with loud commercial pop pumped through the speakers every other night – a place with little relationship to the sort of music they played or the city in which it was located. Upon examination, it is clear that many of the other venues described in this book are unlikely places to be the starting point for global music trends: a hand-decorated house basement in a Liverpool suburb such as the Casbah (Merseybeat) or a first-floor bar in a poor neighbourhood of New York such as Disco Fever (hip hop), yet they are – why?

Importance of place

Places of performance are important in historical terms, not just as a backdrop to the events that happen there, but in real ways that influence those events and are communicated to the performers and audiences. As the theatrical director and producer David Hare has said about the places of performance: 'very few black boxes carry history. They wipe themselves clean with each production. A theatre is partly memory, the residue of the greatness that's passed through ... Certain theatres elevate plays, just by their atmosphere'.[8] Exactly the same can be said for music venues – certain venues elevate performance just by their atmosphere. However, establishing just what it is about the atmosphere that does this is not easy. Micky Hart, drummer with The Grateful Dead, tried to encapsulate what was special about Fillmore East, the 1920s movie theatre that Bill Graham transformed into an important New York rock venue in 1968: 'by day the Fillmore East looked like an innocuous, plain building sitting on the corner of a typical street in the East Village. But at night it came alive. The building became a living organism – breathing, pulsating, vibrating, swaying with the emotional outpouring from within'. This passionate description conveys his feelings about the venue admirably; however, he also described its practical attributes: 'It was small enough that you could hear the room. You could hear the walls, you could hear the music coming back to you, it was a good sounding space, not too big, not too small, kind of intimate.'[9] What makes a venue special is clearly not just its measurable characteristics but its unquantifiable ones too. When a building is professionally designed, for instance by an architect, ideas about appearance and image are consciously addressed in the brief. The client may set the agenda, but the designer will suggest the physical elements that generate the ambience that visitors to the building will experience. This may be in order to create a specific mood, for example comfort or luxury or to address a theme that adds to the venue's individuality, for instance palm trees for the Copacabana, or with even more dubious taste: slave huts and Southern mansions for the Cotton Club. Even without a professional designer, these intentions can be made clear – for example The Twisted Wheel in Manchester not only used a wheel as its logo but also featured a collection of discarded wheels in its interior. These examples are quite crude attempts to generate a unique sense of place, nevertheless they do establish individuality – the clubbers might mock the cheap and simple decoration of a place, but it still does the job of differentiating the building they are in from other venues.

Although many small venues, created with limited budgets and by non-professionals, are naive in the quality of their design, they may still communicate a powerful sense of place. There are also some that have reinforced the image of the music scene with which they are associated through a more sophisticated approach, crafting a creative extension of the music scene with acknowledged high-quality design in the same way that fashion and artwork have done. One example is the Haçienda, Ben Kelly's well-designed interior, which he created specifically to challenge the current standard of club design:

As an architect, being given a massive blank canvas was a dream ... The idea was to create a sense of surprise and discovery: once past this tiny plaque [a granite sign in the red brick façade], you'd emerge into a vast cathedral-like space with yellow-and-black-striped columns rising around the edge of the dancefloor ... It was great to see kids being so taken by surprise when they came in, being made to think about things like architecture. I remember two lads standing there with pint glasses saying: 'Fookin' 'ell!'.[10]

Certainly, the world's most famous venues are known for their individual architectural character as well as the music that happened there: Liverpool's Cavern as an underground cellar bar with bare brick walls and arched ceilings and CBGB for its surfaces plastered in stickers, posters and graffiti. An important feature of the best popular music venues is that, whatever they look like, they successfully address the identity of the peer group that uses them. This is why Dublin's Point may have been 'a kip, but it was our kip' to those who went there, and why Patti Smith would, as a musician, describe 'building' CBGB as a 'place to play', even though the club was created, owned and run by Hilly Kristal. As well as making an ambience that can be adopted by both musicians and audiences, there are other characteristics that can be conveyed through the design of the venue. A venue's design might set out to establish an agenda, as with Kelly's Haçienda – to be something new or to hark back to a past history. In the latter case, the 1970s Grand Ole Opry House building in Nashville utilized visual cues of its former home, the Ryman Auditorium – pews for seats, a brick façade, even a piece of the original stage let into the new one (Plate 16). Similarly, the new Cavern (as we shall see below) reused bricks from the demolished earlier building to replicate its distinctive arches.

One area where innovation is especially important in live popular music performance design is in the creation of large mobile stages. When creating the look of these shows, major touring artists start out with the aspiration to differentiate themselves from what has gone before and to create a novel experience for their audiences – stage sets such as The Claw from U2's 2009–11 360° tour exist solely because of this aspiration. Setting the architectural tone for a new agenda for permanent structures is harder to find in static venue design as the creation of completely new ones are not commissioned very often (although complete interior makeovers such as the Haçienda are more frequent). One example where rather than a conversion an entire new building was constructed is De Vorstin (which means The Queen in English), a new venue constructed in 2010 for the municipality of Hilversum, which is the centre of the Dutch radio and television broadcasting industry. This community venue with rehearsal rooms and recording studio was designed to provide a focus for the existing popular music culture in the city, but also to be a crucible receptive to new musical trends. Replacing an

CONCLUSION 217

FIGURE 12.2 *De Vorstin, Hilversum, The Netherlands (architect: Frits van Dongen with de Archtekten Cie). Source: Photo: Jeroen Musch.*

earlier youth centre that had developed a bad reputation for drug use, the designers de Archtekten Cie's key objective was to indicate change from the immediate past but also to look forward to a new future, and therefore an overtly contemporary architectural set piece was designed with a powerful provocative character.

Although containing performance spaces designed to work acoustically and functionally, the buildings' main circulation space is a dramatic, multi-height volume with dramatic lighting, stairways, balconies and places for informal socializing and small-scale performance. Outside, the building is perhaps even more unusual – angular metal facets with glass and mesh screens that firmly indicate that this is something new. Situated on a major crossroads as you enter the city, De Vorstin is an important statement of social and musical intent. Such investment is rare (De Vorstin cost €8.5

million when built, equal to €9.3 million in 2018); however, the architecture of popular music performance, whether it is created at minimal cost without professional design help or to multimillion-figure budgets by experienced architects, engineers and designers, nevertheless has the same intention – to create a place in which those who use it, musicians and audiences, can feel it is theirs, at least for the duration of the concert.

Venue typologies

This book has examined the history of popular music live performance venues by categorizing them into specific functional types, for example the bar, pub, club, hall, theatre, arena, outside stage. It has also looked at some of the non-venue situations in which popular music is performed: homes, shops, riverboats etc. However, it is clear that these categories cannot always be distinctly separated from each other. Unlike performance for classical music, popular music can work well without the specific acoustic requirements that determine the architectural space formulas usual in classical concert halls and recital rooms. This means that the spaces of popular music performance are more varied in typology and the boundaries between the types more blurred. For example although London's Hope and Anchor is described as a *public house*, its principal venue is a basement below the main bar, very typical of basement *clubs* such as the Cavern or the 100 Club. Similarly, CBGB was essentially a ground-floor *bar* converted to a *club*, only able to operate in that way because it had neighbours indifferent to the noise and disturbance it created. At a larger scale, the music, variety and vaudeville *halls* could also be described as *theatres* (also used for plays or cinema), and most of these buildings were actually designed with this flexibility in mind to lengthen their commercial life – a strategy that clearly worked. It is therefore also useful to examine venue typologies in terms that do not relate to a description of their function, but rather to their physical manifestation – where, how and why they are established.

Where: Venue locations

As commercial ventures, music venue locations are determined by operational factors based on economic reasoning. The most common location for a popular music venue is in the city centre for like any entertainment facility it must be placed in an affordable spot that is convenient for its audience. Many older venues were built in a time when personal transport was not available for most people, so easy access meant being close to where audiences lived or to affordable public transport links. Being in the city centre had other benefits, such as being near other types of entertainment such as drinking and eating establishments, and away from the main residential areas where late-night entertainment might be a disturbance. Many cities developed entertainment zones where different forms of night-time activity took place close together, thereby increasing footfall of likely audiences (New Orleans' Basin Street and Frenchman's Street areas for example). However, cities are constantly changing and the zones of activity shift due to infrastructure improvements or as new development takes place. Venues are forced to close or relocate as property values rise, pricing them out of the area as the mix of building functions change, or the level of complaints increase as noise-sensitive uses (such as residences) take over. Paradoxically, increased popularity of the area is, on occasion, instigated by the success of the same venues that are subsequently forced to close (see later this chapter).

The location of a venue is crucially important in determining its commercial success, but also in terms of what it can offer back to the neighbourhood in which it is based. Venues are usually seen as negative development, bringing in problems with noise and disturbance; however, they also bring in cultural and economic activity, and can be a positive, social, enjoyable resource, particularly for young people. The city of Venlo in South-East Netherlands lies on the Maas River (the Ruhr in German) close to Germany. Grenswerk pop stage is a 550-capacity music venue situated in the city's medieval centre built new in 2014 by architects van Dongen-Koschuch. The name means Border Work – chosen to signify the venue's ambition to draw people across the Dutch/German border region and to be an active place where creative work is done. Replacing an older venue, Perron 55, which had been a commercial venue but was also supported by a regional well-being foundation for the social value it brought to the city, Grenswerk is more than just a space for bands to play, containing rehearsal studios, recording studios and maintaining a big outreach and educational commitment reinforced by other social spaces, including a bar and café.

It was crucial that such an important function be located in the city's heart and the architects therefore had to find solutions to the typical music venue problems of unwanted sound disturbance but also in creating an attractive building that fitted in with the historic warehouse character of the area, buildings now taken over by housing and other uses. Grenswerk's façade is therefore clad in a local brick with gable walls reflecting the pitched rooves that reflect the pattern of the surrounding buildings. The main performance space is set at the first-floor level, allowing much of the ground floor to be an accessible public space, open for most of the day – a large processional staircase with windows onto the other rooms of the building enhances this welcoming atmosphere. Rather than the unrelieved, anonymous walls of most performance spaces, large windows in the façade have the same intention. The performance hall and rehearsal rooms are surrounded on all sides by other spaces, which provide an acoustic buffer to the surrounding area, although acoustically sealed windows look into the rehearsal rooms

FIGURE 12.3 *Grenswerk Poppodium (Border Work Pop Stage), Venlo, The Netherlands (architects and planners: van Dongen-Koschuch). Source: Van Dongen-Koschuch.*

from the public areas to show what's going on there. Like De Vorstin, this rare, built-from-scratch, medium-scale, pop music venue shows that the preconceived problems of venue provision in city centres can be successfully addressed when new architectural ideas are applied to the specific problems of this building type.

Located outside the city centre, some venues can be classed as neighbourhood places, drawing a local crowd rather than a mixed audience from the city, region or beyond. This locality might be a part of the city or a smaller town or village such as Matt Molloy's in Westport, Co. Mayo, Ireland, a venue that is located in a community of 6,000 people, although its clientele also come from the surrounding rural areas as well as some touristic visitors. Floore's Country Store venue and dance hall in Helotes, Texas (8,000 population), operates in a similar way. Venues physically similar to Matt Molloy's and Floore's also operate in the city – the difference for the non-urban venues is only that their reputation is such that audiences, both local and further away, are willing to travel to enjoy what they have to offer.

Remote rural venues are understandably not very common for the access reasons described above; however, those that do exist often have a unique quality that underpins their continued success. The Band Room is a 100-capacity venue located in the remote British North York Moors village

FIGURE 12.4 *The Band Room, Low Mill, North Yorkshire, UK. Source: Robert Kronenburg.*

of Low Mill. Built as a rehearsal room in the 1920s for a traditional brass band, the Farndale Silver Band, it is now operated as a live music venue famous for the intimate quality of its performances, accentuated without doubt by its special location and the subsequent dedication that both the artists and the audiences must show to get there.

The ultimate arboreal popular music location is, however, the festival. Locations such as Worthy Farm, Somerset (Glastonbury Festival), and the Black Rock Desert, Pershing County, Nevada (Burning Man Festival), are remote from the normal infrastructure that a city provides despite enormous audiences (*c.* 135,000 for Glastonbury and *c.* 70,000 for Burning Man). They are located in these remote places specifically because they can thereby provide a large immersive experience in which the destination becomes shaped wholly by the event, the music and the ethos of the organizers, engaging the festival attendees in participation activities that range from the hard work of creating and operating the event to ritualistic ceremonies like the burning of the giant wicker statue that gives Burning Man its name.[11]

However, although they are held in a rural/remote environment, these events do have their own peculiar form of urbanity, as a temporary city is created to make them possible, incorporating all the infrastructure and services necessary for so many people gathered together in one place at one time.

How: Venue creation

Architecture is often described in terms of style as if fashion is the main determinant in its form; however, materiality, function, environment and cost are as important, and in many cases, more so. Analysis of the operation of architectural spaces now means that many areas in which a designer previously had to rely only on experience (or conjecture) can now be carefully predetermined to obtain the ideal environment for the proposed building's performance, something that is particularly of value for rooms in which complex acoustics issues are a factor.[12] What materials are chosen (or available), how the building works for the activities that take place there, how it modifies its environment for users in terms of climate and local conditions (e.g. noise or safety) and what resources are available to invest in its construction (normally estimated in terms of money, but this equates to site value, materials, time, manpower, equipment, energy) are key factors in the design. These factors all determine the approach that is taken in the creation of a new building, some having more influence than others depending on the situation. In terms of popular music, this can be categorized in terms of the approach that must be taken in the venue's realization – either as an adopted, adapted or dedicated building.[13]

Adopted venues are those that have been brought into use without large changes to the character of the original building and without much cost. This usually happens quite quickly, perhaps even informally or without permission. The Band Room, described earlier, is one of these – a simple space created in a different age, which with the simple addition of performers, their instruments and an audience now has a successful life almost hundred years later. Another archetypal music venue is the 100 Club on London's Oxford Street, which was established in 1942 as a restaurant in the basement of a 1930s commercial building. It is a single space 9 metres (30 feet) by 26 meters (85 feet) – the only alteration to its layout in its lengthy existence being the relocation of the bar to the end of the room and the stage to the middle in 1964.

It was also painted red at that time, as it is now. Initially jazz musicians performed for the diners with Sunday nights eventually becoming more about the music than the food. In the late 1950s it became a 'trad' jazz venue hosting all the major British musicians, and so began a pattern of following diverse musical trends within an unchanging venue. Blues followed in the 1960s, many legendary artists travelling from the United States, including Bo Diddley, Muddy Waters and Sunnyland Slim. Later in the 1960s it was British

FIGURE 12.5 *100 Club, Oxford Road, London. Source: Robert Kronenburg.*

pop and early rock: The Kinks, The Who and the Animals. In the 1970s the first ever punk festival was held at the club with the Sex Pistols, The Damned, Siouxsie and The Banshies performing, and punk continued into the 1980s. African jazz, indie and Northern soul are some of the other musical genres that trade nights at this remarkable long-running venue, which is nothing more than a single basement room, a bar, a few plastic chairs and a tremendous (and well-deserved) reputation. Having a dedicated owner/manager as a key factor in its survival as an independent venue cannot be underestimated. Originally partly owned by the current owner Jeff Horton's grandmother, his father Roger ran the club from 1964 and was responsible for the decision to engage with diverse musical genres.[14] The club's legendary status, coupled with Jeff's determination, was pivotal in saving it from closure in 2010 due to rising rents in its central London location, when famous musicians rallied round to create publicity to draw attention to the threat, eventually held off by a sponsorship arrangement with shoe manufacturer Converse.[15]

Adapted venues are buildings that have been significantly modified from their original pattern of use to accommodate music performance. This is the largest category of contemporary music venue; however, the diversity of building type from which that adaptation has taken place is wide. Most common is buildings that were originally designed with some sort of entertainment in mind, including, for example public houses, bars, halls, theatres, ballrooms, cinemas and sports buildings. Making alterations to these adds in another income stream, and this has usually happened in response to changes in demand. The Palais de Dance ballrooms of the 1910s and 20s, where they survive, became the large nightclubs, discotheques and music venues of the 1960s and 70s, sometimes with comparatively little change (new decoration, amplification, lighting, signage). In other cases, the adaptation has been dramatic. Dublin's Point Theatre was converted in 1988 from a group of Victorian railway sheds originally built in 1878, and although a major venue for the most well-known touring artists for nearly thirty years, its further redevelopment into a 9,500-seat arena by specialist architects Populous in 2007–08 was well overdue. Like many adopted buildings, the new venue (named the O2 Arena when it opened, and currently the 3Arena) retains the appeal of the older building and the connection to its history both for the performances that happened there in the past and for the continuity with its older industrial history. However, most adopted venues are not as grand as this one in Dublin – the vast majority are smaller local spaces, developed by owners and promoters and sometimes by enthusiasts or musicians themselves. Created on strict budgets, many are often crudely developed – simple but crucial adjustments are made to the available space that enable them to operate, but also to provide them with a specific identity, for example the decoration with *avant-garde* murals for the interior of the Cave of the Golden Calf in London in 1912, or more humbly, a collection of old wheels enhancing the interior of The Twisted Wheel in Manchester in 1963. For contemporary popular music venues, even ones set up in an existing space, an essential ingredient is a good sound system, the quality of which can make or break success, as artists are today more likely to tour only with their backline (their instruments and their amplifiers) and are reluctant to return to places where they cannot be heard. Venues usually include a technical specification of the equipment available on their website, so artists and their road crew know what to expect before they arrive.

Dedicated venues are those designed from new to fulfil the specific function as a place for live popular music performance. The music halls of the 1800s were among the first of this typology, buildings designed to fulfil the concept of providing live entertainment, and although music was not the only form available (comedy, novelty, juggling etc. also taking place), the differences of the building type from theatres are quite distinct with the lack of accommodation for stagecraft as would be needed for plays (fly systems and storage for scenery, wings for entrances etc.) and the importance of drink and food provision to patrons within the performance space. Some cabaret clubs also fall into this category such as London's Café de Paris, created in 1924 during the height of the fashion for upmarket dining clubs in which the show, featuring music, dance and comedy, and the band providing the music for patrons to dance themselves was a crucial part of the design brief. Opulently decorated, the dance floor is also a performance space, the musicians generally set to one side of the room, and the audience encircling the central area in an intimate embrace. Spaces like this became a model for high fashion and celebrity often seen in popular movies of the 1930s and 40s, which provided an aspirational window into this world for those not fortunate enough to be part of it.

However, most venues are not so glamorous. The original Cavern Club in Liverpool is one of the most famous music venues in the world and an archetype for the cellar club. It started out occupying the basement of an empty nineteenth-century warehouse in the city centre, dark and dank, without windows or reliable plumbing. The addition of lights, a stage, a tea bar, some tables and chairs converted it into first a jazz then a skiffle club, and finally a place where beat music was developed into a form that was exported around the world. This was a typical music venue that had adopted, with very little expense or effort, a building designed for a different function and made it into something special. Its closure in 1973, shortly before the demolition of the building in which it stood now, seems an incredibly short-sighted decision. The re-creation of the venue began just a few years later in the early 1980s. This might also be considered a suspect decision – how could such a unique place with so much history be recreated with any real meaning? However, the architect David Backhouse was someone who was embedded in Beatles history – he had been at the Casbah during the period when the band had first played there and was also a regular at the Cavern's lunchtime sessions in the 1960s.[16] The idea was to create a new development in Liverpool city centre that would recharge efforts to kick-start the city's economic recovery, in the doldrums as port activity had declined in the 1970s, building a new audacious mixed-use development with offices, shops and restaurants with a dedicated design for a new Cavern club at its centre in both branding terms and as an actual venue. The new club was built in the same location as the old one, although at a greater depth than the original. At first the design incorporated one performance space, which followed the form and appearance of the original with long, low, arched, bare brick vaults, even using some of the old warehouse's original bricks.

However, it was soon decided that more space was needed, and a second room was incorporated, with a more conventional nightclub layout with dance floor, raised bar area, green room and kitchen facilities. Opening in 1984, the new club struggled financially, trying to find a niche that was neither a homage to the old Cavern nor a completely new venue ready to create its own image. A new management in the form of music enthusiasts Dave Jones and Bill Heckle turned the club's fortunes around, bringing in live music, which, if not always profitable, was true to the club's original intentions. A pivotal moment happened on 14 December 1999 when Paul McCartney played a live gig in the club, not on the replica stage but on the new larger one, thereby kick-starting a set of its own special memories for

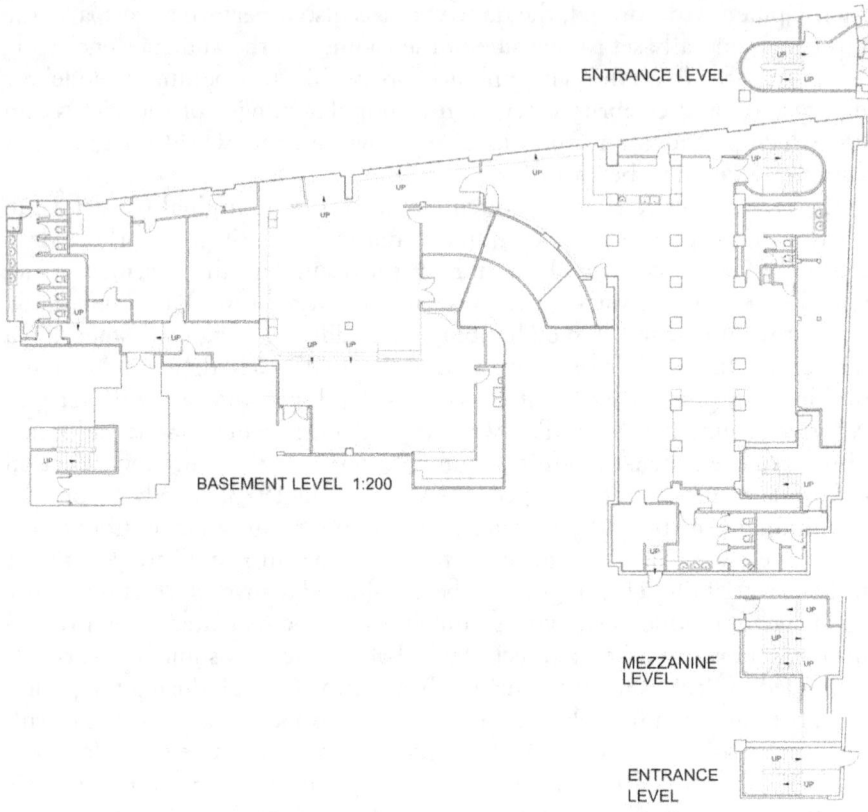

FIGURE 12.6 *Cavern Club, Liverpool, UK. Plan of the new 1980s building with the new performance space to the left and the reproduction of the older space to the right. Source: Courtesy of Dave Jones.*

the new venue, enhanced by the release of the DVD *Live at the Cavern Club* (2003). McCartney played there again in 2018 to promote his new recording. With forty live bands performing in the Cavern each week, the club now mixes tourist-attracting nostalgia sets by local musicians, alongside shows by new artists who have gone on to achieve fame such as K. T. Tunstall, Travis, Adele and the Arctic Monkeys.

A rare mid-size popular music venue that has been designed and constructed from new is AFAS Live (formerly the Heineken Music Hall), in Amsterdam, the Netherlands, located in the Johan Cruyff Arena stadium entertainment and shopping district. It is an example of a flexible venue in which the ability to put on any type of music show with fast turnaround and a high-quality experience for artists and audiences is the key objective.

Designed in 2001 by Frits Van Dongen (who also designed the De Vorstin and Grenswerk music buildings), then working with De Architekten Cie, it contains two spaces, the 5,500-capacity Black Box and the 700-capacity Beat Box. This is a simple shed-type building although extremely well designed with minimal, restrained constructional and interior details including industrial elements like oversize lettering and light fittings. An important design opportunity for new music venues is the ability to create a space that is almost anonymous in acoustic and visual terms, to allow the sound system to be perfectly tuned and the drama of the show the artist brings with them to take over completely. In the case of AFAS Live, special attention was paid to reducing the reverberation time as far as possible by cladding the entire interior with perforated metal plates with sound-absorbing porous material behind: 'Everything is artificial here – the light, the sound, the whole atmosphere.'[17] In addition, the structure is designed as a box within a box so that hardly any of the internal walls touch the external ones, reducing sound transmission to the outside to the minimum. Creating venues from new makes it possible to include such sophisticated responses to acoustic design considerations.

Without doubt the greatest development in venue design that has taken place over the last two decades is the creation of the dedicated entertainment arena: 'The popularity of the arena concert, especially since the turn of the millennium, evidences a radical reshaping of the landscape of popular music, and the meeting of a demand for the actual presence of the global superstar in the global suburbs.'[18] This is now a mature architectural typology, which provides a distinctive environment for a wide range of musical genres (albeit all on a large scale) that has also had a dramatic impact on the urban built environment of many cities across the world, particularly Europe, the Americas and East Asia. Arenas are designed around an economic model that demands flexibility in operation, which is essential as these venues are also designed to accommodate other types of shows including indoor sports, ice shows, motoring events and spectaculars featuring everything from dinosaurs to space monsters. For most arenas (with the possible exception of some in the United States, see below), popular music is the primary focus in their design because of the high proportion of shows and its special functional requirements: the ability to accommodate a speedy changeover for a complex stage setup and the necessity to provide a suitable acoustic environment not only for the audience in terms of sound quality, but also for neighbours in reducing unwanted noise.

The scale of these buildings means that the impact they have on the cities into which they have been inserted is dramatic. For them to be successful, it is desirable that they are located close to the city centre, easily accessible from public transport for the wide variety of people that make up their audience. Being in the city centre has other benefits for the local economy as visitors make use of local hotels and restaurants (see later this chapter).

They also visit other smaller music venues and seek other entertainment such as shopping or tourist attractions. However, inserting a massive building into an urban location is not an easy task; for example Nashville's Bridgestone Arena (opened in 1996) is situated right on Broadway and Memphis' FedExForum (opened in 2004) is on Beale Street, the two central locations synonymous with the live music venue experience these cities are

FIGURE 12.7 *Bridgestone Arena, Nashville (architects HOK Sport and Hart Freeland Roberts). Source: Robert Kronenburg.*

CONCLUSION

famous for. These 20,000-seat arenas feature sport much more than those in Europe as is typical in the United States; however, they also address directly the importance of music in these two cities with regular major concerts, and both are situated on their most famous musical streets. The Bridgestone Arena was designed by HOK Sport and Hart Freeland Roberts just over two decades before the FedExForum, but nevertheless at a time when the importance of retaining a city's distinctive urban character was less recognized. Its design emphasizes its size, even locating a giant tower right on the street.

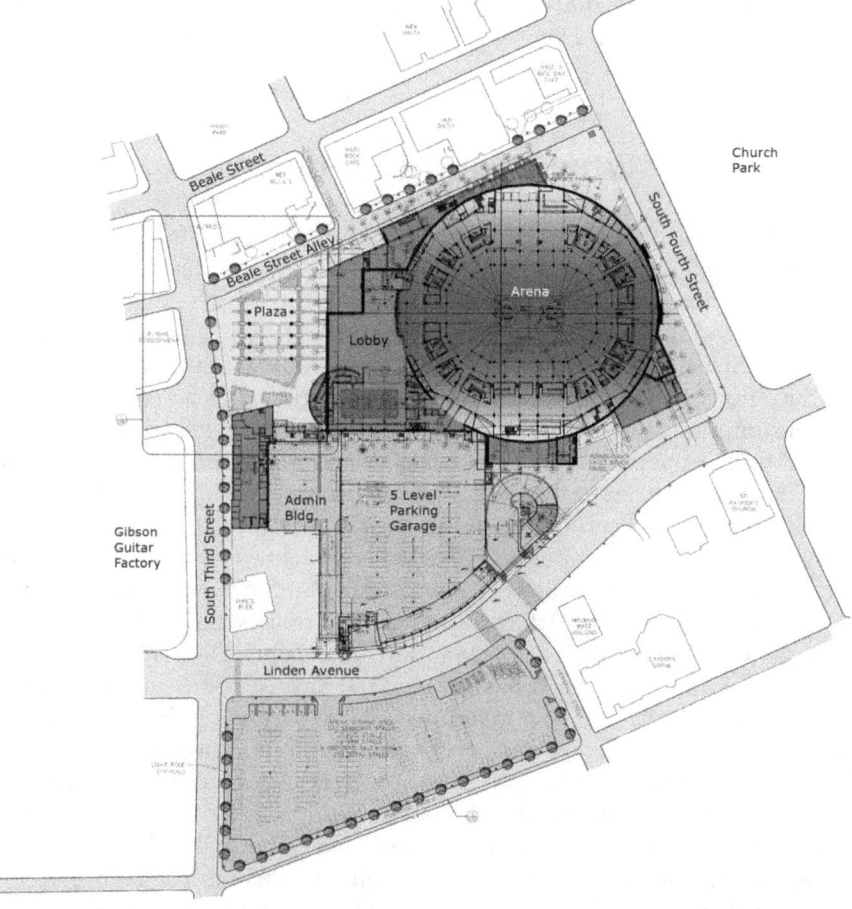

FIGURE 12.8 *Site plan of the FedExForum, Memphis, showing how it is slotted into the existing street pattern surrounded by existing buildings such as St Patrick's Church, and new development of a similar scale to the older buildings along Beale Street (architects Looney Ricks Kiss with Ellerbe Becket). Source: Looney Ricks Kiss.*

The FedExForum takes a more considered approach that has become more common as ideas about urban design have matured. The Memphis building, designed by local architects Ellerbe Becket (now part of AECOM) and Looney Ricks Kiss, was designed to recreate an urban pattern, which had been decimated by inner-city decline, and also to enhance the opportunities for new appropriate development spinning off into the currently underused adjacent areas. The inevitable large mass of the arena space is surrounded by low-rise buildings on three sides, mostly new with some refurbished older properties, which reduce its impact and knits it into the urban street pattern. With brick and cement render façades for the surrounding buildings that contrast with the inevitable steel and glass at the arena's main entrance, despite its scale the new building tries hard to fit in comfortably with the local character.

Why: Venue significance

Music venues embody key aspects of human activity. They are places in which *cultural activity* takes place – creative work that expresses and embodies what people feel and think about themselves and the lives they live. Popular music is an art of the people, made by and for them. Although driven by commercial practice, its audiences proactively engage with it, they are 'not victims of false consciousness, but active participants in consumption, understood as a process of making meaning from, and contributing to popular culture'.[19] People enjoy popular music, but it is also something that taps into the creative force that is in all human beings. At its best it can express potent ideas about society, and therefore ideas that need to be expressed, and communicated to others – venues provide the places for this to happen. John Geddings is a music agent and promoter who has been in the business since the 1970s representing artists such as The Ramones, Genesis, The Rolling Stones, U2, Madonna and Celine Dion. He also revived the Isle of Wight music festival in 2002–03. If anyone could be cynical about the commercial side of the popular music business it would be him; however, talking in the documentary *Hits, Hype and Hustle: An Insider's Guide to the Music Business* (2018) he said: 'In the end, regardless of how the business of live music has changed, when it comes down to it, it's always been about one thing, the joy of the shared experience … when just for a little while you are lost in the moment and that's why I still love this job'.[20]

Music venues are places of *social activity* – where groups of individuals come together to share a common experience. They are sometimes centres for the reinforcement of a groups' commonality – a place to belong. Every city has gathering places set up on the basis of geographic, cultural or political affiliations that simultaneously accentuate togetherness and differentiation, for example social clubs associated with various political and religious associations, for specific employee groups and trade unions, for specific immigrants' associations, sporting, business and arts societies. These are clubs with the general aim of gathering together people of a similar age, gender, ethnic group and social class. In contrast to these, the music venue can (although not universally) be a melting pot where people from different backgrounds meet, drawn together by a shared love of an artist or music genre. For example hip-hop has been a leveller in terms of drawing audiences across racial barriers. Its lyrics and raps frequently express discontent and non-compliance with authority, originally by African American artists for young audiences from that community; however, it has grown into a global musical genre popular with widely differing ethnic and social groups: 'potentially serving as a model for minimizing the impact of race and removing discrimination'.[21] As DJ and broadcaster Annie Mac states: 'I love the way clubs celebrate diversity bringing people from all different backgrounds together with one shared collective love: the music.'[22]

As well as cultural and social activity, music venues are places of *economic activity* – places that people are willing to invest in to maintain their existence. Audiences pay to support their favourite artists, and because music is so often associated with pleasure, they pay for other things that go along with that experience, which make the running of venues viable – entrance fees and ticketing, but also drinks, food and souvenirs. Venues large and small can have a profound impact on their location. Research by UK Music shows that in 2016, popular music performance events made a £4.4 billion annual contribution to UK economy, of which £1 billion, the largest single component, was from live performance. Live performance is by far the fastest growing part of the music industry, increasing by 14 per cent in 2016 and 42 per cent overall between 2011 and 2015 (90 per cent growth in exports) with a 26 per cent increase in employment in this area. The total audience count for 2016 was 30.9 million, 27 million at concerts and the remainder at festivals. This significant growth outpaces the general UK economy.[23] According to international auditors PricewaterhouseCoopers, the US music industry was estimated to generate about $17.2 billion in 2016, of which $9.3 billion was from live performance.[24]

Income can also be analysed by a single event or even a single building. The FedExForum has had a massive impact on the city of Memphis; economic analyses carried out five years after it opened calculated that the building brought in $223 million in extra revenue for the city and was directly responsible for the creation of 1,534 jobs.[25] However, the smaller venues also have a quantifiable economic benefit – in Memphis, 64 per cent of the 11.5 million annual visitors to the city travel there because of its music: 'excited by music legacy attractions [and a] thriving live music scene where emerging musicians still get their start ... 31 per cent ... chose "Beale Street and live music" when asked what they "love most about Memphis"'.[26]

Although in many cases new live entertainment development is welcome, injecting investment to provide new city facilities and employment for its inhabitants, the change it brings can also be viewed as detrimental in terms of musical (and historical) authenticity, eradicating the original qualities of these venues and the neighbourhoods in which they are based in favour of an unauthentic commodified 'image'. This is part of a complex debate regarding the way that commercial tourism is derided, transforming 'real' places into theme-park entertainment venues such as the Hard Rock Cafe and House of Blues (and B. B. King's, which has restaurants on Memphis' Beale Street, but also in New York and Las Vegas). Liverpool's Cavern is now part of a night-time economy, and although it still features live music, it is far removed from the energetic innovations of the 1960s and 70s – for the present-day version of that, you need to look elsewhere in the city. The FedExForum described above is just a short walk from historic Beale Street and makes use of the well-known older address to identify its location. Its proximity also enables patrons to easily access these existing older small venues as part of their night out. However, such a large development dramatically changed the character of this part of the city, and some would criticize this new revitalized Beale Street, stating that it is now simply a tourist location.

FIGURE 12.9 *Beale Street, Memphis – historic music neighbourhood or tourist attraction? Source: Robert Kronenburg.*

The years when Beale Street was a centre for African American-owned bars and restaurants in which blues music was performed as the local community's art form had already been all but wiped from history (despite the street being designated a National Historic Landmark in 1966 and recognized as 'Home of the Blues' by an act of the US Congress in 1977) by earlier disastrous urban renewal projects that demolished whole sections of the area including several buildings on the street itself. Although a vibrant and enjoyable place for a night out featuring much live music, 'authenticity' is not a feature of this part of Memphis. However, as David Grazian argues when discussing the Chicago blues scene:

> Like loaded terms such as 'community', 'authenticity' is not so much an objective quality that exists in time and space as it is a shared belief about the nature of the place and moments most valued in any given social context. Likewise, since authenticity is as subjective as any other social value, it follows that different kinds of audiences measure authenticity according to somewhat divergent criteria ... authenticity, like beauty, can truly exist only in the eye of the beholder.[27]

Those who visit Beale Street today find what they need, being in the same location and effectively saluting rather than reliving the past. The old Beale Street, formed in a period of severe poverty, segregation and extreme racial prejudice, is gone and any reinvention is, thankfully, never going to be truly 'authentic'.

The threat to music venues

Cities like Memphis became famous for their music. As discussed at the beginning of this book, all art needs its place to exist, and for popular music that place is the live music venue. Some of these venues have a long and illustrious history that is closely entwined with the people who have played there and the audiences that experienced their performances. An important venue does not have to be a big venue, nor does it have to be one that was designed and built to the highest architectural standards by professionals. Many of the venues that are loved best have been those created and operated on a minimal budget by people who were simply enthusiastic about what they loved – the music. A cramped, hastily painted cellar, with inadequate toilets, a makeshift stage – this could be the description of many music venues around the world; nevertheless, these places have frequently been the setting for intensely memorable experiences for both audiences and artists. The common feature of all venues, large or small, is that there is a place for musicians to play and be seen and heard by an audience large enough to create a scene. The scene may last only for the duration of that gig or persist for decades. Additional facilities may add to ambience and pleasure, safety and convenience, but the essence of a truly popular music, played live, is redolent in the space, which gives the scene a place to happen.

These spaces are an indicator of changing cultural values. Some underground venues like the typical one described above may be viewed with suspicion by local authorities and police, with concerted efforts being made to close them down or limit their activity, as happened with Eric's club in Liverpool in the 1970s, a seminal venue for the city's alternative music scene that was hounded to closure, despite street protests by local fans.[28] A few years later (if they haven't been run out of business and the building demolished), such places may be recognized as a tourist attraction (with the attendant economic value) or even as places where important historical events occurred that need to be recorded. Blue plaques and popular music trails are, however, a sad, poignant and ultimately frustrating replacement for the destruction of the thing they commemorate. More valuable benefits of changing cultural values are the investment in venues by arts associations and government grants to help preserve places of cultural and historic value as active businesses. Music venues, because of their locations in the heart of our cities, but often in areas that are cheaper and therefore in transition, are especially vulnerable to the cycle of economic activity. They are first to adopt redundant empty spaces and are an early indicator of an emerging fashionable city zone, which can provide vibrant alternative economies in which entrepreneurs can find it easier to establish new businesses that provide employment and enhance city living. However, when the economic potential for the new zone is discovered by developers, places upon which noisy night-time activity is centred are the first to be threatened by gentrification. Changes in attitudes to popular music venues and recognition of both the cultural and economic impact they bring are important, although hard won. When such changes do happen, they eventually lead to local and central government legislation to protect such businesses when new development takes place with 'Agent of Change' policies. The rise in public support for the Tote in Melbourne, Australia, had a pivotal effect on changing both the viewpoints of local government in the city and in the state of Victoria, which was the first to introduce new legislation that would provide some protection for venues like this, placing the responsibility for acoustic improvements that would protect surrounding new developments from noise nuisance.

More recently, after seventeen years of operation, and twice being voted the World's Number 1 club by *DJ* magazine, the popular Fabric club in Farringdon, London, was closed after its licence was withdrawn by Farringdon Council due to two drug-related deaths. Although the problems with drugs cannot and should not be marginalized or underestimated, closing legitimate businesses because some individuals have behaved irresponsibly and illegally will not tackle the issue effectively. After a lengthy campaign widely supported by the club's patrons, DJs and some politicians, including the Mayor of London, Sadiq Khan, the club was allowed to reopen under strict new rules (in addition to those it already had in place) aimed at minimizing drug-related issues.

FIGURE 12.10 *Protests at the Tote Hotel, Collingwood, Melbourne, on 18 January 2010 and 15 March 1980. Source: Nick Carson.*

Thanks to pressure groups like UK Music and the Music Venue Trust, British law is slowly shifting to protect existing night-time businesses like live music venues. In January 2018 the UK Government announced it would alter national planning policy so that the burden of solving sound issues when new housing is built near existing venues will fall on the developer, not the venue.[29] London is also now in the process of introducing local legislation that will protect existing venues and has appointed a 'night czar' with in-depth knowledge of venue operation to advise on mitigating the operational problems that many venues face. This is positive news; however, it will not address an underlying problem that faces all urban entertainment businesses. The sort of commercial development being undertaken in our urban centres focuses on 'acceptable' mixed-use shopping, apartment and offices. In some cases, this creates places that are not busy enough to sustain the regular traffic that pubs and clubs need, placing entertainments like cinemas and restaurants, inside or alongside shopping centres, exacerbating the desertion of our city centres. In prime urban centres like London, this may be less of a problem; however, there is still an issue as when new development takes place, it favours the uses described above and fails to make space available for the night-time businesses it removes. Speaking about the 67-acre Kings Cross development in London, which demolished several popular clubs including Bagleys (Canvas from 2003) and The Cross, Peter Marks, CEO of club owner and management organization, the Deltic Group, states:

> A lot of it [the problem] is to do with property development. If you look at where some of those iconic clubs have gone, Bagleys etc., they are not there anymore, they have been knocked down ... councils have overlooked the importance of the night-time economy as a whole and that includes anything from 6 in the evening to 6 in the morning.[30]

In his article 'What happened to the great London nightclubs?', Will Coldwell lists sixteen memorable venues that closed in the capital between 2008 and 2015, more than half as a direct result of urban development.[31] Statistics from the Association of Licenced Multiple Retailers indicated that nearly half of all nightclubs closed between 2005 and 2015 (from 3,144 to 1,733), partly due to the changing nature of the entertainment scene but mainly because of opposition to late-night licences, problems with gaining planning permission and the risks of being closed due to new development.[32] To solve these problems, city licencing authorities and planners need to appreciate that the loss of a single venue to closure may not have lasting damage on a city's urban character, but repeated losses will.

A key weapon in combating the threat to live music venues is to bring real information to bear to support a positive regard for the industry as: 'previous views of live music as a threat to nightly order, and as an insignificant part of cultural economies, stemmed from an astonishing ignorance of cultural activities (and an astonishing preparedness to act without knowledge)'.[33] Following the example of a live music census carried out in Melbourne, Australia, in 2012 by Music Victoria and the City of Melbourne, in March and June 2017, the UK Live Music census took place, which provided a detailed snapshot of popular music activity across six British city regions.[34] This wide-ranging survey of live music venues in the UK focused not only on the venues' activities in providing entertainment and generating income but also in terms of their social value including education and charity work. The report reinforced the value that live music venues have for society at all the scales they operate, and also the profound threat to their continued existence because of the issues described here – increases in business rates, planning and property development threats, strict licencing laws and dealing with sound complaints. Coming up with a series of recommendations for the stakeholders in the live music experience, musicians, promoters, local and city authorities, national government and the venues themselves, it provides a template for how existing venues can be valued and protected now and in the future. Unlike the architecture that makes up other commercial development – shops, housing, offices, even cinemas and theatres – music venues only rarely result from well-considered planning negotiations, forward-thinking commercial planning and major financial investment. As the examples presented in this book indicate, they are more often the result of ad hoc, creative enthusiasm, which although admirable does not result in the capacity to make the strongest arguments for protection and support when they are threatened. It is therefore not the large arenas that are the dying species of the live music scene but the grass-roots venues, whose loss will nevertheless be felt down the line as these are not only the places from which the next big star will emerge, but also the places for the rest of us to make important memories that will last a lifetime.

The future of music venues

The type and size of popular music performance venues vary dramatically. This book has examined the developmental history of some of the most important; however, it is clear from these individual narratives that this story is ongoing. This is an architectural typology that not only has changed dramatically during its history, but also continues to change, impacted not only by the special pressures and opportunities of the music industry but also by general commercial and societal ones. As we have seen, small independent venues are particularly threatened, and yet because of their crucial importance, they have gathered powerful supporters to aid in their survival. However, they will still need to change to ensure this happens by the venue managers becoming more responsive to the environment in which they operate. In architectural terms, this means focusing more on sound attenuation and on customer safety and other features that will smooth the path of licencing and planning applications. Medium-sized venues are increasingly becoming franchised or chain operations, which brings benefits in terms of coordinated business management and expertise; however, corporate branding risks homogenization. The architectural character of these places should be distinct: physical environments that develop and value their own local character and history. This also applies to the musical curation; local artists stepping up to the next stage in ambition and development need places to play and not be frozen out by restrictive policies only favouring sponsored artists. For the theatres and auditoriums, particularly the older buildings, the risk here is that if they are to survive, they need substantial financial support to keep pace with the more rigorous environmental, safety and technical advancements they require. This is currently accessed more easily for buildings that focus on other cultural activities (e.g. theatre, ballet, opera, fine arts); arts support organizations and charities need to recognize that the cultural significance of these venues is just as important as these more 'polite' arts.

Arenas are currently the largest growth area in permanent popular music venues, and they have fundamentally changed both the nature of the live music experience and its potential to generate income so that it now outstrips that previously provided by recording sales. As this is still a developing area of architectural design, innovations are already present in the most recent examples: environmentally sustainable building systems that are frugal in terms of energy use and other renewable resources; careful acoustic environment design to allow for optimal sound conditions for electronic amplification; engagement with their urban situation not only in sound attenuation to avoid disturbance to neighbours, but also in terms of enabling easy and quiet audience access via integrated public transport as well as private vehicles. Importantly, the best of these buildings contribute to the regeneration and development of urban communities, providing new sources of enterprise and income that include small business and entrepreneurs. They also have the potential to feed into local music scenes as music lovers visiting for the big events stay around to experience small local venues. At some point in time, perhaps not that far away, there will no doubt be an end to this type of development as the number of available seats exceeds demand in a given geographical area. For this reason, it is important that these buildings are designed with flexible design operation in mind. The fact that they might have an ice show on one night, a business conference the next and a pop music concert at the weekend is what will keep them operating and contributing lively cultural opportunities for the city in which they are situated. Festivals are also a major growth area, and these too must pay attention to increasing environmental concerns. Zero impact is the target for non-urban events, although this is difficult to achieve in a situation in which the unavoidable costs of transportation, both for the temporary infrastructure involved and for the audience, provide a huge carbon-deficit hurdle to overcome. The solution to this is the urban festival, which has multiple benefits: the audience can use public transport to attend and local suppliers can be used to temporarily transform the site. In addition, they have crucial additional benefits in providing new income sources for local facilities and businesses and, as with arena development, introducing visitors to the local music scene. All popular music performance, but particularly large events need also to respond to a particularly disturbing problem that has worsened in recent years. During the period that this book has been in preparation, there have been at least three horrific attacks at popular music performance events (on 13 November 2015, ninety people were killed and over 200 injured during an Eagles of Death Metal concert at the Bataclan theatre in Paris, France, as part of a wider series of attacks in the city; on 22 May 2017, twenty-two people were killed and 500 were injured after an Ariana Grande concert at the Manchester Arena, UK; and on 1 October 2017, fifty-eight people were killed and over 800 injured at the Route 92 Harvest music festival in Las Vegas, Nevada). Such events threaten all places where crowds are gathered together, in every country, for every purpose. The design of both the buildings that enable such events (such as entrances and exits, structural systems, security, alarm and fire protection systems) and the facilitation systems (such as ticketing, audience access, screening, event planning) is now a vital part of every organizer's agenda if safety and security without inhibition of personal freedom are to be protected.

Music performance technology is also a crucial aspect of the way that venues will change. Small and medium-sized venues now boast high-quality sound and lighting rigs, enabling artists to travel with just their backline. Standardized systems that use automatic digital technology to allow full customization of the performance at the drop of a downloaded file are surely just around the corner. Recent, more sophisticated analysis of what makes a popular music show sound great has quite rightly come to the conclusion that it is not just the provision of good-quality sound (sometimes call 'transparent') but an acoustic climate in which both the musicians and the audience share in order to experience togetherness.[35] Creating 'the show' in the computer has the danger of reducing spontaneity; however, a counterargument is that the very nature of live performance's energy is what makes it special – what artist would want to give up the vital ingredient that is so integral in communication with the audience? We can be certain that performance technology will change (as it has done throughout its history) in that it will become more adaptable to tune specifically to the venue and it will become smaller, lighter and more affordable. This will be done with much more portable rigs, which not only reduce transportation cost and enable setting up more quickly by less people, but also give more freedom in stage design, as the technical equipment can be hidden away completely if needed. Interaction with the audience via the individual's smart phones as is happening now, directed engagement via social media and dedicated apps are trends that are sure to continue and expand. The search for deeper audience involvement, more satisfying audience experiences and of course continuing novelty where an artist needs to do something different on the next tour compared to the last one is inevitable in live popular music performance: an art form of continuous invention, which simultaneously engages with peoples' deepest natural emotive instincts.

Music venues are a crucial part of the make-up of a vibrant urban society. More than just a place of entertainment for young people, the great variety of venue types caters to many sections of the population, young and old. The income they generate supports the national economy and provides jobs for local people. The cultural activity they create not only provides a voice that translates and communicates issues we all face, but also helps provide an identity that is both local and national. This is a distinct architectural genre that has contributed to the quality and energy of cities all over the world for hundreds of years. Music venues host a crucial creative activity that spans a wide variety of ethnic and social groups, which is both vibrant and proactive. And of course, they are fun places to be. For too long, the popular music venue has been seen as something ephemeral and without cultural significance – it is time that it is recognized for what it is: in all its architectural diversity, a crucially important setting for perhaps the most significant art form of the last hundred years, and one without which that art form would never have existed.

APPENDIX I

Venue Type by Capacity, Music Performance Priority and Geographic Location*

Venue Type (in approximate order of size)	Audience Capacity (typical range)	Frequency of Music Performance	Main Geographic Location
home concerts	25–100	occasional	Urban/suburban/rural
coffee bars	25–150	occasional	Urban/suburban
record shops	25–200	occasional	Urban
juke joints	50–200	regular	Rural/urban
speakeasies	50–300	regular	Urban
honky-tonks	50–400	constant	Rural/urban
jazz clubs	100–300	constant	Urban
blues club	100–300	constant	Urban
public houses	100–400	regular	Urban/suburban/rural
barrooms	100–400	regular	Urban/suburban
music club	100–500	constant	Urban
social clubs	100–600	regular	Urban
ballrooms	150–600	constant	Urban
saloons	150–800	regular	Urban/suburban
cabaret clubs	150–800	constant	Urban
supper clubs	150–800	regular	Urban

*Note: Capacities, performance frequency and locations in this chart are typical but not universal – there are significant examples (some in this book) that break away from the norm.

(*Continued*)

Venue Type (in approximate order of size)	Audience Capacity (typical range)	Frequency of Music Performance	Main Geographic Location
night club	150–1,000	constant	Urban
music halls	150–1,500	regular	Urban
dance halls	200–4,000	constant	Urban/suburban
discotheques	300–4,000	constant	Urban
showboats	500–1,400	constant	Rural/urban
variety	800–4,000	regular	Urban
vaudeville	800–4,000	regular	Urban
riverboats	1,000–4,000	constant	Rural/urban
theatres	1,000–4,000	regular	Urban
concert halls	1,000–5,000	constant	Urban
arenas	5,000–20,000	regular	Urban
tour stages	5,000–70,000	constant	Urban/suburban
stadiums	10,000–70,000	irregular	Urban/suburban
festivals	10,000–150,000	constant	Urban/suburban/rural

APPENDIX II

Principal Buildings Described in the Text (listed in order of appearance) with Type of Operation, Date Original Building Constructed (in brackets, if known), Dates Active as a Music Performance Venue (Regular and Occasional) including Rebuilding or Relocation

Venue	Type	Dates: (built) active
Chapter 1		
Casbah, Liverpool, UK	Home/coffee bar	(1860s) 1959–62, 2009–date
Coach House Folk Club, Liverpool, UK	Home/coffee bar	(1815) 1961–64, 1964–2011
Chapter 2		
Wilton's Music Hall, London, UK	Music hall	(1858) 1858–date
Teatro di San Cassiano, Venice, Italy	Theatre	(1637) 1637–1807
Georgian Theatre, Richmond, UK	Theatre	(1788) 1788–1848, 1963–2002, 2003–date
Bristol Theatre Royal (Old Vic), Bristol, UK	Theatre	(1766) 1766–1800, 1800–1972, 1972–2011, 2012–date
Britannia Music Hall, Glasgow, UK	Music hall	(1859) 1859–1905, 1906–38, 1997–date
Elephant and Castle, London, UK	Variety theatre	(1879) 1879–1932

(*Continued*)

Venue	Type	Dates: (built) active
Liverpool Olympia, Liverpool, UK	Variety theatre	(1905) 1905–30, 1948–64, 1987–90, 1990s–date
Hackney Empire, London, UK	Variety theatre	(1901) 1901–63, 1984–2001, 2004–date
Folies Bergére, Paris, France	Music hall/cabaret	(1869) 1869–1926, 1926–date
Moulin Rouge, Paris, France	Music hall/cabaret	(1889) 1889–1915, 1921–date
Tony Pastor's Opera House, New York, USA	Vaudeville	1865–75, 1875–81, 1881–1908
Grand Opera House (Riley Center), Meridian, USA	Vaudeville	(1889) 1889–1927, 2006–date
Chapter 3		
Robert's Western World, Nashville, USA	Honky-tonk	1993–date
John T. Floore Country Store, Helotes, USA	Honky-tonk	(1942) 1942–date
Broken Spoke, Austin, USA	Honky-tonk	(1964) 1964–date
Po' Monkey's, Merigold, USA	Juke joint	*c.* 1960–2016
Kingston Mines, Chicago, USA	Juke joint/blues bar	*c.* 1968–73, 1973–date
Chapter 4		
Spotted Cat Music Club, New Orleans, USA	Jazz club	2000–09, 2009–date
Eagle Saloon, New Orleans, USA	Saloon/fraternal hall	(1851) 1897–1917
Preservation Hall, New Orleans, USA	Jazz club	(1810s) 1961–date
Perseverance Society Hall, New Orleans, USA	Social club/fraternal hall	(1880s) 1880s–1927
SS Sidney, New Orleans, USA	Riverboat	(1920) 1920–*c.* 1950s

(Continued)

Venue	Type	Dates: (built) active
SS Natchez, New Orleans, USA	Riverboat	(1975) 1975–date
Goldenrod, St. Louis, USA	Showboat (barge)	(1909) 1909–1965, 1989–2017
Birdland, New York, USA	Jazz club	1949–65, 1986–96, 1996–date
Ronnie Scott's, London, UK	Jazz club	1959–65, 1965–date
Chapter 5		
Shakespeare Theatre, Liverpool, UK	Theatre/Cabaret club	(1888) 1963–75
Le Chat Noir, Paris, France	Cabaret club	1881–1920s
Cabaret Voltaire, Zurich, Switzerland	Kabarett	1916–17
Eldorado, Berlin, Gemany	Kabarett	1922–27, 1927–35
Cave of the Golden Calf, London, UK	Cabaret club	1912–14
Ciro's, London, UK	Cabaret club	1915–c. 1940
Café de Paris, London, UK	Cabaret/nightclub	(1920s) 1924–41, 1948–date
Ciro's, Shanghai, China	Cabaret/nightclub	(1936) 1936–c. 1949
Fairmont Peace Hotel (Cathay Hotel), Shanghai, China	Hotel/supper club	(1929) 1929–c. 1949, c. 1979–2007, 2010–date
Café des Beaux Arts, New York, USA	Restaurant/cabaret	1901–21
Reisenweber's 400 Cabaret Club, New York, UK	Restaurant/cabaret	(1850s) 1910–22
300 Club, New York, USA	Speakeasy	1926–28
Cotton Club, New York, USA	Speakeasy/nightclub	1923–35, 1936–40
Copacabana, New York, USA	Supper club/cabaret/disco	1940–c. 1970s, 1970s–92, 1992–2001, 2001–07, 2011–date
Café Society, New York, USA	Supper club/cabaret	1938–47

(*Continued*)

Venue	Type	Dates: (built) active
Chapter 6		
Wellington Rooms (Embassy Rooms, Irish Centre), Liverpool, UK	Ballroom/social club	(1816) 1816–*c.* 1922, 1923–41, 1965–97
The Folly on the Thames (Royal Diversion), London, UK	Riverboat (barge)	1668–1720
Rotunda, Ranelagh Gardens, London, UK	Pleasure pavilion	(1742) 1742–1803
Bath Assembly Rooms, Bath, UK	Ballroom	(1771) 1771–date
Blackpool Tower Ballroom, Blackpool, UK	Ballroom	(1894) 1897–date
Palace Theatre of Varieties (Palais de Danse), Derby, UK	Dance hall	(1862) 1897–1914, *c.* 1919–29
Hammersmith Palais de Danse, London, UK	Dance hall/ concert hall	(1910) 1919–1930s, 1934–2009
Oxford Galleries, Newcastle, UK	Dance hall/disco	(1823, 1923) 1923–1960s, 1960s–2015
Boblo Island Dance Pavilion, Blanc Island, Canada	Dance hall	(1913) 1913–93
Crystal Beach Ballroom, Ontario, Canada	Dance hall	(1924) 1924–1960s, 1975–85
Confitería Ideal, Buenos Aires, Argentina	Dance hall	(1912) 1990s–2016
Chapter 7		
Matt Molloy's, Westport, Ireland	Public house	(1820s)1990s–date
Hope and Anchor, London, UK	Public house	(1880) 1970s–1985, 1996–date
Tote Hotel, Melbourne, Australia	Public house	(1876) 1980–date
Scholz's Hall, Austin, USA	Barroom	(1866) 1866–date
Hole in the Wall, Austin, USA	Barroom	1974–date
Café Wha (Café Feegon), New York, USA	Coffee bar/ nightclub	1959–1968, 1968–87, 1987–date

(Continued)

Venue	Type	Dates: (built) active
Majorica, Kyoto, Japan	Coffee bar/barroom	1974–date
Chapter 8		
Empire Theatre, Liverpool, UK	Theatre/concert hall	(1866, 1879, 1896, 1925, 1999) 1866–date
Birmingham Town Hall, Birmingham, UK	Concert hall	(1834) 1834–1997, 2007–date
Apollo Theater (New Burlesque Theater), New York, USA	Theatre	(1914) 1914–28, 1928–1930s, 1934–76, 1983–date
Rainbow Theatre (Finsbury Park Astoria), Londond, UK	Cinema/concert hall	(1930) 1930–39, 1955–71, 1971–75, 1976–81.
Hammersmith Eventim Apollo (Gaumont Palace), London, UK	Cinema/concert hall	(1932) 1950s–2013, 2013–date
London Astoria, London, UK	Cinema/concert hall	(1927) 1985–2009
O2 Apollo Manchester (Manchester Apollo, Carling Apollo), Manchester, UK	Cinema/concert hall	(1938) 1962–2003, 2003–date
Chapter 9		
The Wall Live stage set, Roger Waters, North and South America, Europe, South America, Australasia	Touring stage set	(2010) 2010–13
Woodstock Music and Art Fair, Woodstock, USA	Festival stage	(1969) 1969
Glastonbury (Pilton Pop, Blues and Folk Festival), Pilton, UK	Festival stage	(1971) 1971, 1978–date
Coachella Music and Arts Festival, Indio, USA	Festival stage	(1999) 1999–date
Burning Man, Black Rock Desert, USA	Festival stage	(1986) 1986, 1987–date
Dark Side of the Moon stage set, Pink Floyd, North America, Europe, Japan,	Touring stage set	(1972) 1972–73

(*Continued*)

Venue	Type	Dates: (built) active
The Wall Live stage set, Pink Floyd, Los Angeles, New York, London, Dortmund	Touring stage set	(1980) 1980–81
The Wall-Live in Berlin, Roger Waters, Germany	Stage set	(1990) 1990
The Joshua Tree Anniversary Tour, U2, North and South America, Europe	Touring stage set	(2017) 2017
Chapter 10		
Earl's Court Exhibition Centre, London, UK	Arena	(1937) 1970s–1991, 1991–2014
SEE Arena (Empire Pool and Sports Arena, Wembley Arena), London, UK	Arena	(1934) 1960s–2005, 2006–date
Spectrum, Philadelphia, USA	Arena	(1967) 1967–2009
Manchester Arena (Nynex Arena, MEN Arena, Phones4U Arena), Manchester, UK	Arena	(1995) 1995–2015, 2015–date
Golden 1 Center, Sacramento, USA	Arena	(2016) 2016–date
T-Mobile Arena, Las Vegas, USA	Arena	(2016) 2016–date
3Arena (O2 Arena, Point Theatre), Dublin, Ireland	Arena	(1878) 1988–2007, 2008–date
Philippine Arena, Manila, Philippines	Arena	(2014) 2014–date
MSG Sphere, Las Vegas, USA	Arena	(predicted 2020)
Chapter 11		
Haçienda, Manchester, UK	Nightclub	1982–97
Disco Fever, New York, USA	Disco/nightclub	1976–86
Twisted Wheel, Manchester, UK	Disco/nightclub	1963–65, 1965–73
Wigan Casino, Wigan, UK	Dance hall/concert hall	(1916) 1916–26, 1926–81
Easy Street Records, Seattle, USA	Record shop	(1925) 1988–date

(*Continued*)

Venue	Type	Dates: (built) active
Chapter 12		
CBGB and OMFUG, New York, USA	Nightclub	1973–2006
Fillmore East (Villageeast), New York, USA	Theatre	(1926) 1968–71, 1972, 1974–75
De Vorstin, Hilversum, The Netherlands	Concert room, rehearsal space	(2010) 2010–date
Grenswerk, Venlo, The Netherlands	Concert room, rehearsal space	(2014) 2014–date
The Band Room, Low Mill, UK	Concert room	(1920s) c. 1995–date
100 Club, London, UK	Music club	(1930s) 1950s–date
Cavern Club, Liverpool, UK	Music club	(1870s) 1957–73, 1973–76, 1984–date
AFAS Live (Heineken Music Hall), Amsterdam, The Netherlands	Concert hall	(2001) 2001–date
Bridgestone Arena, Nashville, USA	Arena	(1996) 1996–date
FedExForum, Memphis, USA	Arena	(2004) 2004–date

NOTES

Chapter 1

1. Daniel Levitin, *This Is Your Brain on Music: The Science of a Human Obsession* (London: Dutton, 2006), 5–6.
2. Lucy Green, 'Ideology', in *Key Terms in Popular Music and Culture*, ed. Bruce Horner and Thomas Swiss (Oxford: Blackwell, 1999), 7–9.
3. Simon Frith, *Performing Rites: On the Value of Popular Music* (Cambridge, MA: Harvard University Press, 1996), 26.
4. Simon Frith, Matt Brennan, Martin Cloonan, and Emma Webster, *The History of Live Music in Britain Volume I: 1950–1967* (Farnham: Ashgate, 2016 [2013]), 2–11.
5. Elizabeth E. Leach, 'Popular Music', in *An Introduction to Music Studies*, ed. John Paul E. Hooper-Scott and Jim Samson (Cambridge: Cambridge University Press, 2009), 194–5.
6. Mark Girouard, *Cities and People: A Social and Architectural History* (London: Yale University Press, 1985), 182.
7. Andy Bennett and Richard A. Peterson, 'Introducing Music Scenes', in *Music Scenes: Local, Translocal and Virtual*, ed. Andy Bennett and Richard A. Peterson (Nashville: Vanderbilt University Press, 2004), 3.
8. Howard S. Becker, 'Jazz Places', in *Music Scenes: Local, Translocal and Virtual*, ed. Andy Bennett and Richard A. Peterson (Nashville: Vanderbilt University Press, 2004), 17.
9. Frith et al., *The History of Live Music in Britain Volume I*, x.
10. David Byrne, *How Music Works* (Edinburgh: Canongate, 2012), 221.
11. Sara Cohen, '"The gigs I've gone to": Mapping Memories and Places of Live Music', in *Coughing and Clapping: Investigating Audience Experience*, ed. Karen Burland and Stephanie Pitts (Farnham: Ashgate, 2014), 141.
12. Patti Smith, *Just Kids* (London: Bloomsbury, 2012 [2010]), 245.
13. Emma Webster, Matt Brennan, Adam Behr, Martin Cloonan, and Jake Ansell *Valuing Live Music: The UK Live Music Census 2017 Report Executive Summary* (Edinburgh: University of Edinburgh, ECA, Reid School of Music, 2018), 11.
14. Sara Cohen and Robert Kronenburg, *Liverpool's Musical Landscapes* (Swindon: Historic England, 2018), 61.

15 Richard A. Peterson, *Creating Country Music: Fabricating Authenticity* (Chicago: University of Chicago Press, 1997), 98.
16 Dave Haslam, *Life After Dark: A History of British Nightclubs and Music Venues* (London: Simon and Schuster, 2015), 398.
17 Tess Reidy and Vanessa Thorpe, 'Secret gigs place the next big thing right into your room', *The Guardian*, 27 April 2014, accessed 2 February 2018, https://www.theguardian.com/music/2014/apr/27/secret-gigs-pop-music-prince-batille
18 Byrne, *How Music Works*, 78.

Chapter 2

1 John Earl, *British Theatres and Music Halls* (Princes Risborough: Shire, 2005), 16.
2 David Cornforth, 'The Theatre Royal Fire-1887', Exeter Memories, 2005, accessed 4 May 2018, http://www.exetermemories.co.uk/em/theatre_fire.php.
3 Earl, *British Theatres and Music Halls*, 26.
4 *The ERA*, 'The Elephant and Castle Theatre', London, 8 June 1879, accessed 24 July 2017, http://www.arthurlloyd.co.uk/ElephantAndCastleTheatre.htm.
5 *The Stage*, 'The Olympia Theatre, West Derby Road, Everton, Liverpool', London, 27 April 1905, accessed 28 July 2017, http://www.arthurlloyd.co.uk/Liverpool/OlympiaTheatreLiverpool.htm.
6 Max Thompson, 'Theatre architect receives blue plaque', *Architects' Journal*, 23 November 2007, accessed 25 July 2017, https://www.architectsjournal.co.uk/news/theatre-architect-receives-blue-plaque/296348.article.
7 Danny Varney, 'Hackney Empire Memories', Arthur Lloyd, 1991 (revised 2010), accessed 25 July 17, http://www.arthurlloyd.co.uk/HackneyEmpireMemories.html.
8 Programme from the Hackney Empire, week commencing Monday 30 January 1956, accessed 28 July 2017, http://www.arthurlloyd.co.uk/HackneyEmpireTheatre.htm.
9 Brooks McNamara, *The New York Concert Saloon: The Devil's Own Nights* (Cambridge, UK: Cambridge University Press, 2002), 3.
10 Alan Lomax, *The Land Where the Blues Began* (New York: New Press, 1993), 189.
11 Donald T. Stewart, *No Applause – Just Throw Money: The Book That Made Vaudeville Famous* (New York: Farrar, Strauss and Giroux, 2006).
12 Sandra L. Tatman, 'McElfatrick, John Bailey (1826–1906)', Philadelphia Architects and Buildings, The Athaneum of Philadelphia, 2018, accessed 31 July 2017, https://www.philadelphiabuildings.org/pab/app/ar_display.cfm/23155.
13 Dennis J. Mitchell, 'Grand Opera House of Mississippi', Jackson: Mississippi Historical Society, September 2006, accessed 31 July 2017, http://www.mshistorynow.mdah.ms.gov/articles/167/grand-opera-house-of-mississippi.
14 Ibid.

15 'History of the Ed Sullivan Show', 2010, accessed 29 July 2017, http://www.edsullivan.com/show-history/.

16 John Koblin, 'Stephen Colbert's Shiny New Home on Broadway Reflects Its Past', *The New York Times*, 9 September 2015, accessed 4 May 2018, https://www.nytimes.com/2015/09/10/arts/television/stephen-colberts-shiny-new-home-on-broadway-reflects-its-past.html.

Chapter 3

1 Juliet Gorman, 'Jukin' it out: Contested visions of Florida in New Deal narratives', May 2001, accessed 2 August 2017, http://www2.oberlin.edu/library/papers/honorshistory/2001-Gorman/default.html.

2 Barry Popik, 'Honky Tonk (not from Tonk pianos)', 2006, accessed 9 August 2017, http://www.barrypopik.com/index.php/new_york_city/entry/honky_tonk_not_from_tonk_pianos/.

3 Bill Porterfield, *The Greatest Honky Tonks in Texas* (Dallas: Taylor Publishing Company, 1983), 16.

4 Ibid., 17.

5 Ibid., 98.

6 Michelle Burgess, 'There's No Place Like Floore's: Texas honky-tonk heaven in Heliote', *Texas Highways*, November 2013, accessed 9 August 2017, http://www.texashighways.com/travel/item/476-there-s-no-place-like-john-t-floores-country-store-helotes.

7 Michael Hall, 'Accommodating an Old Honky-Tonk in Austin', *The New York Times*, 12 January 2013, accessed 1 December 2017, http://www.nytimes.com/2013/01/13/us/in-new-austin-accommodating-the-broken-spoke-honkey-tonk.html?_r=0.

8 Francine Prose, *The Photographs of Marian Post Wolcott: The Library of Congress (Fields of Vision)* (London: D. Giles Ltd., 2008).

9 Lomax, *The Land Where the Blues Began*, 7.

10 Live From Memphis, *See Where the Backroads Take You: Merigold, outside Cleveland, MS*, 2011, accessed 29 May 2018, https://www.youtube.com/watch?v=0f2Qrc_ZArE#t=144.665367582.

11 Lomax, *The Land Where the Blues Began*, 439.

12 Adam Green, 'Blues', in *Electronic Encyclopedia of Chicago*, Chicago Historical Society (Chicago: The Newberry Library, 2005), accessed 10 August 2017, http://www.encyclopedia.chicagohistory.org/pages/151.html.

13 James Rooney, *Bossmen: Bill Monroe and Muddy Waters* (New York: Dial Press, 1971), 126.

14 Lomax, *The Land Where the Blues Began*, 447.

15 HTV33 Campus Housing Television, *Live Chicago Episode 2: Kingston Mines Blues Club*, 2011, accessed 10 August 2017, https://www.youtube.com/watch?v=oqZ3-QgpYLs.

16 'Gilley's BBQ, Finger Licking BBQ, ice cold beer and the Gilley Girls!', accessed 10 August 2017, http://www.treasureisland.com/restaurant/3/gilleys-bbq.

17 Lomax, *The Land Where the Blues Began*, 203.

Chapter 4

1 Mervyn Cooke, *Jazz* (London: Thames and Hudson World of Art, 1998), 50.

2 Alan Lomax, 'Mister Jelly Roll', in *Reading Jazz*, ed. Robert Gottlieb (New York: Vintage, 1996 [1950]), 3–7.

3 Musician and composer Dave Torkanowsky speaking in *Bring Back Eagle Saloon* (Alexander John Glustrom, 2016) promotional fund-raising video. Accessed 27 May 2018, http://www.bringbackeaglesaloon.com.

4 Louis Armstrong, *Satchmo: My Life in New Orleans* (Boston: De Capo Press, 1986 [1954]).

5 B. Stuckey, '"Kid" Jazzmen Play to Preserve Art Form', *New Orleans Times Picayune*, 24 July 1961 (courtesy Hogan Jazz Archive, Tulane University).

6 Claude F. Jacobs, 'Benevolent Societies of New Orleans Blacks during the Late Nineteenth and Early Twentieth Centuries', *Louisiana History: The Journal of the Louisiana Historical Association* 29, no. 1 (Winter 1988): 22.

7 Ann Woodruff, 'Society Halls in New Orleans: A Survey of Jazz Landmarks, Part II', *Jazz Archivist* XXI (2008): 19–36.

8 Karen Armagost, *New Orleans Jazz Sites: Then and Now*. New Orleans Jazz National Historic Park, National Park Service, USA, May 2012, accessed 5 May 2018, https://www.nps.gov/jazz/learn/historyculture/upload/New-Orleans-Jazz-Sites-Then-and-Now.pdf.

9 Sidney Bechet, 'Treat It Gentle', in *Reading Jazz*, ed. Robert Gottlieb (New York: Vintage, 1996 [1960]), 13.

10 Ibid.

11 Cooke, *Jazz*.

12 Woodruff, 'Society Halls in New Orleans', 29.

13 Bruce B. Raeburn, 'Riverboats and Jazz', Hogan Jazz Archive, Tulane University, New Orleans, 2000, accessed 21 November 2017, https://library.tulane.edu/exhibits/exhibits/show/riverboats_jazz.

14 Ibid.

15 United States Department of the Interior. 'Nomination Form for the showboat *Goldenrod*. National Register of Historic Places Inventory, Historic Sites Survey. Washington D.C.: National Park Service, 15 February 1977

16 Miles Davis with Quincy Troupe, *Miles: The Autobiography* (London: Picador, 2012 [1989]), 88.

17 Ibid., 62.

Chapter 5

1. Pete Price and Adrian Butler, *Namedropper* (Liverpool: Trinity Mirror, 2007).
2. Anna Meakin, 'Le Chat Noir: Historic Montmartre Cabaret', *Bonjour Paris*, 19 December 2011, accessed 22 November 2017, https://bonjourparis.com/archives/chat-noir-montmartre-cabaret/.
3. Jennifer Llewellyn, Jim Southey, and Steve Thompson, 'Weimer cabaret', Alpha History, 2014, accessed 5 May 2018, http://alphahistory.com/weimarrepublic/weimar-cabaret/.
4. Robert Upstone, 'Study for a Mural Decoration for "The Cave of the Golden Calf" 1912 by Spencer Gore', in *The Camden Town Group in Context*, ed. Helena Bonett, Ysanne Holt, Jennifer Mundy (London: Tate Research Publication, May 2012), accessed 5 May 2018, https://www.tate.org.uk/art/research-publications/camden-town-group/spencer-gore-study-for-a-mural-decoration-for-the-cave-of-the-golden-calf-r1139297.
5. British Pathé (8 February 1932), [Film] *London's Famous Clubs and Ciro's*. Available online: https://www.britishpathe.com/video/ciros-club/query/nightclubs (accessed 18 January 2018).
6. Prince with Chaka Khan, Larry Graham, and Doug E., Café de Paris, London (28 August 1998), [TV programme] Channel 4 Television. https://www.youtube.com/watch?v=Q3fWVAYQO-0 (accessed 10 January 2018).
7. Andrew Field, *Shanghai's Dancing World: Cabaret Culture and Urban Politics, 1919–1954* (Honk Kong: Chinese University Press, 2010), 104–6.
8. James Farrar and Andrew Field, *Shanghai Nightscapes: A Nocturnal Biography of a Global City* (Chicago: University of Chicago Press, 2015), 133–4.
9. Louis A. Erenberg, *Steppin' Out: New York Nightlife and the Transformation of American Culture, 1890–1930* (Chicago: University of Chicago Press, 1984 [1981]), 87.
10. Newspaper advertisement, c.1920. http://www.brighteningglance.org/reisenwebers-columbus-circle.html (accessed 5 January 2018).
11. Peter J. Brown, 'Liquor Licenses, Steelworkers and the British Navy – an Unlicensed History and Etymology of "Speakeasies"', Early Sports and Pop Culture History Blog, 2014, accessed 7 December 2018, https://esnpc.blogspot.co.uk/2014/08/liquor-licenses-steelworkers-and.html.
12. Daniel Okrent, *Last Call: The Rise and Fall of Prohibition* (New York: Scribner, 2010), 209.
13. *1928-Toasts by Texas Guinan at Prohibition-era Speakeasy, New York City* (1928) [Film]. Available online: https://www.youtube.com/watch?v=CSqk4m4W_3E (accessed 9 January 2018).
14. Cab Calloway and Bryant Rollins, *Of Minnie the Moocher and Me* (New York: Crowell, 1976).
15. Pete Denis, 'The Copacabana, New York City: The Hottest Spot North of Havana', Disco-Disco, 2008, accessed 10 January 2018, http://www.disco-disco.com/clubs/copacabana.shtml.

16 David Margolick, *Strange Fruit: Billie Holiday, Café Society, and an Early Cry for Civil Rights* (Philadelphia: Running Press, 2000).
17 *The Cotton Club* (trailer) (1984) [Film] Dir. Francis Ford Coppola. Available online: https://www.youtube.com/watch?v=fru1zRGhs-Y (accessed 5 May 2018).
18 Anne Thompson, 'Francis Ford Coppola: Why He Spent $500K to Restore His Most Troubled Film, "The Cotton Club"', *IndieWire*, 1 September 2017, accessed 9 January 2018, http://www.indiewire.com/2017/09/francis-coppola-recut-the-cotton-club-telluride-1201872249/2/

Chapter 6

1 Roy Shuker, *Understanding Popular Music Culture* (Abingdon: Routledge, 2013), 169.
2 Lawrence M. Zbikowski, 'Music, Dance and Meaning in the Early Nineteenth Century', *Journal of Musicological Research* 31 (2012): 151.
3 'Bachelors' Fancy Ball at the Wellington Rooms, Liverpool', in *The Kaleidoscope: Literary and Scientific Mirror*, vol. 1 (Liverpool: E. Smith, 20 March 1821), 302.
4 Joseph Sharples and Richard Pollard, *Liverpool; Pevsner Architectural Guides* (New Haven and London: Yale University Press, 2004), 212.
5 Sarah J. Downing, *The English Pleasure Garden 1660–1860* (Oxford: Shire, 2011), 8.
6 Ibid., 29.
7 Zbikowski, 'Music, Dance and Meaning in the Early Nineteenth Century', 152.
8 Historic England, 'Tower Buildings, Grade 1 listing report no. 183675', 1973 (amended 1983), accessed 16 January 2018, https://historicengland.org.uk/listing/the-list/list-entry/1205810.
9 From the caption to a painting by Fortunino Matania featured in a Winter Gardens Complex programme, 1938, showing the Blackpool Tower Ballroom. Accessed 16 January 2018, http://www.arthurlloyd.co.uk/BlackpoolTheatres/TowerBallroomBlackpool.htm.
10 James Nott, *Going to the Palais: A Social and Cultural History of Dancing and Dance Halls in Britain, 1918–1960* (Oxford: Oxford University Press, 2015).
11 Ibid.
12 Björn Englund, 'The London Sonora Band's Favorite Recordings. A revised discography', Nottingham: *Vintage Jazz Mart*, no. 169 (2014): 12–15.
13 Paul Kassay, Friends of Crystal Beach (interview) *The Crystal Ballroom* (2009), [TV programme] Buffalo, FM/WNYMedia.net, accessed 22 January 2018, https://www.youtube.com/watch?v=-hkKkscp0tA.
14 Christopher Popa, 'Do Big Bands Today Stand a Ghost of a Chance?' Big Band Library, 2004, accessed 13 February 2018, http://www.bigbandlibrary.com/dobigbandstodaystandaghostofachance.html.

Chapter 7

1. Historic England, 'Hope and Anchor Public House, Grade II listing report no. 1195774', 1994, accessed 29 January 2018, https://www.historicengland.org.uk/listing/the-list/list-entry/1195774.
2. Mark Blunden, 'Infamous Tales from Rock Haven The Hope', *Camden New Journal*, 5 April 2007, accessed 29 January 2018, http://www.thecnj.com/review/040507/feat040507_01.html.
3. Chas de Collis, 'Hope & Anchor: History', accessed 29 January 2018, https://www.punk77.co.uk/punkhistory/hope_and_anchor.htm.
4. Nick Tester, 'Joy Division, Hope and Anchor', *Sounds*, 1979, accessed 29 January 2018, https://www.joydiv.org/c271278.htm.
5. 'U2-3 London Tour 1979', The U2 Setlist Archive, accessed 29 January 2019, http://www.u2setlists.com/earlydays_u23.shtml.
6. Andy S review on Yelp as quoted on 'Hope and Anchor – History 2', accessed 29 January 2018, https://www.punk77.co.uk/punkhistory/hope_and_anchor_history2.htm.
7. Shane Homan, '"I Tote and I Vote": Australian Live Music and Cultural Policy', *Arts Marketing* 1, no. 2 (2011): 102–4.
8. Pete Blackstock, 'Street Survivor: Hole in the Wall Celebrates 40 Years down on the drag', *Austin American-Statesman*, 18 June 2014, accessed 30 January 2018, http://www.mystatesman.com/entertainment/street-survivor-hole-the-wall-celebrates-years-down-the-drag/hrAyDGUQB4oqBhpYfmUHzN/.
9. David Sackllah, 'The Crisis of Gentrification Hits the Austin Music Scene', *Pitchfork*, 9 July 2015, accessed 20 January 2018, https://pitchfork.com/thepitch/836-the-crisis-of-gentrification-hits-the-austin-music-scene/.
10. ATX Music also helps: 'Mediate agreements between permitted venues and neighbourhood groups to find equitable, win-win solutions and compromises related to outdoor music issues'. Accessed 30 January 2019, http://www.austintexas.gov/department/venues.
11. Frith et al., *The History of Live Music in Britain Volume I*, 123.
12. 'Artists Stories', Musicstorytellers, accessed 9 February 2018, https://musicstorytellers.wordpress.com/33/.
13. Ibid.
14. 'The Topic Folk Club: An Outline of History', accessed 30 July 2018, http://www.nawaller.com/topicfc/Site/history.html.
15. Rob Young, 'Folk – the "music of the people" is now hip again', *The Guardian*, 31 July 2010, accessed 30 July 2018, https://www.theguardian.com/culture/2010/jul/31/folk-music-of-people-young.
16. Kim Stravers, 'Majorica Jazz Bar', *The Guardian, Travel*, 24 December 2016, 8–9.

Chapter 8

1. Joseph Sharples and Richard Pollard, *Liverpool; Pevsner Architectural Guides* (New Haven and London: Yale University Press, 2004), 13.
2. *The ERA*, 'The New Empire Theatre Liverpool', London, 12 December 1896, accessed 5 March 2018, http://www.arthurlloyd.co.uk/Liverpool/EmpireTheatreLiverpool.htm.
3. Nigel Williamson, *The Rough Guide to Bob Dylan* (London: Rough Guides, 2004).
4. Simon Robinson, 'The Deep Purple Appreciation Society, Deep Purple Atlas, Liverpool Empire Theatre', accessed 5 March 2018, http://www.deep-purple.net/archive/a-z/liverpool/liverpool.htm.
5. Helen Soteriou, 'Why is the Harlem Apollo Theatre so important?', *BBC News*, 15 June 2014, accessed 9 March 2014, http://www.bbc.co.uk/news/entertainment-arts-27813129.
6. Garrett Felber, 'Apollo Theater', in *The Encyclopedia of New York City*, ed. Kenneth T. Jackson, 2nd edn. (New Haven: Yale University Press, 2010), 46–7.
7. Soteriou, 'Why is the Harlem Apollo Theatre so important?'
8. Lucinda Moore, 'Show Time at the Apollo', *Smithsonian*, November 2010, accessed 15 March 2018, https://www.smithsonianmag.com/arts-culture/show-time-at-the-apollo-64658902/.
9. Eve M. Kahn, 'The Restoration of Harlem's Apollo Theater', *Traditional Building*, 28 September 2017, accessed 9 February 2018, https://www.traditionalbuilding.com/projects/apollo-theater-restoration.
10. NYCEDC Press Release, 15 December 2005, 'Mayor Bloomberg Unveils Phase I restoration of Apollo Theater in Harlem', accessed 9 March 2018, https://www.nycedc.com/press-release/mayor-bloomberg-unveils-phase-i-renovation-apollo-theater-harlem.
11. Historic England, 'Numbers 232 to 238 (even) Rainbow Theatre, former, Grade II* listing report no. 1297977', 1974, accessed 12 March 2018, https://historicengland.org.uk/listing/the-list/list-entry/1297977.
12. *Programme of a Gala Performance upon the occasion of the opening of Finsbury Park Astoria*, 29 September 1930 (Islington Local History Centre collection).
13. Rick Burton, 'A History of the Rainbow Theatre', 2011, accessed 13 March 2018, http://www.rainbowhistory.x10.mx/index.htm.
14. Michael Palin, *The Python Years: Diaries 1969–79: Volume One* (London: Orion Publishing Co., 2006).
15. Islington Heritage Services and Rick Burton, *From Coleman to Costello: A history of the Astoria Cinema and Rainbow Theatre* (Finsbury Park, London: Islington Heritage Services, 2013).

16 Owen Gibson, 'The Astoria, legendary venue for acts from Kylie to the Killers, falls silent for final time', *The Guardian*, 15 January 2009, accessed 13 March 2018, https://www.theguardian.com/music/2009/jan/15/astoria-final-gigs.

Chapter 9

1 Jack Doyle, 'Elvis on the Road 1955–56', The Pop History Dig, 9 August 2017, accessed 22 March 2018, http://www.pophistorydig.com/topics/tag/elvis-presley-concerts-1955-1956/.
2 Mark Cunnigham, 'A Short History of Rock Touring', in *U2 Show*, ed. Diana Scrimgeour (London: Orion, 2004), 197.
3 Bob Spitz, *Barefoot in Babylon: The Creation of the Woodstock Music Festival, 1969* (New York: Plume, 2014 [1979]), 92.
4 Cunnigham, 'A Short History of Rock Touring', 198.
5 Spitz, *Barefoot in Babylon*, 305.
6 Ibid., 439.
7 *Front of House (FOH) online*, 'Parnelli Innovator Honoree, Father of Festival Sound', September 2006, accessed 20 January 2013, http://www.fohonline.com/index.php?option=com_content&task=view&id=579&Itemid=1.
8 Marian Sandberg, 'Q&A: Andrew Gumper, Owner and CEO of AG Light and Sound', *Live Design*, 10 November 2017, accessed 24 April 2018, http://www.livedesignonline.com/business-people-news/qa-andrew-gumper-owner-and-ceo-ag-light-and-sound.
9 Dave Brooks, 'Coachella Grossed Record-Breaking $114 Million This Year: Exclusive', *Billboard*, 18 October 2017, accessed 24 April 2018, https://www.billboard.com/articles/business/8005736/coachella-festival-2017-114-million-gross.
10 Robert Kronenburg, *Live Architecture: Popular Music Venues, Stages and Arenas* (Oxford: Routledge, 2012), 56–67.
11 Robert Edgar and Kirsty Fairclough-Isaacs, Ben Halligan, and Nicola Spelman, 'A Stately Pleasure-Dome', in *The Arena Concert: Music Media and Mass Entertainment*, ed. Robert Edgar, Kirsty Fairclough-Isaacs, Ben Halligan and Nicola Spelman (New York: Bloomsbury, 2015), 3.
12 Kelefa Sanneh, 'The Persistence of Prog Rock', *The New Yorker*, 19 June 2017, accessed 30 March 2018, https://www.newyorker.com/magazine/2017/06/19/the-persistence-of-prog-rock.
13 Mark Blake, *Pigs Might Fly: The Inside Story of Pink Floyd* (London: Aurum Press, 2007), 60.
14 Ibid., 215–16.
15 Roger Waters, *The Solo Years, Volume 1: The Flickering Flame*, 2002, CD booklet sleeve notes.

16 Steve Turner, 'Roger Waters: The Wall in Berlin', *Radio Times*, 25 May 1990. Reprinted in *Classic Rock*, no. 148, August 2010, 76.
17 Sutherland Lyall, *Rock Sets: The Astonishing Art of Rock Concert Design* (London: Thames and Hudson, 1992), 95.
18 Kronenburg, *Live Architecture: Popular Music Venues, Stages and Arenas*, 166–89.
19 Cunnigham, 'A Short History of Rock Touring', 197.
20 Stephen Armstrong, 'Inside the Amish town that builds U2, Lady Gaga, and Taylor Swift's live shows', *Wired*, 5 January 2018.
21 Daniel Sanchez, 'What Streaming Music Services Pay (updated for 2018)', *Digital Music News*, 16 January 2018, accessed 30 March 2018, https://www.digitalmusicnews.com/2018/01/16/streaming-music-services-pay-2018/.
22 1999 figures from the Recording Industry Association of America. 2015 figures from PwC Auditors (as quoted in Armstrong, 'Inside the Amish town that builds U2, Lady Gaga, and Taylor Swift's live shows').
23 Willie Williams, 'Art, Commerce and Logistics: Designing a U2 Show', in *U2 Show*, ed. Diana Scrimgeour (London: Orion, 2004), 15.
24 Michael Bracewell, 'U2 and Rock Music as Spectacle', in *U2 Show*, ed. Diana Scrimgeour (London: Orion, 2004), 9.
25 Kimi Kärki, 'Evolutions of the Wall: 1979–2015', in *The Arena Concert: Music Media and Mass Entertainment*, ed. Robert Edgar, Kirsty Fairclough-Isaacs, Ben Halligan, and Nicola Spelman (New York: Bloomsbury, 2015), 62.
26 George McKay, ed., *The Pop Festival: History, Music, Media, Culture* (New York: Bloomsbury Academic, 2015), 8–9.

Chapter 10

1 This chapter is based in part on the author's essay 'From Shed to Venue: The Arena Concert Event Space' in *The Arena Concert: Music Media and Mass Entertainment*, ed. Robert Edgar, Kirsty Fairclough-Isaacs, Ben Halligan, and Nicola Spelman (New York: Bloomsbury, 2015), 73–85.
2 Sounes Howard, *Down the Highway: The Life of Bob Dylan* (New York: Grove Press, 2001), 314–16.
3 Robert Kronenburg, *Flexible: Architecture that Responds to Change* (London: Lawrence King, 2007), 78–87.
4 August Brown, 'Bruce Springsteen's last stand at the Sports Arena: "We gotta play this one for the old Building"', *Los Angeles Times*, 20 March 2016, accessed 15 May 2018, http://www.latimes.com/entertainment/music/posts/la-et-ms-springsteen-sports-arena-20160320-story.html.
5 Richard Rys, 'The Full Spectrum: an oral history', *Philadelphia*, 24 June 2009, accessed 17 November 2014, http://www.phillymag.com/articles/the-full-spectrum/?all=1.

6 Ibid.

7 Ibid.

8 There are several well-supported fan appreciation websites for the Spectrum, for example www.rememberthespectrum.com and www.facebook.com/pages/The-Philadelphia-Spectrum-Concert-Appreciation-Group.

9 W. Mandel, 'Led Zeppelin's Music Needs the Spectrum', *Philadelphia Bulletin*, 14 June 1972, accessed 3 July 2017, http://www.ledzeppelin.com/show/june-13-1972.

10 Ibid.

11 'Pollstar 2016 Year End Worldwide Ticket Sales Top 200 Arena Venues', Pollstar, 2017, accessed 14 May 2018, https://www.pollstar.com/Chart/2017/01/2016YearEndWorldwideTicketSalesTop200ArenaVenues_350.pdf.

12 Clare Hartwell, Matthew Hyde, and Nikolaus Pevsner, *Buildings of England. Lancashire: Manchester and the South-East* (New Haven: Yale University Press, 2004), 301.

13 See Pollstar Awards Archive. Accessed 26 February 2015, http://www.pollstarpro.com/PCIA-Static/.

14 James Ferguson, 'Manchester Arena signs deal with Phones4U', *Manchester Evening News*, 31 July 2013, accessed 21 November 2014, http://www.manchestereveningnews.co.uk/business/business-news/manchester-arena-signs-deal-phones-5385660.

15 Roscanuck83, November 2012. Comment. Nirvana – The Point Theatre, Dublin, Ireland 1992, accessed 10 January 2013, http://www.youtube.com/watch?v=74bKupYf4N8.

16 Kronenburg, *Live Architecture: Popular Music Venues, Stages and Arenas*, 69–73.

17 D. Quentin, 3Arena blog entry, 9 June 2011, accessed 19 February 2018, https://www.yelp.co.uk/biz/3arena-dublin-2.

18 John Barrow, Senior Principle and project architect for the O2 Greenwich, Populous. Interview with the author, 2010.

19 Eli Blumenthal, 'How Madison Square Garden Co. is aiming to make every seat the best in the house', *USA Today*, 9 February 2018, accessed 16 July 2018, https://eu.usatoday.com/story/money/2018/02/08/how-madison-square-garden-co-aiming-make-every-seat-best-house/318516002/.

20 'Falling Attendances Hit Profits at Manchester Arena Operator SMG'. Insider Media Ltd., North West News, 9 September 2013, accessed 14 November 2014, http://www.insidermedia.com/insider/north-west/98014-falling-attendances-hit-profits-manchester-arena-operator-smg/.

21 Maria Armental, 'Live Nation Profit Falls as Attendance Drops', *Market Watch*, 31 July 2014, accessed 22 November 2014, http://www.marketwatch.com/story/live-nation-profit-falls-as-attendance-drops-2014-07-31.

22 'Live Nation Entertainment Reports First Quarter 2018 Financial Results', Live Nation Entertainment, 3 May 2018, accessed 14 May 2018, http://investors.

livenationentertainment.com/news-center/news-center-details/2018/Live-Nation-Entertainment-Reports-First-Quarter-2018-Financial-Results/default.aspx.

23 Robert Kronenburg, 'Safe and Sound: Audience Experience in New Venues for Popular Music Performance', in *Coughing and Clapping: Investigating Audience Experience*, ed. Karen Burland and Stephanie Pitts (Farnham: Ashgate, 2014b), 35–52.

24 Edgar et al., 'A Stately Pleasure-Dome', 1.

Chapter 11

1 Tim Jonze, 'Cunard Yanks: The Sailors Who Taught Britain How to Rock "n" Roll', *The Guardian*, 1 July 2015, accessed 2 January 2018, https://www.theguardian.com/music/2015/jul/01/liverpool-merseybeat-cunard-yanks-sailors-taught-britain-to-rocknroll.

2 Haslam, *Life After Dark: A History of British Nightclubs and Music Venues*, 130.

3 Ibid., 40.

4 John Williamson and Martin Cloonan, *Player's Work Time: A History of the British Musicians' Union, 1893–2013* (Manchester: Manchester University Press, 2016), 11.

5 Andrew Boryga, 'A Museum Quest Spins On and On', *New York Times*, 3 September 2010, accessed 18 May 2018, https://www.nytimes.com/2010/09/05/nyregion/05hiphop.html?scp=3&sq=1520%20Sedgwick%20Avenue&st=cse.

6 Robbie, 'An Oral History of New York's Early Hip-Hop Clubs', *Easey*, 14 May 2014, accessed 14 February 2018, http://www.unkut.com/2014/05/an-oral-history-of-new-yorks-early-hip-hop-clubs/.

7 Carol Cooper, 'Remembering the Fever', Liner notes from the CD *Night at the Fever*. Fever Records, 2000, accessed 14 February 2018, http://carolcooper.org/music/fever-00.php.

8 Bill Adler, 'The South Bronx was getting a bad rap until a club called Disco Fever came along', *People*, 16 May 1983, accessed 14 February 2018, http://people.com/archive/the-south-bronx-was-getting-a-bad-rap-until-a-club-called-disco-fever-came-along-vol-19-no-19/.

9 Haslam, *Life After Dark: A History of British Nightclubs and Music Venues*, 139.

10 Daniel Jones, 'a brief history of … Wigan Casino', *The Skinny*, 6 April 2015, accessed 9 February 2018, http://www.theskinny.co.uk/clubs/interviews/a-brief-history-of-wigan-casino.

11 Elaine Constantine and Gareth Sweeney, *Northern Soul: An Illustrated History* (London: Virgin Books, 2013), 105.

12 Ibid., 106.

13 Shuker, *Understanding Popular Music Culture*, 179.
14 Ben Kelly, 'The Haçienda, Factory Records', accessed 12 January 2018, http://benkellydesign.com/hacienda/.
15 Tony Wilson, *24 Hour Party People (FAC424)* (London: Channel 4 Books, 2002), 139.
16 Peter Hook, *How Not to Run a Club* (London: Simon and Schuster, 2009) 301–2.
17 Holly Kruse, *Site and Sound: Understanding Independent Music Scenes* (New York: Peter Lang, 2003), 94.
18 Shuker, *Understanding Popular Music Culture*, 118.
19 Florence Lentz and Sarah J. Martin, 'City of Seattle, Landmarks Preservation Board, city landmark submission for the Crescent-Hamm Building, 4302 SW Alaska Street/4559 California Avenue SW, Seattle, Washington 98116', SW Seattle Historical Society, 15 February 2017, accessed 3 February 2018, http://www.seattle.gov/Documents/Departments/Neighborhoods/HistoricPreservation/Landmarks/CurrentNominations/LPBCurrentNom_CrescentHamm.pdf.
20 Easy Street Records, 'About Us', accessed 3 February 2018, : http://easystreetonline.com/CustomPage/5825.
21 David Fricke, 'Pearl Jam: Live at Easy Street', *Rolling Stone*, 21 September 2006, accessed 3 February 2018, https://www.rollingstone.com/music/albumreviews/live-from-easy-street-20060921.
22 Jonze, 'Cunard Yanks: The Sailors Who Taught Britain How to Rock "n" Roll'.

Chapter 12

1 Hilly Kristal, 'History of CBGB & OMFUG'. CBGB & OMFUG Home of Underground Rock, 1998, accessed 15 February 2018, http://www.cbgb.com/history-by-hilly.
2 David Steinfeld, 'Our Hole in the Wall: An Oral History of the CBGB Scene', *Cuepoint*, 12 February 2015, accessed 15 February 2018, https://medium.com/cuepoint/our-hole-in-the-wall-an-oral-history-of-the-cbgb-scene-33dc69a1f7c8.
3 Byrne, *How Music Works*, 16–17.
4 Smith, *Just Kids*, 240.
5 Sara Cohen, 'Scenes', in *Key Terms in Popular Music and Culture*, ed. Bruce Horner and Thomas Swiss (Oxford: Blackwell, 1999), 241.
6 Steinfeld, 'Our Hole in the Wall'.
7 Haslam, *Life After Dark: A History of British Nightclubs and Music Venues*, 405.
8 David Hare, 'Such Stuff as Dreams Are Made Of', *The Guardian Review*, 30 December 2017, 2.

9   Mickey Hart, 'Foreword', in *Live at Fillmore East: A Photographic Memoir*, ed. Amelie R. Rothschild and Ruth Ellen Graber (New York: Thunder's Mouth Press, 1999), 5–6.
10 Dave Simpson, 'How We Made: Ben Kelly and Peter Hook on the Haçienda club', *The Guardian*, 3 July 2012, accessed 19 February 2018, https://www.theguardian.com/culture/2012/jul/02/how-we-made-hacienda-club.
11 Roxy Robinson, 'No Spectators! The Art of Participation, from Burning Man to Boutique Festivals in Britain', in *The Pop Festival: History, Music, Media, Culture*, ed. George McKay (New York: Bloomsbury, 2015), 165–82.
12 Only as recently as 2014 has a detailed scientific analysis of rock and pop concert hall acoustics been published with recommendations for the creation of new spaces and the adaptation of existing ones (Adelman-Larsen, *Rock and Pop Venues*).
13 Kronenburg, *Live Architecture: Popular Music Venues, Stages and Arenas*, 5.
14 Jeff Horton, Interview with the author, 2011.
15 Sean Michaels, '100 Club Saved by Converse Deal', *The Guardian*, 15 February 2011, accessed 26 February 2018, https://www.theguardian.com/music/2011/feb/15/100-club-saved-converse.
16 David Backhouse, interview with the author, 2011.
17 Fred Feddes and Allard Jolles, *Frits van Dongen: Designing for Culture* (Rotterdam: 010 Publishers, 2006), 81.
18 Edgar et al., 'A Stately Pleasure-Dome', 1.
19 Anahid Kassabian, 'Popular', in *Key Terms in Popular Music and Culture*, ed. Bruce Horner and Thomas Swiss (Oxford: Blackwell, 1999), 115.
20 *Hits, Hypes and Hustle: An insider's Guide to the Music Business* (2018), [TV programme] Episode 2: 'On the Road', 19 January 2018, Colin Murray, Pacific Quay Productions BBC.
21 Jonah Hahn, 'The Politics of Race and Rap', *Harvard Political Review*, 8 June 2014, accessed 23 February 2018, http://harvardpolitics.com/books-arts/politics-race-rap/.
22 *Annie Mac: Who Killed The Night* (2017), [TV programme] Paul Haydock, Rumpus Media BBC.
23 UK Music, *Measuring Music 2017 Report* (London: UK Music, 2017), 9–13.
24 Paul Resnikoff, 'Live Concerts + Streaming = 73% of US Music Industry', *Digital Music News*, 7 June 2017, accessed 3 May 2018, https://www.digitalmusicnews.com/2017/06/07/music-industry-concerts-streaming/.
25 Don Wade, 'Memphis measures local sports impact in dollars – and desire', *Memphis Daily News*, 23 January 2016, accessed 23 February 2018, https://www.memphisdailynews.com/news/2016/jan/23/in-the-game/.
26 Memphis Convention and Visitors Bureau, *The Memphis Tourism Industry* (Memphis: Memphis Convention and Visitors Bureau, 2017), accessed 23 February 2018, http://www.memphistravel.com/economic-impact.

27 David Grazian, 'The Symbolic Economy of Authenticity in the Chicago Blues Scene', in *Music Scenes: Local, Translocal and Virtual*, ed. Andy Bennett and Richard A. Peterson (Nashville: Vanderbilt University Press, 2004), 32.

28 Cohen and Kronenburg, *Liverpool's Musical Landscapes*, 92–3.

29 Rowena Mason, 'Planning Rules to be strengthened in UK to protect music venues', *The Guardian*, 18 January 2018, accessed 2 May 2018, https://www.theguardian.com/music/2018/jan/18/planning-rules-protect-music-venues-developers-soundproofing-homes.

30 Peter Marks, from an interview in; Annie Mac, *Who Killed The Night*, BBC, 2017.

31 Chris Coldwell, 'What happened to the great London nightclubs?' *The Guardian*, 13 August 2015, accessed 26 February 2018, https://www.theguardian.com/music/2015/aug/13/what-happened-to-the-great-london-nightclubs.

32 Lucy Clarke-Billings, 'Half of UK nightclubs close in ten years a Brits abandon rave culture', *The Telegraph*, 10 August 2015, accessed 26 February 2018, http://www.telegraph.co.uk/news/uknews/11794636/Half-of-UK-nightclubs-close-in-ten-years-as-Brits-abandon-rave-culture.html.

33 Homan, '"I Tote and I Vote": Australian Live Music and Cultural Policy', 104.

34 Webster et al., *Valuing Live Music: The UK Live Music Census 2017 Report Executive Summary*.

35 Niels W. Adelman-Larsen, *Rock and Pop Venues: Acoustic and Architectural Design* (Springer: Berlin, 2014), xiii.

BIBLIOGRAPHY

Adelman-Larsen, Niels W. *Rock and Pop Venues: Acoustic and Architectural Design*. Springer: Berlin, 2014.
Adler, Bill. 'The South Bronx was getting a bad rap until a club called Disco Fever came along'. *People*, 16 May 1983. Available online: http://people.com/archive/the-south-bronx-was-getting-a-bad-rap-until-a-club-called-disco-fever-came-along-vol-19-no-19/ (accessed 14 February 2018).
Anderton, Chris, Andrew Dubber, and Martin James. *Understanding the Music Industries*. London: Sage, 2013.
Armagost, Karen. *New Orleans Jazz Sites: Then and Now*. New Orleans Jazz National Historic Park, National Park Service, USA, May 2012. Available online: https://www.nps.gov/jazz/learn/historyculture/upload/New-Orleans-Jazz-Sites-Then-and-Now.pdf (accessed 5 May 2018).
Armental, Maria. 'Live Nation Profit Falls as Attendance Drops'. *Market Watch*, 31 July 2014. Available online: http://www.marketwatch.com/story/live-nation-profit-falls-as-attendance-drops-2014-07-31 (accessed 22 November 2014).
Armstrong, Louis. *Satchmo: My Life in New Orleans*. 1954. Boston: De Capo Press, 1986.
Armstrong, Stephen. 'Inside the Amish town that builds U2, Lady Gaga, and Taylor Swift's live shows'. *Wired*, 5 January 2018.
'Bachelors' Fancy Ball at the Wellington Rooms, Liverpool'. In *The Kaleidoscope: Literary and Scientific Mirror*. Liverpool: E.Smith, 20 March 1821, vol. 1, 302.
Bechet, Sidney. 'Treat It Gentle'. 1960. In *Reading Jazz*, edited by Robert Gottlieb, 8–16. New York: Vintage, 1996 (this edition 1999).
Becker, Howard S. 'Jazz Places'. In *Music Scenes: Local, Translocal and Virtual*, edited by Andy Bennett and Richard A. Peterson, 17–30. Nashville: Vanderbilt University Press, 2004.
Bennett, Andy and Richard A. Peterson. 'Introducing Music Scenes'. In *Music Scenes: Local, Translocal and Virtual*, edited by Andy Bennett and Richard A. Peterson, 1–16. Nashville: Vanderbilt University Press, 2004.
Blackstock, Pete. 'Street Survivor: Hole in the Wall Celebrates 40 Years down on the drag'. *Austin American-Statesman*, 18 June 2014. Available online: http://www.mystatesman.com/entertainment/street-survivor-hole-the-wall-celebrates-years-down-the-drag/hrAyDGUQB4oqBhpYfmUHzN/ (accessed 30 January 2018).
Blake, Mark. *Pigs Might Fly: The Inside Story of Pink Floyd*. London: Aurum Press, 2007.
Blunden, Mark. 'Infamous Tales from Rock Haven The Hope'. *Camden New Journal*, 5 April 2007. Available online: http://www.thecnj.com/review/040507/feat040507_01.html (accessed 29 January 2018).

Blumenthal, Eli. 'How Madison Square Garden Co. is aiming to make every seat the best in the house'. *USA Today*, 9 February 2018. Available online: https://eu.usatoday.com/story/money/2018/02/08/how-madison-square-garden-co-aiming-make-every-seat-best-house/318516002/ (accessed 16 July 2018).

Boryga, Andrew. 'A Museum Quest Spins On and On'. *New York Times*, 3 September 2010. Available online: https://www.nytimes.com/2010/09/05/nyregion/05hiphop.html?scp=3&sq=1520%20Sedgwick%20Avenue&st=cse (accessed 18 May 2018).

Bracewell, Michael. ' U2 and Rock Music as Spectacle'. In *U2 Show*, edited by Diana Scrimgeour, 9–14. London: Orion, 2004.

Brooks, Dave. 'Coachella Grossed Record-Breaking $114 Million This Year: Exclusive'. *Billboard*, 18 October 2017. Available online: https://www.billboard.com/articles/business/8005736/coachella-festival-2017-114-million-gross (accessed 24 April 2018).

Brown, August. 'Bruce Springsteen's last stand at the Sports Arena: "We gotta play this one for the old building"'. *Los Angeles Times*, 20 March 2016. Available online: http://www.latimes.com/entertainment/music/posts/la-et-ms-springsteen-sports-arena-20160320-story.html (accessed 15 May 2018).

Brown, Peter J. 'Liquor Licenses, Steelworkers and the British Navy – an Unlicensed History and Etymology of "Speakeasies"'. Early Sports and Pop Culture History Blog, 2014. Available online: https://esnpc.blogspot.co.uk/2014/08/liquor-licenses-steelworkers-and.html (accessed 7 December 2018).

Buckland, Theresa J. *Society Dancing: Fashionable Bodies in England, 1870–1920*. Basingstoke: Palgrave Macmillan, 2011.

Burgess, Michelle. 'There's No Place Like Floore's: Texas honky-tonk heaven in Heliote'. *Texas Highways*, November 2013. Available online: http://www.texashighways.com/travel/item/476-there-s-no-place-like-john-t-floores-country-store-helotes (accessed 9 August 2017).

Burton, Rick. 'A History of the Rainbow Theatre'. 2011. Available online: http://www.rainbowhistory.x10.mx/index.htm (accessed 13 March 2018).

Byrne, David. *How Music Works*. Edinburgh: Canongate, 2012.

Calloway, Cab and Bryant Rollins. *Of Minnie the Moocher and Me*. New York: Crowell, 1976.

Clarke-Billings, Lucy. 'Half of UK nightclubs close in ten years a Brits abandon rave culture'. *The Telegraph*, 10 August 2015. Available online: http://www.telegraph.co.uk/news/uknews/11794636/Half-of-UK-nightclubs-close-in-ten-years-as-Brits-abandon-rave-culture.html (accessed 26 February 2018).

Cohen, Sara. 'The gigs I've gone to': Mapping Memories and Places of Live Music'. In *Coughing and Clapping: Investigating Audience Experience*, edited by Karen Burland and Stephanie Pitts, 131–46. Farnham: Ashgate, 2014.

Cohen, Sara. 'Scenes'. In *Key Terms in Popular Music and Culture*, edited by Bruce Horner and Thomas Swiss, 239–49. Oxford: Blackwell, 1999.

Cohen, Sara and Robert Kronenburg. *Liverpool's Musical Landscapes*. Swindon: Historic England, 2018.

Coldwell, Chris. 'What happened to the great London nightclubs?' *The Guardian*, 13 August 2015. Available online: https://www.theguardian.com/music/2015/aug/13/what-happened-to-the-great-london-nightclubs (accessed 26 February 2018).

Connell, John and Chris Gibson. *Sound Tracks: Popular Music, Identity and Place.* 2003. Abingdon: Routledge, 2006.

Constantine, Elaine and Gareth Sweeney. *Northern Soul: An Illustrated History.* London: Virgin Books, 2013.

Cooke, Mervyn. *Jazz.* London: Thames and Hudson World of Art, 1998.

Cooper, Carol. 'Remembering the Fever'. Liner notes from the CD *Night at the Fever.* Fever Records, 2000. Available online: http://carolcooper.org/music/fever-00.php (accessed 14 February 2018).

Cornforth, David. 'The Theatre Royal Fire 1887'. Exeter Memories. 2005. Available online: http://www.exetermemories.co.uk/em/theatre_fire.php (accessed 4 May 2018).

Cunnigham, Mark. 'A Short History of Rock Touring'. In *U2 Show*, edited by Diana Scrimgeour, 196–9. London: Orion, 2004.

Davis, Miles, with Quincy Troupe. *Miles: The Autobiography.* 1989. London: Picador, 2012.

Denis, Pete. 'The Copacabana, New York City: The Hottest Spot North of Havana'. Disco-Disco, 2008. Available online: http://www.disco-disco.com/clubs/copacabana.shtml (accessed 10 January 2018).

Downing, Sarah J. *The English Pleasure Garden 1660–1860.* Oxford: Shire, 2011.

Doyle, Jack. 'Elvis on the Road 1955–56'. The Pop History Dig, 9 August 2017. Available online: http://www.pophistorydig.com/topics/tag/elvis-presley-concerts-1955-1956/ (accessed 22 March 2018).

Earl, John. *British Theatres and Music Halls.* Princes Risborough: Shire, 2005.

Edgar, Robert and Kirsty Fairclough-Isaacs, Ben Halligan, and Nicola Spelman. 'A Stately Pleasure-Dome'. In *The Arena Concert: Music Media and Mass Entertainment*, edited by Robert Edgar, Kirsty Fairclough-Isaacs, Ben Halligan and Nicola Spelman, 1–12. New York: Bloomsbury, 2015.

Englund, Björn. 'The London Sonora Band's Favorite Recordings. A revised discography'. Nottingham: *Vintage Jazz Mart*, no. 169 (2014): 12–15.

ERA, The. 'The Elephant and Castle Theatre'. London, 8 June 1879. Available online: http://www.arthurlloyd.co.uk/ElephantAndCastleTheatre.htm (accessed 24 July 2017).

ERA, The. 'The New Empire Theatre Liverpool'. London, 12 December 1896. Available online: http://www.arthurlloyd.co.uk/Liverpool/EmpireTheatreLiverpool.htm (accessed 5 March 2018).

Erenberg, Louis A. *Steppin' Out: New York Nightlife and the Transformation of American Culture, 1890–1930.* 1981. Chicago: University of Chicago Press, 1984.

'Falling Attendances Hit Profits at Manchester Arena Operator SMG'. Insider Media Ltd., North West News, 9 September 2013. Available online: http://www.insidermedia.com/insider/north-west/98014-falling-attendances-hit-profits-manchester-arena-operator-smg/ (accessed 14 November 2014).

Farrar, James and Andrew Field. *Shanghai Nightscapes: A Nocturnal Biography of a Global City.* Chicago: University of Chicago Press, 2015.

Feddes, Fred and Allard Jolles. *Frits van Dongen: Designing for Culture.* Rotterdam: 010 Publishers, 2006.

Felber, Garrett. 'Apollo Theater'. In *The Encyclopedia of New York City*, 2nd edn., edited by Kenneth, T. Jackson, 46–7. New Haven: Yale University Press, 2010.

Ferguson, James. 'Manchester Arena signs deal with Phones4U'. *Manchester Evening News*, 31 July 2013. Available online: http://www.manchestereveningnews.co.uk/business/business-news/manchester-arena-signs-deal-phones-5385660 (accessed 21 November 2014).

Field, Andrew. *Shanghai's Dancing World: Cabaret Culture and Urban Politics, 1919–1954*. Honk Kong: Chinese University Press, 2010.

Fricke, David. 'Pearl Jam: Live at Easy Street'. *Rolling Stone*, 21 September 2006. Available online: https://www.rollingstone.com/music/albumreviews/live-from-easy-street-20060921 (accessed 3 February 2018).

Frith, Simon. *Performing Rites: On the Value of Popular Music*. Cambridge, MA: Harvard University Press, 1996.

Frith, Simon, Matt Brennan, Martin Cloonan, and Emma Webster. *The History of Live Music in Britain Volume I: 1950–1967*. Farnham: Ashgate, 2013.

Gibson, Owen. 'The Astoria, legendary venue for acts from Kylie to the Killers, falls silent for final time'. *The Guardian*, 15 January 2009. Available online: https://www.theguardian.com/music/2009/jan/15/astoria-final-gigs (accessed 13 March 2018).

Girouard, Mark. *Cities and People: A Social and Architectural History*. London: Yale University Press, 1985.

Gorman, Juliet. 'Jukin' it out: Contested visions of Florida in New Deal narratives'. May 2001. Available online: http://www2.oberlin.edu/library/papers/honorshistory/2001-Gorman/default.html (accessed 2 August 2017).

Grazian, David. 'The Symbolic Economy of Authenticity in the Chicago Blues Scene'. In *Music Scenes: Local, Translocal and Virtual*, edited by Andy Bennett and Richard A. Peterson, 31–47. Nashville: Vanderbilt University Press, 2004.

Green, Adam. 'Blues'. In *Electronic Encyclopedia of Chicago*, Chicago Historical Society. Chicago: The Newberry Library, 2005. Available online: http://www.encyclopedia.chicagohistory.org/pages/151.html (accessed 10 August 2017).

Green, Lucy. 'Ideaology'. In *Key Terms in Popular Music and Culture*, edited by Bruce Horner and Thomas Swiss, 5–17. Oxford: Blackwell, 1999.

Hahn, Jonah. 'The Politics of Race and Rap'. *Harvard Political Review*, 8 June 2014. Available online: http://harvardpolitics.com/books-arts/politics-race-rap/ (accessed 23 February 2018).

Hall, Michael. 'Accommodating an Old Honky-Tonk in Austin'. *The New York Times*, 12 January 2013. Available online: http://www.nytimes.com/2013/01/13/us/in-new-austin-accommodating-the-broken-spoke-honkey-tonk.html?_r=0 (accessed 1 December 2017).

Hare, David. 'Such Stuff as Dreams Are Made Of'. *The Guardian, Review*, 30 December 2017, 2–3.

Hart, Mickey. 'Foreword'. In *Live at Fillmore East: A Photographic Memoir*, edited by Amelie R. Rothschild and Ruth Ellen Graber, 5–8. New York: Thunder's Mouth Press, 1999.

Hartwell, Clare, Matthew Hyde, and Nikolaus Pevsner. *Buildings of England. Lancashire: Manchester and the South-East*. New Haven: Yale University Press, 2004.

Haslam, Dave. *Life After Dark: A History of British Nightclubs and Music Venues*. London: Simon and Schuster, 2015.

Historic England. 'Hope and Anchor Public House, Grade II listing report no. 1195774'. 1994. Available online: https://www.historicengland.org.uk/listing/the-list/list-entry/1195774 (accessed 29 January 2018).
Historic England. 'Numbers 232 to 238 (even) Rainbow Theatre, former, Grade II* listing report no. 1297977'. 1974. Available online: https://historicengland.org.uk/listing/the-list/list-entry/1297977 (accessed 12 March 2018).
Historic England. 'Tower Buildings, Grade 1 listing report no. 183675'. 1973 (amended 1983). Available online: https://historicengland.org.uk/listing/the-list/list-entry/1205810 (accessed 16 January 2018).
Homan, Shane. '"I Tote and I Vote": Australian Live Music and Cultural Policy'. *Arts Marketing* 1, no. 2 (2011): 96–107.
Hook, Peter. *How Not to Run a Club*. London: Simon and Schuster, 2009.
Islington Heritage Services and Rick Burton. *From Coleman to Costello: A history of the Astoria Cinema and Rainbow Theatre*. Finsbury Park, London: Islington Heritage Services, 2013.
Inglis, Ian, ed. *Performance and Popular Music: History, Place and Time*. London: Ashgate, 2006.
Jacobs, Claude F. 'Benevolent Societies of New Orleans Blacks during the Late Nineteenth and Early Twentieth Centuries'. *Louisiana History: The Journal of the Louisiana Historical Association* 29, no. 1 (Winter 1988): 21–33.
Jones, Daniel. 'a brief history of … Wigan Casino'. *The Skinny*, 6 April 2015. Available online: http://www.theskinny.co.uk/clubs/interviews/a-brief-history-of-wigan-casino (accessed 9 February 2018).
Jonze, Tim. 'Cunard Yanks: The sailors who taught Britain how to rock "n" roll'. *The Guardian*, 1 July 2015. Available online: https://www.theguardian.com/music/2015/jul/01/liverpool-merseybeat-cunard-yanks-sailors-taught-britain-to-rocknroll (accessed 2 January 2018).
Kahn, Eve M. 'The Restoration of Harlem's Apollo Theater'. *Traditional Building*, 28 September 2017. Available online: https://www.traditionalbuilding.com/projects/apollo-theater-restoration (accessed 9 February 2018).
Kärki, Kimi. 'Evolutions of the Wall: 1979–2015'. In *The Arena Concert: Music Media and Mass Entertainment*, edited by Robert Edgar, Kirsty Fairclough-Isaacs, Ben Halligan, and Nicola Spelman, 57–70. New York: Bloomsbury, 2015.
Kassabian, Anahid. 'Popular'. In *Key Terms in Popular Music and Culture*, edited by Bruce Horner and Thomas Swiss, 113–23. Oxford: Blackwell, 1999.
Koblin, John. 'Stephen Colbert's Shiny New Home on Broadway Reflects Its Past'. *The New York Times*, 9 September 2015. Available online: https://www.nytimes.com/2015/09/10/arts/television/stephen-colberts-shiny-new-home-on-broadway-reflects-its-past.html (accessed 4 May 2018).
Kristal, Hill. 'History of CBGB & OMFUG'. CBGB & OMFUG Home of Underground Rock, 1998. Available online: http://www.cbgb.com/history-by-hilly (accessed 15 February 2018).
Kronenburg, Robert. *Flexible: Architecture that Responds to Change*. London: Lawrence King, 2007.
Kronenburg, Robert. *Live Architecture: Popular Music Venues, Stages and Arenas*. Oxford: Routledge, 2012.
Kronenburg, Robert. *Architecture in Motion: The History and Development of Portable Building*. Oxford: Routledge, 2014.

Kronenburg, Robert. 'Safe and Sound: Audience Experience in New Venues for Popular Music Performance'. In *Coughing and Clapping: Investigating Audience Experience*, edited by Karen Burland and Stephanie Pitts, 35–52. Farnham: Ashgate, 2014.

Kronenburg, Robert. 'From Shed to Venue: The Arena Concert Event Space'. In *The Arena Concert: Music Media and Mass Entertainment*, edited by Robert Edgar, Kirsty Fairclough-Isaacs, Ben Halligan, and Nicola Spelman, 73–85. New York: Bloomsbury, 2015.

Kruse, Holly. *Site and Sound: Understanding Independent Music Scenes*. New York: Peter Lang, 2003.

Leach, Elizabeth E. 'Popular Music'. In *An Introduction to Music Studies*, edited by John Paul E. Hooper-Scott and Jim Samson, 188–200. Cambridge: Cambridge University Press, 2009.

Lentz, Florence and Sarah J. Martin. 'City of Seattle, Landmarks Preservation Board, city landmark submission for the Crescent-Hamm Building, 4302 SW Alaska Street/4559 California Avenue SW, Seattle, Washington 98116'. SW Seattle Historical Society, 15 February 2017. Available online: http://www.seattle.gov/Documents/Departments/Neighborhoods/HistoricPreservation/Landmarks/CurrentNominations/LPBCurrentNom_CrescentHamm.pdf (accessed 3 February 2018).

Levitin, Daniel. *This Is Your Brain on Music: The Science of a Human Obsession*. London: Dutton, 2006.

'Live Nation Entertainment Reports First Quarter 2018 Financial Results'. Live Nation Entertainment, 3 May 2018. Available online: http://investors.livenationentertainment.com/news-center/news-center-details/2018/Live-Nation-Entertainment-Reports-First-Quarter-2018-Financial-Results/default.aspx (accessed 14 May 2018).

Llewellyn, Jennifer, Jim Southey, and Steve Thompson. 'Weimer cabaret'. Alpha History, 2014. Available online: http://alphahistory.com/weimarrepublic/weimar-cabaret/ (accessed 5 May 2018).

Lomax, Alan. *The Land Where the Blues Began*. New York: New Press, 1993.

Lomax, Alan. 'Mister Jelly Roll'. 1950. In *Reading Jazz*, edited by Robert Gottlieb, 3–7. New York: Vintage, 1996 (this edition 1999).

Lyall, Sutherland. *Rock Sets: The Astonishing Art of Rock Concert Design*. London: Thames and Hudson, 1992.

Mandel, W. 'Led Zeppelin's Music Needs the Spectrum'. *Philadelphia Bulletin*, 14 June 1972. Available online: http://www.ledzeppelin.com/show/june-13-1972 (accessed 3 July 2017).

Margolick, David. *Strange Fruit: Billie Holiday, Café Society, and an Early Cry for Civil Rights*. Philadelphia: Running Press, 2000.

Mason, Rowena. 'Planning Rules to be strengthened in UK to protect music venues'. *The Guardian*, 18 January 2018. https://www.theguardian.com/music/2018/jan/18/planning-rules-protect-music-venues-developers-soundproofing-homes (accessed 2 May 2018).

McKay, George, ed. *The Pop Festival: History, Music, Media, Culture*. New York: Bloomsbury Academic, 2015.

McNamara, Brooks. *The New York Concert Saloon: The Devil's Own Nights*. Cambridge, UK: Cambridge University Press, 2002.

Meakin, Anna. 'Le Chat Noir: Historic Montmartre Cabaret'. *Bonjour Paris*, 19 December 2011. Available online: https://bonjourparis.com/archives/chat-noir-montmartre-cabaret/ (accessed 22 November 2017).

Memphis Convention and Visitors Bureau. *The Memphis Tourism Industry*. Memphis: Memphis Convention and Visitors Bureau, 2017. Available online: http://www.memphistravel.com/economic-impact (accessed 23 February 2018).

Michaels, Sean. '100 Club Saved by Converse Deal'. *The Guardian*, 15 February 2011. Available online: https://www.theguardian.com/music/2011/feb/15/100-club-saved-converse (accessed 26 February 2018).

Mitchell, Dennis J. 'Grand Opera House of Mississippi'. Jackson: Mississippi Historical Society, September 2006. Available online: http://www.mshistorynow.mdah.ms.gov/articles/167/grand-opera-house-of-mississippi (accessed 31 July 2017).

Moore, Lucinda. 'Show Time at the Apollo'. *Smithsonian*, November 2010. Available online: https://www.smithsonianmag.com/arts-culture/show-time-at-the-apollo-64658902/ (accessed 15 March 2018).

Nott, James. *Going to the Palais: A Social and Cultural History of Dancing and Dance Halls in Britain, 1918–1960*. Oxford: Oxford University Press, 2015.

Okrent, Daniel. *Last Call: The Rise and Fall of Prohibition*. New York: Scribner, 2010.

Palin, Michael. *The Python Years: Diaries 1969–79: Volume One*. London: Orion Publishing Co. 2006.

Peterson, Richard A. *Creating Country Music: Fabricating Authenticity*. Chicago: University of Chicago Press, 1997.

Peterson, Richard A. and Andy Bennett. 'Introducing Music Scenes'. In *Music Scenes: Local, Translocal and Virtual*, edited by Andy Bennett and Richard A. Peterson, 1–16. Nashville: Vanderbilt University Press, 2004.

'Pollstar 2016 Year End Worldwide Ticket Sales Top 200 Arena Venues'. Pollstar 2017. Available online: https://www.pollstar.com/Chart/2017/01/2016YearEndWorldwideTicketSalesTop200ArenaVenues_350.pdf (accessed 14 May 2018).

Popa, Christopher. 'Do Big Bands Today Stand a Ghost of a Chance?' Big Band Library, 2004. Available online: http://www.bigbandlibrary.com/dobigbandstodaystandaghostofachance.html (accessed 13 February 2018).

Popik, Barry. 'Honky Tonk (not from Tonk pianos)'. 2006. Available online: http://www.barrypopik.com/index.php/new_york_city/entry/honky_tonk_not_from_tonk_pianos/ (accessed 9 August 2017).

Porterfield, Bill. *The Greatest Honky Tonks in Texas*. Dallas: Taylor Publishing Company, 1983.

Price, Pete and Adrian Butler. *Namedropper*. Liverpool: Trinity Mirror, 2007.

Prose, Francine. *The Photographs of Marian Post Wolcott: The Library of Congress (Fields of Vision)*. London: D. Giles Ltd., 2008.

Raeburn, Bruce B. 'Riverboats and Jazz'. Hogan Jazz Archive, Tulane University, New Orleans, 2000. Available online: https://library.tulane.edu/exhibits/exhibits/show/riverboats_jazz (accessed 21 November 2017).

Reidy, Tess and Vanessa Thorpe. 'Secret gigs place the next big thing right in your room'. *The Guardian*, 27 April 2014. Available online: https://www.theguardian.com/music/2014/apr/27/secret-gigs-pop-music-prince-batille (accessed 2 February 2018).

Resnikoff, Paul. 'Live Concerts + Streaming = 73% of US Music Industry'. *Digital Music News*, 7 June 2017. Available online: https://www.digitalmusicnews.com/2017/06/07/music-industry-concerts-streaming/ (accessed 3 May 2018).

Robbie. 'An Oral History of New York's Early Hip-Hop Clubs'. *Easey*, 14 May 2014. Available online: http://www.unkut.com/2014/05/an-oral-history-of-new-yorks-early-hip-hop-clubs/ (accessed 14 February 2018).

Robinson, Roxy. 'No Spectators! The Art of Participation, from Burning Man to Boutique Festivals in Britain'. In *The Pop Festival: History, Music, Media, Culture*, edited by George McKay, 165–82. New York: Bloomsbury, 2015.

Rooney, James. *Bossmen: Bill Monroe and Muddy Waters*. New York: Dial Press, 1971.

Rys, Richard. 'The Full Spectrum: an oral history'. *Philadelphia*, 24 June 2009. Available online: http://www.phillymag.com/articles/the-full-spectrum/?all=1 (accessed 17 November 2014).

Sanchez, Daniel. 'What Streaming Music Services Pay (updated for 2018)'. *Digital Music News*, 16 January 2018. Available online. https://www.digitalmusicnews.com/2018/01/16/streaming-music-services-pay-2018/ (accessed 30 March 2018).

Sandberg, Marian. 'Q&A: Andrew Gumper, Owner and CEO of AG Light and Sound'. *Live Design*, 10 November 2017. Available online: http://www.livedesignonline.com/business-people-news/qa-andrew-gumper-owner-and-ceo-ag-light-and-sound (accessed 24 April 2018).

Sanneh, Kelefa. 'The Persistence of Prog Rock'. *The New Yorker*, 19 June 2017. Available online: https://www.newyorker.com/magazine/2017/06/19/the-persistence-of-prog-rock (accessed 30 March 2018).

Sackllah, David. 'The Crisis of Gentrification Hits the Austin Music Scene'. *Pitchfork*, 9 July 2015. Available onlne: https://pitchfork.com/thepitch/836-the-crisis-of-gentrification-hits-the-austin-music-scene/ (accessed 20 January 2018).

Scott, Derek. *Sounds of the Metropolis: The 19th Century Popular Music Revolution in London, New York, Paris and Vienna*. Oxford: Oxford University Press, 2011.

Sharples, Joseph and Richard Pollard. *Liverpool; Pevsner Architectural Guides*. New Haven and London: Yale University Press, 2004.

Shuker, Roy. *Understanding Popular Music Culture*. Abingdon: Routledge, 2013.

Simpson, Dave. 'How We Made: Ben Kelly and Peter Hook on the Haçienda club'. *The Guardian*, 3 July 2012. https://www.theguardian.com/culture/2012/jul/02/how-we-made-hacienda-club (accessed 19 February 2018).

Sounes, Howard. *Down the Highway: The Life of Bob Dylan*. New York: Grove Press, 2001.

Smith, Patti. *Just Kids*. London: Bloomsbury, 2011.

Spitz, Bob. *Barefoot in Babylon: The Creation of the Woodstock Music Festival, 1969*. 1979. New York: Plume, 2014.

Stage, The. 'The Olympia Theatre, West Derby Road, Everton, Liverpool'. London, 27 April 1905. Available online: http://www.arthurlloyd.co.uk/Liverpool/OlympiaTheatreLiverpool.htm (accessed 28 July 2017).

Steinfeld, David. 'Our Hole in the Wall: An Oral History of the CBGB Scene'. *Cuepoint*, 12 February 2015. Available online: https://medium.com/cuepoint/our-hole-in-the-wall-an-oral-history-of-the-cbgb-scene-33dc69a1f7c8 (accessed 15 February 2018).

Stravers, Kim. 'Majorica Jazz Bar'. *The Guardian, Travel*, 24 December 2016, 8–9.
Stuckey, B. '"Kid" Jazzmen Play to Preserve Art Form'. *New Orleans Times Picayune*, 24 July 1961 (courtesy Hogan Jazz Archive, Tulane University).
Tatman, Sandra L. 'McElfatrick, John Bailey (1826–1906)'. Philadelphia Architects and Buildings, The Athaneum of Philadelphia, 2018. Available online: https://www.philadelphiabuildings.org/pab/app/ar_display.cfm/23155 (accessed 31 July 2017).
Taylor, Paul. 'The Arena put Manchester on top of the world'. *Manchester Evening News*, 13 July 2010. Available online: http://menmedia.co.uk/manchestereveningnews/life_and_style/s/1301523_the_arena_put_manchester_on_top_of_the_world (accessed 19 January 2013).
Tester, Nick. 'Joy Division, Hope and Anchor'. *Sounds*, 1979. Available online: https://www.joydiv.org/c271278.htm (accessed 29 January 2018).
Thompson, Anne. 'Francis Ford Coppola: Why He Spent $500K to Restore His Most Troubled Film, "The Cotton Club"'. *IndieWire*, 1 September 2017. Available online: http://www.indiewire.com/2017/09/francis-coppola-recut-the-cotton-club-telluride-1201872249/2/ (accessed 9 January 2018).
Thompson, Max. 'Theatre architect receives blue plaque'. *Architects' Journal*, 23 November 2007. Available online: https://www.architectsjournal.co.uk/news/theatre-architect-receives-blue-plaque/296348.article (accessed 25 July 2017).
Trav S. D. *No Applause – Just Throw Money: The Book That Made Vaudeville Famous*. New York: Farrar, Strauss and Giroux, 2006.
Turner, Steve. 'Roger Waters: The Wall in Berlin'. *Radio Times*, 25 May 1990. Reprinted in *Classic Rock*, no. 148, August 2010, 76.
UK Music. *Measuring Music 2017 Report*. London: UK Music, 2017.
United States Department of the Interior. 'Nomination Form for the showboat Goldenrod. National Register of Historic Places Inventory, Historic Sites Survey. Washington D.C.: National Park Service, 15 February 1977.
Upstone, Robert. '*Study for a Mural Decoration for "The Cave of the Golden Calf"* 1912 by Spencer Gore'. In *The Camden Town Group in Context*, edited by Helena Bonett, Ysanne Holt, Jennifer Mundy. London: Tate Research Publication, May 2012. Available online: https://www.tate.org.uk/art/research-publications/camden-town-group/spencer-gore-study-for-a-mural-decoration-for-the-cave-of-the-golden-calf-r1139297 (accessed 5 May 2018).
Varney, Danny. 'Hackney Empire Memories'. Arthur Lloyd, 1991 (revised 2010). Available online: http://www.arthurlloyd.co.uk/HackneyEmpireMemories.html (accessed 25 July 17).
Wade, Don. 'Memphis measures local sports impact in dollars – and desire'. *Memphis Daily News*, 23 January 2016. Available online: https://www.memphisdailynews.com/news/2016/jan/23/in-the-game/ (accessed 23 February 2018).
Webster, Emma, Matt Brennan, Adam Behr, Martin Cloonan, and Jake Ansell. *Valuing Live Music: The UK Live Music Census 2017 Report Executive Summary*. Edinburgh: University of Edinburgh, ECA, Reid School of Music, 2018.
Williams, Willie. 'Art, Commerce and Logistics: Designing a U2 Show'. In *U2 Show*, edited by Diana Scrimgeour, 15–18. London: Orion, 2004.
Williamson, Nigel. *The Rough Guide to Bob Dylan*. London: Rough Guides, 2004.

Williamson, John and Martin Cloonan. *Player's Work Time: A History of the British Musicians' Union, 1893–2013*. Manchester: Manchester University Press, 2016.
Wilson, Tony. *24 Hour Party People (FAC424)*. London: Channel 4 Books, 2002.
Woodruff, A. 'Society Halls in New Orleans: A Survey of Jazz Landmarks, Part II'. *Jazz Archivist* XXI (2008): 19–36.
Wright, Jade. 'Remembering 50 Years of Jacqui and Bridie's folk club'. *Liverpool Echo*, 19 January 2011 (updated 7 May 2013). Available online: https://www.liverpoolecho.co.uk/news/liverpool-news/remembering-50-years-jacqui-bridies-3385531 (accessed 30 July 2018).
Young, Rob. 'Folk – the "music of the people" is now hip again'. *The Guardian*, 31 July 2010. Available online: https://www.theguardian.com/culture/2010/jul/31/folk-music-of-people-young (accessed 30 July 2018).
Zbikowski, Lawrence M. 'Music, Dance and Meaning in the Early Nineteenth Century'. *Journal of Musicological Research* 31 (2012): 147–65.

INDEX

Absolute Beginners (film) 131
AC/DC 172
Adele (Laurie Blue Adkins) 172, 226
AECOM (architectural design practice) 191, 230
AFAS Live, Amsterdam, The Netherlands 226–7
Afrika Bambaataa (Kevin Donovan) 199
AG Light and Sound (music industry specialist) 164
Agent of Change principle 121, 234
Air, Birmingham, England 206
alehouses. *See* public houses
Alexandra Palace, London, England 179
Alice Cooper (Vincent Damon Furnier) 148, 167
Animals (travelling set) 169. *See also* Pink Floyd
Animals, The 223
Annabel's, London, England 197
Anschutz Entertainments Group (AEG) 4, 182, 187
Antone's, Austin, USA 122
Antwerp Sportspaleis, Belgium 180
Apollo Theater, New York, USA 4, 140–4, **143**, 153, **Plate 10**
Apple Music. *See* streaming
Arcade Fire 55, **185**
architects 16, 17, 19, 21–2, 27, 30, 33, 77, 92, 97, 102, 103, 104, 136, 139, 141, 142, 149, 182, 190–3, 208, 215, 216, 217–18, 219, 227
architectural styles and design 9, 24, 27, 32, 47, 69, 74, 77, 83, 86–7, 97, 99, 102, 103, 108, 113, 116, 136, 141, 146, 155, 169, 195, 205, 210, 215, 222, 224, 238
Arctic Monkeys 179, 226
arenas xvi, 3, 10, 166, 177–94, 177, 182, 186, 227, 238
Armadillo World Headquarters, Austin, USA 125
Armstrong, Louis 54, 57, 60, 64
audiences 1, 32, 39, 53, 57, 106, 119, 139, 140–1, 156, 160–1, 164–6, 168, 175, 177–8, 185, 187, 189, 203, 210, 221
Austin City Limits (television show) 122
Austin, Texas, USA 9, 41, 122–6, 165
authenticity. *See* heritage
awards 163, 179, 181, 186

B.B. King's, (multiple locations), USA 232
Back to the Future (film) 127
Badly Drawn Boy (Damon Michael Gough) 214
Bagleys, London, England 236
Baker, Chesney 'Chet' 67
Baker, Josephine 27
ballad opera. *See* opera
ballrooms 3, 6, 10, 91–4, 97–100, 224
Band Room, The, Yorkshire, England 220–1, **221**, 222
bandstands (park and garden) 3, 97
Barber, Chris 140
barrooms xvi, 9, 52, 121–6. *See also* public houses
Basie 'Count' (William James Basie) 64, 65, 106, 141
Bataclan Theatre, Paris, France 150, 239

Bath Assembly Rooms, Bath, England 97, **98**
BBC Television Dancing Club (television show) 104
Beach Boys, The 147, 181
Beatles, The x, xv, 6, 33, 102, 140, 147, 157–8, **157**, 158, 181, 197, 209
Bechet, Sidney 58–9, 64, 102
beer parlours (Canada) 119
Berlin 73–4, 169–70
Berry, Charles 'Chuck' 167, 197
Beyoncé, Giselle Knowles Carter 172
Birdland, New York, USA 64–5, **66**, 67, **67**, **Plate 6**
Birmingham Town Hall, England 139
Black Abbots, The 69
Black Patti Troubadours 32
Black Sabbath 140, 148, 172
Blackpool Tower Ballroom, Blackpool, England 24, 98–100, 107, **Plate 8**
Blakey, Arthur 'Art' 65, 142
Blondie 211, 213
Blue Note, New York, USA 65, 211
bluegrass 38, 55
blues
    clubs 44–50, 51, 121
    music 6, 38, 44–5, 131, 196, 199, 222
Blues Brothers (film) 50
Boblo Dancing Pavilion, Ontario, Canada 104–5, **105**
Bolden, Charles 'Buddy' 53, 55, 58
Bombay Bicycle Club 179
boogie-woogie 38, 45
Bowie, David (David Robert Jones) 102, 148, 179
Bridgestone Arena, Nashville, USA 187, 228–30, **228**
Bristol Theatre Royal (Bristol Old Vic), USA 17
Brit Awards 179
Britannia Music Hall (Britannia Panoptican), Glasgow, Scotland 19, **20**
British Summer Time festival, London, England 165
Brixton Academy, London, England 150

broadcasting 2, 104, 165–6, 216
    radio 5, 6, 37, 38, 83, 99, 126
    television 26, 29, 33–4, 76, 88, 99, 104, 113, 122, 127, 131, 147, 150, 160, 170, 205
Broken Spoke, The, Austin, USA 41–3, **42**, **43**, 122, 125
Brooks, Garth 43
Brown, James 142, 203
Brown, Willie 45
Brubeck, Dave 140, 142
burlesque 29, 141
burletta 17
Burning Man festival, Nevada, USA 165, 221
Bush, Kate xvi, 137, 140, 150–1, **151**, 167
Buzzcocks, The 149
Byrds, The 147

cabaret 27, 69–71, 86–9, 152. *See also* kabarett
Cabaret (film) 89
Cabaret Voltaire, Zurich, Switzerland 72
café chantants. *See* cabaret
café concert. *See* cabaret
Café de Paris, London, England 75–6, **76**, 100, 224
Café des Beaux Arts, New York, USA 78–9, 81
Café Society, New York, USA 87–8
Café Wha!, New York, USA 132, **133**
cafés. *See* coffee bars
Calloway, Cabell 'Cab' 83, 85, 88, 141
Candlestick Park stadium, San Francisco, USA xv
Canned Heat 135
Carnegie Hall, New York, USA 55
Carpenters, The 138
Carter Family, The 38
Casbah, Liverpool, England 6–7, **7**, 214, 225
Cash, Johnny 123, 184
Casino de Paris, Paris, France
Castle Clinton, New York, USA. *See* Castle Garden
Castle Garden, New York, USA 179

Cathay Hotel, Shanghai, People's Republic of China. *See* Peace Hotel
Cave of the Golden Calf, London, England 74, **75**, 224
Cavern Club, Liverpool xv, **xvi**, 4, 11, 216, 218, 225–6, **226**, 232
CBGB and OMFUG, New York, USA 4, 11, 12, 211–14, **212**, 216, 218, **Plate 15**
CBS Studio 50, New York, USA 33
céilí music 91–2, 109–12
CenturyLink Field stadium, Seattle, USA **Plate 12**
charity 161, 171
Charles, Ray (Charles Ray Robinson) 147, 184
Chateau Impney, Droitwich, England 201
Cheers (television show) 113
Chevalier, Maurice 29
Chicago, USA 48–50, 64
Chieftains, The 111
cinema
    buildings 24, 29, 34, 100, 102, 144–7, 150, 153, 218
    films 29, 33, 50, 79, 82, 88–9, 127, 131, 146, 148, 160, 167, 175, 198, 199, 205
circus 24, 148
Ciro's, London, England 74–5, 100
Ciro's, Shanghai, People's Republic of China 76–8, **77**
Clash, The 117, 149
classical music xvii, 2, 99, 139
Cline, Patsy (Virginia Patterson Hensley) 37, 38
Clinton, George 142
Coach House Folk Club, Liverpool, England 7–8
Coachella Music and Arts Festival, California, USA 163–4, 174, **Plate 11**
Coasters, The 197
Cochran, Eddie 147
coffee bars 9, 10, 111, 126–32
Cohen, Leonard xvi
Cole, Nat 'King' 147

Coltrane, John 64
Come Dancing (television show) 99
commercial pressures on venues xvi, 4–5, 17, 34, 81, 94, 150–3, 156, 188, 193–4, 206, 208, 218–19, 223, 231–2, 234–7
concert rooms 3, 18, 113
Condemned to Devil's Island (film) 146
Confitería Ideal, Buenos Aires, Argentina 108
Cooke, Sam (Samuel Cook) 87
Copacabana, New York, USA 86–7, 215, **Plate 7**
Costello, Elvis (Declan Patrick MacManus) 115, 149, 208
Cotton Club, The (film) 88
Cotton Club, The, New York, USA 82–7, **83**, **84**, **86**, 104
country and western 35–43, 52, 122, 239
Coward, Noel 76, 87
Cream (musicians) 184
Cream, Liverpool, England. *See* Nation
Crosby, 'Bing' (Harry Lillis Crosby) 138
Crystal Beach Amusement Park ballroom, Ontario, Canada 105–6, **106**
Cure, The 102

Dada (art movement) 72
Damned, The 117, 212, 223
dance 2, 79, 83. *See also céilí; milonga*
    ballet 17, 21, 92, 153
    Can-Can 27
    dance hall 3, 6, 38–47, 69, 93, 100–8, 201–3
    Northern soul 201–3
    social dancing 39–47, 79, 91–108, 195, 203–6
Dark Side of the Moon (travelling set) 168–9. *See also* Pink Floyd
Davis, Miles 64
Davis, Sammy Jr. 87
De Vorstin, Hilversum, The Netherlands 216–18, **217**, 219
Dean Martin Show, The 34

decoration. *See* architectural styles and design
Deejay. *See* disc jockey
Deep Purple 135, 140
Dekker, Desmond (Saint Andrew Parish) 197
Delaney and Bonnie 140
Derby Palais de Danse, Derbyshire, England 101
Detroit, USA 48
Diddley, Bo (Elias McDaniel) 222
Die Katakombe (The Catacombs), Berlin, Germany 73
Dietrich, 'Marlene' (Mary Magdalene Dietrich) 73, 76
diners (USA) 127–8, **128**
Dion, Celine 230
disc jockey 196–203
Disco Fever, New York, USA 198–9, 214
discotheque 87, 104, 195, 197, 210, 224
Dixon, Reginald 99–100
DJ. *See* disc jockey
Doors, The 167
Doves 214
Down Under, Manchester, England 214
Dr. Feelgood 115, 119
Drifters, The 201
drugs 205, 234
Drury, Ian 115
Drury Lane Theatre, London, England 17
Dublin Arena, Republic of Ireland **188**, 189–90, **190**, 224
Durutti Column 203
Dylan, Bob (Robert Zimmerman) 39, 132, 138, 140, 177–8, 184

Eagle, Roger 197, 199
Eagle Saloon, New Orleans, USA 53–5, **54**
Eagles of Death Metal 150, 239
Earls Court arena, London, England 168–9
Earls Court Exhibition Centre, London, England 177–8, **178**

Easy Street Records, Seattle, USA 207–8, **208**
Ed Sullivan Show, The (television show) 33
Eddie and the Hot Rods 115, 149
Eddy, Duane 142
808 State 206
Elbow 214
Eldorado, Berlin, Germany 73–4, **73**
electronic music 165, 193, 195, 203–6
Elephant and Castle Theatre, London, England 22, **23**
Ellington, Edward 'Duke' 84–5, 88, 107, 141
emcee. *See* MC
Emerson, Lake and Palmer 135, 167
Empire Pool and Sports Arena, London, England. *See* Wembley Arena
Empire Theatre, Liverpool, England 135–9, **136**, **137**, 140, 152
Empress Hall, Wigan, England. *See* Wigan Casino
environment (internal) 23–4, 34, 119, 180, 189, 213, 222, 227
environmental impact 161, 191, 238
equipment (music performance) xvii, 10, 105, 155–63, 171, 175, 178, 184–5, 192–3, 197, **198**, 205, 238–40. *See also* jukebox
Eric's club, Liverpool, England xv, 9, 213, 234
Eurovision Contest 150
Evans, Gilmore 'Gil' 140
Expresso Bongo (film) 131

Fabric, London, England 206
FAC251, Manchester, England 207
Facebook. *See* social media
Factory Records, Manchester, England 195, 203–7
fairs 2, 15
Fall, The 102, 203
Family (musicians) 148
fans (music) 11, 135, 138–9, 175, 189, 214, 230–1. *See also* audiences

FedExForum, Memphis, USA 187, 228–30, **229**, 231, 232
festivals (music) 3, 10, 55, 59, 60, 108, 118, 122, 139, 158–66, **159**, **162**, **163**, 184
Fillmore East, New York, USA 144, 147, 158, 215
film. *See* cinema
Finsbury Park Astoria, London, England. *See* Rainbow Theatre
fire escape and prevention 15, 17, 21, 34. *See also* safety
Fisher, Mark (architectural design practitoner) 155, 169–73
Fitzgerald, Ella 67, 142
Folies Bergére, Paris, France 27, 71
folk 2, 7–8, 10, 92, 94, 109–11, 131–2
Folly on the Thames, The, London, England 95
Formby, George (George Hoy Booth) 26
funk music 51

Garland, Judy (Frances Ethel Gumm) 138
Gaye, Marvin 87, 137
Generation X 149
Genesis 135, 148, 149, 167, 173, 230
gentrification 118, 121, 125, 219. *See also* urban regeneration and development
Georgian Theatre Royal, Richmond, England 16, **16**
Getz, Stan (Stanley Gayetski) 64, 142
Gillespie, 'Dizzy' (John Birks Gillespie) 64, 141
Gilley's, Texas 50
Gilmour, David. *See* Pink Floyd
Glastonbury Festival, Somerset, England 161–3, **162**, **163**, 164, 165, 174, 221
Globe Theatre, London, England 16, 69
Godskitchen, Birmingham, England. *See* Air
Golden Torch, Stoke-on-Trent, England 201–2
Golden1 Center, Sacramento, USA 187

Good Old Days, The (television show) 33
gospel music 50
Graham, Bill 147, 158, 215
Grand Ole Opry House 216, **Plate 16**
Grand Ole Opry radio show 37
Grand Opera House, Meridian, USA 30–3, **32**
Grand Theatre, Blackpool, England 24
Grandmaster Flash (Joseph Saddler) 198
grassroots venues 5, 119–21
Grateful Dead 184, 215
Grease (film) 127
Great Depression, The 38, 45, 62, 63, 74
Green Day 212
Grenswerk Poppodium, Venlo, The Netherlands 219–20, **220**
Griffith, Nanci 123
guerrilla gigs 8. *See also* home performance
Guinan, Mary Louise Cecilia 'Texas' 81
Guns and Roses 212
Gypsy Rose Lea (Rose Louise Hovick) 29

Haçienda, Manchester, England 195, 203–7, **204**, 215, **Plate 14**
Hackney Empire, London, England 24–7, **25**, **Plate 3**
Haley, Bill and His Comets 167
Hall, Adelaide (musician) 85, 102, 141
Hamersmith Palais de Danse, London, England 101–2, **103**
Hammersmith Eventim Apollo, London, England 150–1, **151**, 152
Hammerstein's Theatre, New York, USA 33
Hamp's Place, Arkansas, USA 45
Hampton Court Palace, Richmond upon Thames, England 16
Hanley, Bill 159–60
Happy Days (television show) 127
Happy Mondays, The 205

Hard Rock Café (multiple locations) 50, 232
Harris, Emmy Lou 123
Harrison, George. *See* Beatles, The
Harvest country music festival, Las Vegas, USA 239
Havens, Richie 160
Hawkins, 'Screamin' Jay (Jalacy Hawkins) 200
Helpyourself Manchester 8
Hendrix, James 'Jimi' 67, 132, 138, 142, 147, 160
heritage 7, 142, 144, 148, 189, 216, 233
hip-hop 2, 55, 165, 198–9, 231
Hipgnosis (graphic design practice) 168
Hole on the Wall, Austin, USA 123–6, **124, 125**, 126
Holiday, Billie (Eleanora Fagan) 87
Hollies, The 200
Holly, 'Buddy' (Charles Hardin Holley) 140, 142
Hollywood Bowl, Los Angeles, USA 55, 168
home performance 2, 5–9, 97
honky-tonk 35–43, 104, 121
Hooker, John Lee 197, 200
Hooton Tennis Club (musicians) 209
Hope and Anchor, London, England 115–19, **116, 117**, 126, 218
House, 'Son' (Eddie James House) 45
house music. *See* electronic music
House of Blues (multiple locations) 50, 232
Howlin' Wolf (Chester Burnett) 46, 48, **48**
Humperdinck, Engelbert (Arnold George Dorsey) 138
100 Club, London, England 11, 218, 222–3, **223**

I Am Kloot 214
Incredible String Band 160
Indiana State Fair, Indianapolis, USA 164. *See also* safety
indie rock 55
inns. *See* public houses
insider music events 8–9
interior design. *See* architectural styles and design
Irish Centre, Liverpool, England. *See* Wellington Rooms
Iron Maiden 148
Isle of Wight festival, England 3

Jackson, Mahalia 142
Jackson, Michael xvi
Jacqui and Bridie (Jacqueline McDonald and Bridget O'Donnell) 7–8
Jam, The 149
Jamaica 197, **198**
Jay Z (Shawn Corey Carter) 172
jazz
 clubs 63–8, 121, 133–4, 139, 222, 225
 music 2, 38, 50, 51–68, 78, 99, 100, 103, 106–7, 141–2, 222
Jethro Tull 148
Joe Loss Orchestra 102
John T. Floore Country Store, Helotes, Texas, USA 39–40, **40, 41**, 50, 104, 220
Johnson, Robert 46
Jones, George 39
Joshua Tree, The (travelling set) 173. *See also* U2
Joy Division 118, 203
juke joints 37, 44–50, **44, 46**, 121
jukebox 126–8, 196

kabarett 71–4, 89
Kansas City, Kansas, USA 64
Kelly, Ben (architectural design practitioner) 205, 216, **Plate 14**
Killers, The 187
King Crimson 140
Kingston Mines, Chicago, USA 49–50, **49**
Kinks, The 223
kissaten 132–3. *See also* jazz, clubs
klezmer 51
Knitting Factory 211
Kool DJ Red Alert (Frederick Crute) 199
Kool Herc (Clive Campbell) 198–9

INDEX

Koster and Bial's Music Hall, New York, USA 29
Krall, Diane 65
Kristopherson, Kris 43
Krush Groove (film) 199
Krystal, Hilly 4, 211, 216
Kursall Flyers, The 117
Kurtis Blow (Kurtis Walker) 199

Lafayette Theatre, New York, USA 142
Las Vegas, USA 50, 180, 192–3, 239
Laughing Dogs, The 214
Le Chat Noir, Paris, France 71, 72
Led Zeppelin 135, 140, 179, 184–5
Left Wing, Manchester, England. *See* Twisted Wheel
legislation and licensing 5, 21, 81, 84, 107, 112, 118, 120–1, 123, 125, 206, 234, 237
Lennon, John. *See* Beatles, The; Plastic Ono Band
Lewis, Jerry Lee 39, 167
Libertines, The 8
licensing. *See* legislation and licensing
Little Gem Saloon, New Orleans, USA 54–5
Little Richard (Richard Wayne Penniman) 138, 167
Live Nation Entertainment 4, 50, 187, 189, 194
Liverpool, England 6–8, 11, 20–4, 52, 69–71, 91–4, 115, 135–9, 206, 225–6, 135–9, 234
Liverpool Olympia, England 24, **Plate 2**
Locarno, Glasgow, Scotland 102–3
London, England 13–14, 16–17, 21–7, 66–7, 74–6, 95–7, 101–2, 115–19, 128–31, 144–50, 150–1, 165, 168–9, 177–82, 191–3, 197, 206, 222–3, 236
London Sonora Band 103
Los Angeles Memorial Sports Arena, USA 169, 180
Lovett, Lyle 123
Lymon, Franklin 'Frankie' and the Teenagers 138

Madison Square Garden, New York, USA 180
Madonna (Madonna Louise Ciccone) 172, 205, 230
Majorica, Kyoto, Japan 132–4
Manchester Arena, England 155–6, **156**, 185–7, **185**, 239
Manchester, England 8, 155–6, 185–7, 199–207, 214
Marable, Fate 60, **60**
Marley, Robert 'Bob' and the Wailers 148, 197
Marquee, The, London, England 197
Marsden, Gerry and the Pacemakers 196
Martin, Dean (Dino Paul Crocetti) 87
Marvin, Hank. *See* Shadows, The
Matcham, Frank (architectural design practitioner) 21–7, 102, 136
Mathis, Johnny 138
Matt Molloy's, Westport, Republic of Ireland 109–11, **110**, **111**, 220, **Plate 9**
MC 198–9
McCartney, Paul 187, 225. *See also* Beatles, The; Wings
M.C. Chill (Kevin Heard) 199
McColl, Ewan 8
McTell, Ralph 8
Memphis, USA 48, 62, 228–30, 232–3
Methany, Pat 65
Middle Temple Hall, London, England 16
Miller, Glenn 106–7
milonga 107
Ministry of Sound, London, England 206
minstrel
 show 29
 tunes 50
Mississippi Blues Trail, USA 47
Mistinguett (Jeane Florentine Bourgeois) 27
Modern Jazz Quartet 140
Monk, Thelonius 64, 140
Monterey festival, California, USA 3
Monty Python's Flying Circus 148
Moore, Christopher 'Christy' 8

281

Moore, Scott 'Scotty' 123
Morecambe and Wise Show, The (television show) 33–4
Morgan, Helen 82
Morton, Jelly Roll (Ferdinand Joseph LaMothe) 53
Moss Empires 21, 139
Mott the Hoople 148
Moulin Rouge, The, Paris, France 27–9, **28**, 71
MSG Sphere, Las Vegas, USA and London, UK 192–3, **193**
Mudhoney 209
Music Hall Preservation Society 18
music halls 3, 5, 10, 13–14, 18–20, 37, 71, 113, 224
musical notation 1
musical theatre xvi, 63, 82, 92, 138, 153, 196
Musician's Union (United Kingdom) 197
Music Venue Trust (United Kingdom) 236

Nashville, USA 35–8, 52, 228–30
Nassau Coliseum, New York, USA 169
Nation, Liverpool, England 206
Nelson, Willie 39, 40, 43, 122
New Order 203, 205, 206
New Orleans Brass Band **59**
New Orleans, Louisiana, USA 51–64, **Plate 5**
New Orleans Society for the Preservation of Jazz 55
New York, USA 3, 29–33, 55, 64–5, 78–81, 86–8, 132, 140–4, 157–8, 179–80, 197–9, 211–14
Nickelback 172
night-time economy 5, 232
nightclubs 3, 10, 75–88, 198, 203–7, 234–6
Nippon Budokan Hall, Tokyo, Japan 178
Northern soul 199–203, 223

O'Day, Anita 142
O2 Apollo Manchester, England 153

O2 Arena, Greenwich, London, England xvi, 4, 165, 179, 182, 186, 187, 191, **191**
Odyssey Centre, Belfast, Northern Ireland 189
Old Jazz Band, Shanghai, People's Republic of China. *See* Peace Hotel
Oliver, Joe 'King' 58, 64
opera
  houses 15, 24
  music 15–16, 99, 141, 146, 153, 175
  rock opera 147
Opeth 167
Orbison, Roy 140
Orbital 206
Original Dixieland Jazz (Jass) Band 79, 80, 102
Orpheum Circuit, USA 30

Palais de Danse, Glasgow, Scotland 103
Pantages Circuit, USA 30
Paris, France 27–9, 71, 74, 78
Parker, Charlie 'Yardbird' 64
Parker, Graham and the Rumour 117
Parton, Dolly 149
Patton, Charlie 45
Paxton, Tom 8
Peace Hotel, Shanghai, People's Republic of China 76–8
Pearl Jam 184, 209
Peppermint Lounge, New York, USA 197
Perseverance Society Hall, New Orleans, USA 57–8, **58**
Peter, Paul and Mary 132
Peterson, Oscar 65, 140
Philippine Arena, Manila, Philippines 191–2, **192**
Pilton Pop, Blues and Folk Festival, Somerset, England. *See* Glastonbury Festival
Pink Floyd 135, 140, 148, 155, 167–72, 178, 179. *See also* Animals; *Dark Side of the Moon*; *Wall, The*
Planet, Coventry, England 206

planning control. *See* legislation and licensing
Plastic Ono Band 167
pleasure gardens 3, 10, 95–7
Po' Monkey's, Merigold, Mississippi, USA 46–7, **47**, 50
Point, The, Dublin, Republic of Ireland. *See* Dublin Arena
Police, The (musicians) 102, 117, 152
popular music
  definition 2, **Plate 1**
  scenes 2, 6–8, 114–19, 126–34, 195–210, 214–15, 230–1
  significance 1, 230–3, 240
Populous (architectural design practice) 190–1, 224
Porter, Cole 75
Prefects, The 149
Preservation Hall Jazz Band 55–7
Preservation Hall, New Orleans, USA 55–7, **56**
Presley, Elvis 39, 157, 158
Primal Scream **Plate 2**
Procol Harum 148
Prohibition Act 1919, USA 81, 84
pub rock 114–19
public houses 9, 10, 13, 15, 18, 109–21, **115**, 234
public space performance 2, 58–9, **59**, 107, 165
punk rock 117–19, 149, 211–13, 223

Quarrymen, The 199. *See also* Beatles, The
Queen 135, 148, 172, 178

Radio City Music Hall, New York, USA 144
Radiohead 167, 172
ragtime 38, 45, 50, 79
Rainbow (musicians) 135, 138, 139
Rainbow Theatre, London, England 144–50, **145**, **146**, 153
Ramones, The 117, 149, 211–13, 230
Ranalegh Gardens, London, England 95–6, **96**
rap music 198–9
rave (event) 206

record shops 37, 202, 207–9, **208**
recording studios xvi, 216–17, 219–20
recordings xvi, 5, 6, 10, 26, 45, 49, 79, 103, 127, 132–4, 160, 166, 170, 193–4, 209. *See also* jukebox
records. *See* recordings
Reed, Jimmy 197
Reed, Lewis 'Lou' 132, 208
rehearsal rooms xvi, 216–17, 219–20
Reisenweber's Café, New York, USA 79–81, 80
rhythm and blues 134, 196–7, 199–203. *See also* blues; soul music
Richard, Cliff (Harry Webb) 6, 131, 140, 147
Riley Center, Meridian, USA. *See* Grand Opera House
Ritter, 'Tex' (Woodward Maurice Ritter) 122
Ritz Hotel, London, England 100
riverboats 60–3, **60**, **61**
Rob's Place, Robstown, Texas, USA 39
Robert's Western World, Nashville, USA 35–8, **36**, **Plate 4**
rock 'n' roll 2, 6, 10, 33, 55, 106, 112
rock 2, 50, 118, 135, 138–40, 139. *See also* indie rock; pub rock; punk rock; rock 'n' roll
Rogers (Richard) and Hammerstein (Oscar) 63, 196
Rolling Stones, The 102, 140, 147, 172, 181, 184, 197, 202, 230
Rollins, Walter Theodore 'Sonny' 65
Ronnie Scott's, London, England 65–7, **68**
Rose Theatre, London, England 16
Ross, Diana 142
Rotunda, London, England 95–6, **96**
Royal Albert Hall of Arts and Sciences, London, England 179
Royal Diversion, London. *See Folly on the Thames, The*
Royal Liverpool Philharmonic Hall, England 8
Royal Variety Performance, England 150
Run-DMC 199

Russell Lillian (Helen Louise Leonard) 30, 79
Ryman Auditorium, Nashville, USA 37, 216

safety 95, 152, 160, 164, 206, 234, 239
saloon. *See* barroom
Saturday Night Fever (film) 198
Savoy Hotel, London, England 100
Scene, The, London, England 197
Scholz's Hall, Austin, USA 122
Scofield, John 65, **67**
Screaming Trees 209
Sedaka, Neil 138
Seeger, Peggy 8
Sex Pistols 223
Shadows, The 131. *See also* Richard, Cliff
Shakespeare Theatre, Liverpool, England 69–71, **70**
Sham 69 149
Shea Stadium, New York, USA xv, 157–8, **157**
Showboat (film) 82
showboats (vessel) 63
Siberry, Jane 9
Silver, Horace 142
Silvester, Victor 104
Silvio's, Chicago, USA 48, **48**
Sinatra, Frank 76, 106, 138, 147
Siouxsie and the Banshees 149, 223
Six-Five Special (television show) 131
skiffle 10, 131, 225
Slaughter and the Dogs 203
SMG (venue property management) 188
Smith, Patricia 'Patti' 208, 211, 213, 216
Smiths, The 205
social change 3, 78, 79, 85, 100–1, 118–19, 128, 234, 237
social clubs 57–60, **58**, 101
social media 11, 139, 175, 240
Sofarsounds 8
Sonics, The 209
soul music 2, 134, 196, 199–203
Soundgarden 209
South by South West festival, Austin, USA 165
Space, Ibiza, Spain 206

speakeasy 81–5, 121
Spectrum Arena, Philadelphia, USA 182–5, **183**
Spice Girls, The 179
Spillers Records, Cardiff, Wales 207
Spiritualized 205
spirituals 30, 50
sponsor naming rights 188, 194, 223. *See also* commercial pressures on venues
Spoon 123
Spotify. *See* streaming
Spotted Cat Music Club, New Orleans, USA 51, **52**
Springsteen, Bruce 132, 180
SSE Arena, London, England. *See* Wembley Arena
St. Vincent (Ann Erin Clark) 123
stadiums 3, 10, 166, 179
StageCo (music industry specialist) 172–3
stages (mobile). *See* travelling sets
Starr, Edwin (Charles Edwin Hatcher) 201, 203
Starr, Ringo (Richard Starkey). *See* Beatles, The
Steele, Tommy (Tony Hicks) 130
Stevens, Guy 197
Sting (Gordon Matthew Thomas Sumner). *See* Police, The
Strait, George 43
Stranglers, The 117–18, **117**, 149
streaming 6, 11, 165–6, 174
Streckfus, John. *See* riverboats
street music. *See* public space performance
Strictly Come Dancing (television show) 99
Stubb's, Austin, USA 9
StuFish (architectural design practice). *See* Fisher, Mark
Subway Sect 149
Sum 42 212
Summer, Donna (LaDonna Adrian Gaines) 149
Sunnyland Slim (Albert Luandrew) 222
Superbowl, USA 172
superclubs 11, 203–7

supper clubs 19, 86–8
Supremes, The 87. *See also* Ross, Diana
sustainability. *See* environmental impact
Swift, Taylor 174–5, **Plate 12**
swing music 106–7, 142. *See also* jazz

T-Mobile Arena, Las Vegas, USA 180, **Plate 13**
Tait Towers (music industry specialist) 172–3
Talking Heads 12, 211–13
tango 107–8
taverns. *See* public houses
Teatro di San Cassiano, Venice, Italy 15
Television (musicians) 211–12
Temptations, The 87
Ten Years After 148
terrorism. *See* safety
Tharpe, Sister Rosetta 139–40, 142
theatre buildings 3, 10, 15–17, 29, 135–53
Theatre Royal, Exeter, England. *See* fire escape and prevention
Theatres Act (Great Britain 1843) 17–18
Thin Lizzy 148
This Is Spinal Tap (film) 167
ticketing 3–4, 239
Ticketmaster 4
Tokyo Dome, Japan 179
Tony Pastor's Theatre (Tony Pastor's Opera House), New York, USA 30, **31**
Topic Folk Club, Bradford, England 131
Tote, The, Melbourne, Australia 119–21, **120, 121**, 126, 234, **235**
Town and Country Club, London, England 150
Townsend, Pete. *See* Who, The
travelling sets 3, 10, 95, 152, 155–75, 216
Tubb, Ernest 37, 38, 39
Tube, The (television show) 205
Tucker, Sophie (Sophie Abuza) 79
Tunnel, New York, USA 206

Tunstall, K. T. (Kate Victoria Tunstall) 226
Turner, 'Big' Joe 87
24 Hour Party People (film) 205
Twisted Wheel, Manchester, England 199–203, **200**, 206, 215, 224
twitter. *See* social media
2i's coffee bar, London, England 6, 128–31, **129, 130**
typologies, music venues xvi–xviii, 218–33, 237

U2 xvi, 102, 118, 172, 173, 174, 178–9, 230. *See also Joshua Tree, The*; U2 360°
U2 360° (travelling set) 172, 216. *See also* U2
UK Live Music census 237
UK Music 231
UNESCO City of Music 11
Urban Cowboy (film) 50
urban music festivals 165–6. *See also* festivals
urban regeneration and development 41, 121, 125, 143–4, 152, 165, 194, 219, 234–7

variety 3, 10, 21–7, 33, 37, 70, 101, 138, 218, 225
vaudeo 33. *See also* broadcasting
vaudeville 3, 5, 10, 27–33, 78, 79, 141, 218
Vaughan, Sarah 87
Vaughan, Stevie Ray and Double Trouble 122, 123
Vincent, Gene (Vincent Eugene Craddock) and the Wild Cats 147, 167
Vipers, The 129

Wachovia Center, Philadelphia, USA 184
Walker Brothers, The 147
Walker, Junior (Autry DeWalt Mixon Jr.) 203
Wall, The (travelling sets) 155–6, **156**, 169–72, **170, 171**
Washington Coliseum arena, Washington D.C., USA xv

Waters, Muddy (McKinley Morganfield) 46, 48, 222
Waters, Roger. *See* Pink Floyd; *Wall, The*
Webster, Ben 67
Wellington Rooms, Liverpool, England 91–4, **93**, **94**, 100
Wells, Kitty (Ellen Muriel Deason) 43
Wembley Arena, London, England 179, 180–2, **181**, **182**, 187, 188
Wembley Stadium, London, England 179, 181
West, Kanye 172
western swing 38
Westfalenhallen, Dortmund, Germany 169
White, John 'Jack' 209
Who, The 102, 147, 197, 223
Wigan Casino, Wigan, England 201–3, **201**, **202**, 210
Williams, 'Hank' (Hiram King Williams) 39
Williams, Lucinda 123
Williams, Robbie 172
Williamson, Sonny Boy (Alex Miller) 200
Wills, Robert 'Bob' 43
Wilson, Jackie (Jack Leroy) 203
Wilton's Music Hall, London, England 13–14, **14**, 18–20, **19**
Wings 135. *See also* McCartney, Paul
Wishbone Ash 148
Wonder, Stevie (Stevland Hardaway Morris) 142, 172
Woodstock (film) 160
Woodstock festival, New York, USA 3, 147, 158–61, **159**, 165
WSB Atlanta radio station 6. *See also* broadcasting
WSM Radio Station, Nashville, USA 37, 38. *See also* broadcasting

Yes 135, 148, 167, 184
Yoakam, Dwight 40
YouTube 6. *See also* streaming

Zims, 'Zoot' (John Haley Zims) 65
Zulu Social Aid and Pleasure Club, New Orleans, USA 59–60
zydeco 51

www.ingramcontent.com/pod-product-compliance
Lightning Source LLC
Chambersburg PA
CBHW071805300426
44116CB00009B/1208